THE BUSINESS OF WOMEN

The Business of Women

Female Enterprise and Urban Development in Northern England 1760–1830

HANNAH BARKER

OXFORD

UNIVERSITY PRESS

OXFORD
UNIVERSITY PRESS

Great Clarendon Street, Oxford ox2 6dp

Oxford University Press is a department of the University of
It furthers the University's objective of excellence in research, s
and education by publishing worldwide in

Oxford New York

Auckland Cape Town Dar es Salaam Hong Kong Kar
Kuala Lumpur Madrid Melbourne Mexico City Nai
New Delhi Shanghai Taipei Toronto

With offices in

Argentina Austria Brazil Chile Czech Republic France Greece
Guatemala Hungary Italy Japan Poland Portugal Singapore
South Korea Switzerland Thailand Turkey Ukraine Vietnam

Oxford is a registered trade mark of Oxford University Press
in the UK and in certain other countries

Published in the United States
by Oxford University Press Inc., New York

© Hannah Barker 2006

The moral rights of the author have been asserted
Database right Oxford University Press (maker)

First published 2006

British Library Cataloguing in Publication Data
Data available

Library of Congress Cataloging in Publication Data
Data available

Typeset by Newgen Imaging Systems (P) Ltd., Chennai, India
Printed in Great Britain
on acid-free paper by
Biddles Ltd., Kings Lynn, Norfolk

ISBN 0–19–929971–4   978–0–19–929971–3

1 3 5 7 9 10 8 6 4 2

This book is dedicated with much love to my mother,
Diana Leonard

Acknowledgements

THIS project would not have been possible without funding from the Economic and Social Research Council (award number R000223187) and the Arts and Humanities Research Council. Many individuals also provided invaluable help. I am particularly grateful to Karen Harvey, who worked as a Research Associate compiling the project database, and to Vicky Brookes, who acted as a Research Assistant. The database itself was constructed with the help of Sarah Davnall and Ann Sharrock of Manchester Computing, and its findings were accessed with the patient aid of Albert Freeman. Others who provided valuable assistance and advice include Maxine Berg, Leonore Davidoff, Joanna Innes, Rebecca Jennings, Keith McClelland, Colin Phillips, Olga Shipperbottom, and Terry Wyke. The staff of various libraries and Record Offices were also immensely helpful. I am grateful to those at the Brotherton Library, John Rylands Library, Lancashire Country Record Office, Leeds Central Library, Manchester Central Reference Library, National Archives, Sheffield Archives, Sheffield Central Reference Library, and the West Yorkshire Archive Service at Leeds and Wakefield. I am especially thankful to the staff of Chetham's Library, and Michael Powell, Fergus Wilde, and Jane Foster in particular, to Nigel Taylor of the National Archives for his help in wading through Georgian court records, to Peter Nockles of the John Rylands Library for directing me to George Heywood's diary, and to the Map Room counter staff of the National Archives for repackaging massive Exchequer rolls for me with cheerful good humour. I would also like to thank Sophie and Jeremy Archdale for access to their family archives, housed in their working snuff mill at Sharrow, and Simon Barley, for his help negotiating the company's voluminous ledgers. The following were kind enough to comment on earlier drafts of individual chapters: Helen Berry, Andrew Hann, Stuart Jones, Peter Kirby, Nicola Pullin, Helen Roberts, and Bob Shoemaker, whilst the participants of seminars at the Institute of Historical Research and the Universities of Leeds, Manchester, Warwick, and York offered valuable comments and ideas. My anonymous OUP readers made many extremely useful and incisive suggestions, while Rodney Barker, Elaine Chalus, and Rosemary Sweet also proved their generosity by reading and commenting on the manuscript as a whole. I am particularly grateful to Rosemary, and to the other editors of *Urban History*, for permission to reprint material that forms the basis of Chapter 1, and which appeared in the journal as ' "Smoke cities' ": Northern Industrial Towns in Late Georgian England' in 2004. Finally, I would like to thank my colleagues at the Universities of Manchester and Keele for supporting my research, as well as family and friends for putting up with me while I beavered away. I am particularly grateful to Stephen for frequent cups of tea and chocolate biscuits, and to Mimi and Jess for providing the most delightful of distractions.

December 2005
Manchester

Contents

List of Tables

List of Maps

Introduction

IN 1832, Robert Ayrey, a milliner and straw hat and stay maker,[1] wrote to fellow Independents and missionaries in Jamaica. Ayrey was clearly concerned for his friends, and pleaded with them to return home to Leeds despite the ongoing cholera epidemic. His greatest anxiety was reserved for three girls that the couple had taken with them: one of whom was their eldest daughter, Hannah, whilst the other two were unnamed and apparently orphans. All three, according to Ayrey, should be sent home immediately to learn a trade:

iff you are Determined not to Come you Ought by all means to Send them two girls you tooke with you because they should now be able to lern some buisness but iff they stay any longer, they will be too Old and as Mr [?] Armitage informs me that therre is a provision made for them to the amount of 30 shillings per weeke so that it will lern them a buisness and afterward set them up in buisness so that you should by no means neglect sending them before there habits gets formed indeed they Should have beene Sent Some years ago and they would have been better to lern Therefore trust you will Send them the Very first Oportunity and it is allso Quite time that you should Send your Oldest Daughter Hannah the proper age to lern a buisness Should not be later than 12 years to begin With you had better send Hannah to Leeds and I will take care for her that she getts her buisness lernt if we all be Spared I therefore hope iff you Cannot See your Way Clear to Come yourselves you Will looke at your Childrens Wellfair and Send them of the Very first Oportunity that you have . . . [2]

Ayrey's concern that these girls were properly equipped to run a business tells us much about lower middle-class life in the early nineteenth

---

[1] Listed in William Parson, *General and Commercial Directory of the Borough of Leeds* (Leeds, 1826) as 'London millinery, patent stay and straw bonnet warehouse, 31 Commercial St and stay mfr 5 Upperhead Row', and in the 1834 edition as 'Straw and Tuscan Hat mfr. and milliner, 30 Park Row'.

[2] Leeds Central Library, MS letter book of Robert Ayrey, SR826.79 AY 74, fos. 16–17.

century. There is no suggestion that any of them might hope for, or aspire to, a more domesticated life away from the concerns of the commercial world (even with almost £80 a year to live on). On the contrary, he clearly expects that all three girls would need to provide for their own livings in the future. His assumption sits uneasily with accounts of gender and work in this period that suggest middling women were less likely to labour outside the home as time went on. In contrast to such a model of increasing domestication, Ayrey's letter suggests that even in the 1830s, lower middle-class women were expected to prepare for working life from childhood. Robert Ayrey was not alone in his belief that girls should learn a trade, and newspaper advertisements for apprenticeships for middle-class girls—especially in millinery and dress and hat making—were common. In 1809, for example, E. Haley informed parents and guardians in Leeds that she could teach 'the manufacturing of Thread Lace' to 'Young Ladies', which they could supplement with learning 'the Straw hat business'.[3]

This study argues that businesswomen were central to urban society and to the operation and development of commerce in the late eighteenth and early nineteenth centuries. It presents a rich and complicated picture of lower middling life and female enterprise in three northern English towns: Manchester, Leeds, and Sheffield. A systematic examination of trade directories and newspaper advertisements offers new insights into women's work during the period: challenging existing models of change and revealing the ways in which gender was constructed amongst the lower middling sorts. Gendered identities are further explored through court records and family papers, which offer up more detailed information about the experiences of individual women, and, in particular, tell us about both their place within family firms and their relationships with the wider commercial world. The stories told by these disparate sources demonstrate the very differing fortunes and levels of independence that businesswomen enjoyed. Yet as a group, their involvement in the economic life of

---

[3] *Leeds Mercury*, 4 February 1809.

towns, and, in particular, the manner in which they exploited and facilitated commercial development, force us to reassess our understanding of both gender relations and urban culture in late Georgian England. In contrast to the traditional historical consensus that the independent woman of business during this period—particularly those engaged in occupations deemed 'unfeminine'—was insignificant and no more than an oddity, businesswomen are presented here not as footnotes to the main narrative, but as central characters in a story of unprecedented social and economic transformation.

Concentrating on the efforts of modest property-owners to make a living constitutes a new direction in the history of women's work, which has been dominated by the study of the labouring poor, or conversely, the lives of the comparatively wealthy middle class.[4] Moreover, this study challenges traditional assumptions that the development of capitalism acted to marginalize female workers both socially and economically, limiting middle-class women to their role as consumers. Instead, they are represented here as significant economic agents and not just as the providers of a 'hidden investment' in the family firm, or as wives increasingly alienated from the world of business.

The subjects in this study of lower middle-class women are small-scale manufacturers, artisans, traders, and service providers. The development of the urban middle classes as a whole during the 'long' eighteenth century has attracted much historical interest in recent years. Its size, wealth, culture, and politics have all been subjected to scrutiny by scholars keen to map the fortunes of the 'polite and commercial people' of the eighteenth century and trace the emergence of

---

[4] Women's 'work' is defined here as work that generated income. There is no doubt that this excludes some important forms of women's work, such as housework, making it harder to measure women's work in family enterprises, since these were often based in the home. In such circumstances it is difficult to say where 'home' work stopped and work for the market began. Focusing only on paid work (for monetary reward or in kind) arguably undervalues women's work as a whole. Yet this is a distinction that we are used to drawing in modern-day society, and which eighteenth- and nineteenth-century contemporaries would have found familiar. On the problems of defining women's work, see the introduction to the revised edition of Leonore Davidoff and Catherine Hall's, *Family Fortunes: Men and Women of the English Middle Class 1780–1850* (London, 2002), pp. xxxvi–xxxviii.

the assertive bourgeoisie of the nineteenth.[5] Yet despite this interest in the 'middling sorts', class is often considered anachronistic by eighteenth-century historians, who see little evidence for the existence of class consciousness or identity before around 1800, despite contemporaries' fascination for rank, status, and classification.[6] The model of a 'modern' class society seems more convincing in the nineteenth century—the 'locus classicus of class conflict'[7]—and it is only at the very end of the period described in this book that either the sort of associational culture or political outlook required to formulate a sense of middle-class identity has been identified by historians, and even then the use of class is a contested one.[8] The term 'middle class' is therefore used guardedly here, and less specific descriptors such as 'middling sort' and 'middle classes' are preferred, acknowledging the slippery nature of both social structures, and the ways in which they were described and understood by contemporaries.

Urban society during the later Georgian period was extremely diverse and in a constant state of flux. Nowhere was this more apparent than in burgeoning 'industrial' towns such as Manchester, Leeds, and Sheffield where immigration, commercial uncertainty, and religious and political division were particularly marked. In such conditions, the middling sort were especially prominent, as the unique

[5] See, among others, Peter Earle, *The Making of the English Middle Class: Business, Society and Family Life in London, 1660–1830* (London, 1989); Paul Langford, *A Polite and Commercial People: England, 1727–1783* (Oxford, 1989); and *Public Life and the Propertied Englishman* (Oxford, 1991); Margaret Hunt, *The Middling Sort: Commerce, Gender and the Family, 1680–1780* (Berkeley and Los Angeles, 1996); G. Crossick and H.-G. Haupt (eds.), *The Petite Bourgeoisie in Europe 1780–1914: Enterprise, Family and Independence* (London, 1995).

[6] P. J. Corfield, 'Class by Name and Number in Eighteenth-Century Britain', *History* 72 (1987), 38–61.

[7] Nicholas Rogers, 'Introduction' to special edition of *Journal of British Studies*, 'Making of the English Middle Class, ca. 1700–1850', 32/4 (1993), 299–304, p. 299.

[8] R. J. Morris, *Class, Sect and Party: The Making of the British Middle Class, Leeds 1820–1850* (Manchester, 1990). Postmodernists' readings of class have questioned the role of class-consciousness in forging social alliances in the nineteenth century: see Gareth Stedman Jones, *Languages of Class: Studies in Working-Class History 1832–1982* (Cambridge, 1983); Patrick Joyce, *Visions of the People: Industrial England and the Question of Class, 1840–1914* (Cambridge, 1992). Also Dror Wahrman, *Imagining the Middle Class: The Political Representation of Class in Britain, c.1780–1840* (Cambridge, 1995).

opportunities offered by rapidly expanding urban economies encour-aged commercial speculation and frequently rewarded those embark-ing on new business ventures, particularly the buyers and sellers of goods and providers of services.[9] Yet even here, the middling sort was neither a unified nor a stable social group. As Rosemary Sweet has pointed out, the urban middling sort consisted of individuals sepa-rated by subtle gradations of status: 'wholesale shopkeepers, such as mercers, drapers and hosiers, were of higher status than the retail shopkeepers, and among the shopkeepers, the dealers in luxury fin-ished goods, such as china or silverware, occupied a position above those who dealt in foodstuffs and other basic goods'.[10]

Women of all social classes predominated in Georgian towns owing, at least in part, to the particular attractions that an urban lifestyle offered them, including the lure of better employment.[11] Yet a powerful body of scholarship on gender relations in the eighteenth and nineteenth cen-turies, and the middle classes in particular, suggests that women of the middling sort were increasingly unlikely to labour outside the home as the period progressed.[12] In line with recent work attacking models of 'domestication' or 'separate spheres',[13] much of what follows appears to contradict such a finding. In part, this can be ascribed to a difference of focus, since this book concentrates on rather lower down the social scale than do most accounts of middle-class women in this period. But it is

[9] The rise of shopkeeping is particularly noteworthy in this respect: Ian Mitchell, 'The Development of Urban Retailing 1700–1815', in Peter Clark (ed.), *The Transformation of English Provincial Towns 1600–1800* (London, 1984); Hoh-Cheung and Lorna H. Mui, *Shops and Shopkeeping in Eighteenth-Century England* (London, 1989).

[10] Rosemary Sweet, *The English Town, 1680–1840: Government, Society and Culture* (Harlow, 1999), 180.

[11] Pamela Sharpe, 'Population and Society 1700–1840', in Peter Clark (ed.), *The Cambridge Urban History of Britain*, ii. *1540–1840* (Cambridge, 2000), 495–500.

[12] Most importantly, Davidoff and Hall, *Family Fortunes*, 1st edn. (London, 1987).

[13] Critiques of separate spheres theory include Jane Lewis, 'Separate Spheres: Threat or Promise?', *Journal of British Studies* 30/1 (1991), 105–15; Amanda Vickery, 'Golden Age to Separate Spheres? A Review of the Categories and Chronology of English Women's History', *Historical Journal* 36/2 (1993), 383–414; Lawrence E. Klein, 'Gender and the Public/Private Distinction in the Eighteenth Century: Some Questions about Evidence and Analytic Procedure', *Eighteenth-Century Studies* 29/1 (1995), 97–109.

also the result of differing methodologies: in terms of the sources used and by adopting an approach that is frequently quantitative rather than qualitative in nature. The use of trade directories and newspaper advertisements in particular allows us to assess developments in a less impressionistic way than do accounts based solely on small groups of individuals or families, or on didactic literature.

Much of this study concerns the ways in which women appeared in the 'public' commercial world, but it also considers personal and familial relations at some length. The family was crucial to the urban lower middling sorts: being the site of most economic, as well as social, activity. Historians are divided as to whether the eighteenth and early nineteenth centuries witnessed profound changes in the nature of the family and in the ways in which familial hierarchies operated.[14] The evidence from this study suggests that the bulk of the lower middling sorts experienced 'companionate' or 'co-dependent' models of familial and marital relations, rather than those principally founded on patriarchy. Within marriages wives were, as Rosemary O'Day notes, for the most part 'helpmeets, not dependents'.[15] The maintenance of the family was seen as a shared concern, not one where men took sole or primary responsibility. Women's contribution to the family economy could be significant,[16] and gave them a sense of entitlement while helping to ensure the family's social standing and creditworthiness.[17] As Bailey has argued in her study of early modern marriages amongst the middling and lower orders, 'the predicament of wives without their husbands is

[14] See e.g. Lawrence Stone, *The Family, Sex and Marriage in England, 1500–1800* (London, 1977); Randolph Trumbach, *The Rise of the Egalitarian Family: Aristocratic Kinship and Domestic Relations in Eighteenth-Century England* (London, 1978); Bridget Hill, *Women, Work and Sexual Politics in Eighteenth-Century England* (Oxford, 1989); Anna Clark, *The Struggle for the Breeches: Gender and the Making of the British Working Class* (London, 1995), ch. 14; Hunt, *Middling Sort*, 166–70; Joanne Bailey, *Unquiet Lives: Marriage and Marriage Breakdown in England, 1660–1800* (Cambridge, 2003).

[15] Rosemary O'Day, *The Family and Family Relationships, 1500–1900: England, France and the United States of America* (Basingstoke, 1994), 204.

[16] Davidoff and Hall, *Family Fortunes*, ch. 6; Hunt, *The Middling Sort*.

[17] Margaret Hunt, 'Wives and Marital "Rights" in the Court of Exchequer', in P. Griffiths and M. S. R. Jenner (eds.), *Londinopolis: Essays in the Cultural and Social History of Early Modern London* (Manchester, 2000), 118–21; Shani D'Cruze, 'The Middling Sort in Eighteenth-Century Colchester: Independence, Social Relations and the Community

well known, but without their wives, husbands faced the loss of income, property, household management, child care and reputation'.[18]

Family unity was arguably particularly important during periods of intense economic and social upheaval. The late eighteenth and early nineteenth centuries in England have been traditionally associated with rapid change brought about during a period of 'Industrial Revolution'. Although many economic historians now question such a model, and argue instead that industrialization was a gradual process that was extremely diverse in its impact between regions, industries, and over time,[19] marked economic and social transformations still took place in certain sectors of the economy and in particular regions.[20] Urban centres such as Manchester, Leeds, and Sheffield experienced striking and unusual levels of economic growth and urban development compared with much of the rest of the country, and here—if not elsewhere—descriptions of revolutionary change seem justified. This picture of rapid change also holds true for patterns of consumption in these towns, as it seems that their populations were not only producing more, but also consuming in increasing amounts.

The extent to which the type of rapid growth and social and economic transformation witnessed in Manchester, Leeds, and Sheffield affected middling women's experience of work is open to question. However, it seems likely that these places allowed female manufacturers and traders greater independence than more established and less

Broker', in Jonathan Barry and Christopher Brooks (eds.), *The Middling Sort of People: Culture, Society and Politics in England 1550–1800* (Basingstoke, 1994); Craig Muldrew, *The Economy of Obligation: The Culture of Credit and Social Relations in Early Modern England* (London, 1998), 148–59.

[18] Bailey, *Unquiet Lives*, 203–4.

[19] See N. F. R. Crafts, *British Industrial Growth During the Industrial Revolution* (Oxford, 1985); E. A. Wrigley, *Continuity, Chance and Change: The Character of the Industrial Revolution in England* (Cambridge, 1989); Pat Hudson, *The Industrial Revolution* (London, 1992); Patrick O'Brien and Roland Quinault (eds.), *The Industrial Revolution and British Society* (Cambridge, 1993); Maxine Berg, *The Age of Manufactures, 1700–1820*, 2nd edn. (London, 1994); Steven King and Geoff Timmins (eds.), *Making Sense of the Industrial Revolution: English Economy and Society 1700–1850* (Manchester, 2001), ch. 2.

[20] Maxine Berg and Pat Hudson, 'Rehabilitating the Industrial Revolution', *Economic History Review* 45/1 (1992), 24–50.

dynamic market towns, such as Oxford.[21] Recent research on other urban centres in this period that experienced fast growth, notably London and towns in the Midlands, also present more extensive pictures of middling women's economic activity.[22] Britain, and England in particular, is often celebrated for the precocity of its urban and industrial development in the late eighteenth and early nineteenth centuries. But this does not mean that the picture of female economic activity presented here was unique. Middling women could be found operating freely in the French guild system,[23] trading independently in Edinburgh, Glasgow, and Geneva,[24] and acting as merchants in northern German and Scandinavian towns.[25] Across Europe examples can be found of bourgeois women assisting in the family firm well into the nineteenth century.[26] A lack of broad statistical evidence makes it difficult to make direct comparisons between towns in Europe and

[21] Wendy Thwaites, 'Women in the Marketplace: Oxfordshire c. 1690–1800', *Midland History* 9 (1984), 23–42; Mary Prior, 'Women and the Urban Economy: Oxford 1500–1800', in Prior (ed.), *Women in English Society 1500–1800* (London, 1985).

[22] Nicola Pullin, '"Business is Just Life": The Practice, Prescription and Legal Position of Women in Business, 1700–1850', Ph.D. thesis (London, 2001). A revised version of the thesis will appear as Nicola Phillips, *Women in Business, 1700–1850* (Woodbridge, 2006); Maxine Berg, 'Women's Property and the Industrial Revolution', *Journal of Interdisciplinary History* 24/2 (1993), 233–50; Christine Wiskin, 'Women, Finance and Credit in England, c. 1780–1826', Ph.D. thesis (Warwick, 2000); Penelope Lane 'Women in the Regional Economy, the East Midlands 1700–1830', Ph.D. thesis (Warwick, 1999).

[23] Margaret Darrow, *Revolution in the House: Family, Class and Inheritance in Southern France, 1775–1825* (Princeton, NJ, 1989); Cynthia Maria Truant, 'Parisian Guildswomen and the (Sexual) Politics of Privilege: Defending Their Patrimonies in Print', in Elizabeth C. Goldsmith and Dena Goodman (eds.), *Going Public: Women and Publishing in Early Modern France* (Ithaca, NY, 1995); Carolyn Sargentson, *Merchants and Luxury Markets: The Marchands Merciers of Eighteenth-Century Paris* (London, 1996); Daryl Hafter, 'Female Masters in Eighteenth-Century Rouen', *French Historical Studies* 20/1 (1997), 1–54.

[24] Elizabeth Sanderson, *Women and Work in Eighteenth-Century Edinburgh* (Basingstoke, 1996); E. Monter, 'Women in Calvinist Geneva, 1550–1800', *Signs* 6 (1980), 189–209, pp. 199–204.

[25] Daniel A. Rabuzzi, 'Women as Merchants in Eighteenth-Century Northern Germany: The Case of Stralsund, 1750–1830', *Central European History* 28/4 (1995), 435–56; see p. 441 for a discussion of Scandinavian towns.

[26] Bonnie Smith, *Ladies of the Leisure Class: The Bourgeoises of Northern France in the Nineteenth Century* (Princeton, NJ, 1981), ch. 3; Deborah Simonton, *A History of Women's Work, 1700 to the Present* (London, 1998), 156–9. Other accounts contradict this picture of middling women's economic freedom: see e.g. Merry Weisner, 'Guilds, Male Bonding and Women's Work in Early Modern Germany', *Gender and History* 1/2 (1989), 125–37.

north America during the eighteenth and nineteenth centuries.[27] It seems likely, however, that middling women's involvement in business was most prevalent in towns that were undergoing the early stages of modern industrial development and consumer growth. In such relatively fluid and changing environments, businesswomen found themselves able to participate in great numbers and with a sort of independence that may well have been curtailed in subsequent years.[28]

In order to assess this process, the book begins with an examination of the ways in which Manchester, Leeds, and Sheffield were transformed between 1760 and 1830. The first chapter explores the development of urban society through a study of newspaper advertisements, the writings of contemporary commentators, and patterns of urban building and improvement. It argues for the existence of strong provincial identities, and describes the emergence of a self-confident middling, consumerist culture in each of the three towns. Chapter 2 introduces the subject of women's work with a detailed examination of trade directories in Manchester, Leeds, and Sheffield. This suggests that middling women were a significant and consistent feature of commercial life in these towns during the late eighteenth and early nineteenth centuries. While women of the lower middling sorts were most likely to be involved in certain sectors of the economy traditionally associated with women's work—namely clothing, food and drink, and shopkeeping and dealing—they could be found running most types of lower middling business throughout the period. Chapter 3 builds upon this

---

[27] Though see Claudia Goldin, 'The Economic Status of Women in the Early Republic: Quantitative Evidence', *Journal of Interdisciplinary History* 16/3 (1986), 375–404, which describes women's labourforce participation in Philadelphia between the 1790s and 1860s in great detail. However, her categories of occupational analysis do not easily lend themselves to a comparison with this study.

[28] This suggests a model of change in middling female economic activity during the eighteenth and nineteenth centuries that echoes the findings of Maxine Berg, 'What Difference Did Women's Work Make to the Industrial Revolution?', *History Workshop Journal* 35 (1993), 22–44; and Katrina Honeyman and Jordan Goodman, 'Women's Work, Labour Markets and Gender Conflict in Europe, 1500–1900', *Economic History Review* 44 (1991), 608–28, on those lower down on the social scale. See also Jean H. Quataert, 'The Shaping of Women's Work in Manufacturing: Guilds, Households, and the State in Central Europe, 1648–1870', *American Historical Review* 90/5 (1985), 1122–48; Rabuzzi, 'Women as Merchants in Eighteenth-Century Northern Germany'.

depiction of the ubiquity of women in business, and examines their appearance in advertising, at the centre of business networks and their physical presence as traders in town centres. It also examines the ways in which businesswomen represented themselves in public, and suggests that occupation could be central to middling notions of femininity, in addition to those 'domestic' qualities that we are used to associating with women in this period. The final two chapters concern women's involvement in different types of enterprise: principally family firms, but also as independent traders and in partnerships with others. In Chapter 4, evidence from directories, court records, and correspondence suggests the variety of forms that female engagement with commerce could take, and the differing hierarchies within small businesses. It shows that women were not always subordinate to men, and that considerations of age, wealth, and skill could override those of gender. Chapter 5 explores the issue of female power more closely, using legal documents to examine women's relationship to property and the law, and diaries and correspondence to judge the degree to which businesswomen could operate independently of their menfolk. Here again a broad spectrum of female experience is uncovered, with evidence of female agency as common as material describing their subjugation.

This book reveals a complex picture of female participation in business. As we shall see, factors traditionally thought to discriminate against women's commercial activity—particularly property laws and ideas about gender and respectability—did have significant impacts upon female enterprise. Yet it is also evident that women were not automatically economically or socially marginalized as a result, and that individuals could experience a great variety of opportunities and obstacles as they sought to achieve financial security. Being female might greatly affect the ways in which women took part in commerce and manufacturing, but this does not mean that gender entirely predetermined the nature of their involvement. The woman of business might be subject to various constraints, but at the same time, she could be blessed with a number of freedoms, and a degree of independence, that set her apart from most other women—and many men—in late Georgian society.

1

Manchester, Leeds, and Sheffield in the Later Georgian Age

As the 'shock' cities of their age, northern industrial towns feature prominently in most accounts of Victorian England. Whether viewed as dynamic, productive, and self-confident, or squalid, dangerous, and exploitative, they appear central to both contemporary and historical narratives. Yet these same places have been largely overlooked in the period leading up to large-scale industrial development. Towns such as Manchester, Leeds, and Sheffield have generally been presented as factory- or at least manufacturing-based societies, whose rise to prominence was a largely nineteenth-century phenomenon.[1] Despite the work of economic historians which suggests that industrial development in the early decades of the nineteenth century was mostly 'traditional' in form—small-scale and workshop- or domestically based, without the rapid introduction of new technology, and accompanied by a proliferation of service activities[2]—we have learnt

[1] E. J. Connell and M. Ward, 'Industrial Development, 1780–1914', in Derek Fraser (ed.), *A History of Modern Leeds* (Manchester, 1980); Geoffrey Tweedale, *Steel City: Entrepreneurship, Strategy, and Technology in Sheffield 1743–1993* (Oxford, 1995); David Hey, *A History of Sheffield* (Lancaster, 1998); Alan Kidd, *Manchester*, 2nd edn. (Keele, 1996); R. Lloyd-Jones and M. J. Lewis, *Manchester in the Age of the Factory* (London, 1988); S. Pollard, *A History of Labour in Sheffield* (Liverpool, 1959).

[2] Raphael Samuel, 'Workshop of the World: Steam Power and Hand Technology in Mid-Victorian Britain', *History Workshop Journal* 3 (1977), 6–72; N. F. R. Crafts, *British Economic Growth During the Industrial Revolution* (Oxford, 1985); E. A. Wrigley, *Continuity, Chance and Change: The Character of the Industrial Revolution in England* (Cambridge, 1988); Maxine Berg, *The Age of Manufactures, 1700–1820: Industry, Innovation and Work in Britain*, 2nd edn. (London, 1994).

surprisingly little about service, retailing, and small-scale manufacturing industries in the industrial towns of the north of England.
Moreover, we remain largely ignorant of the ways in which society in
these places operated more generally: about, for example, the rise of
the middling sorts, cultural consumption, sociability, and the emergence of a widening public sphere.[3]

Recent historical work has provided a serious challenge to more traditional views. One of the major concerns of the second volume of the
Cambridge Urban History of Britain was to demonstrate that many of
the pivotal changes of the early nineteenth century derived from
developments that took place in the previous period.[4] This shift in
chronological focus to the 'long' eighteenth century of 1700–1840 is
particularly critical in the case of the industrial or manufacturing
towns, which could appear lost in social and cultural history accounts
(in contrast to the work of political historians) which focused on
'short' versions of the eighteenth or nineteenth centuries, but which
failed to examine the transition between the two.[5] A new approach
that encompasses the late eighteenth and early nineteenth centuries
allows us to explore a crucial period in the development of provincial
industrial towns. By examining public building and improvement,
local guides and directories, and newspaper advertising, this chapter
suggests some new ways of viewing the histories of towns such as
Manchester, Leeds, and Sheffield during the later Georgian period.

---

[3] Though see Helen Berry, 'Promoting Taste in the Provincial Press: National and Local
Culture in Eighteenth-Century Newcastle upon Tyne', *British Journal for Eighteenth-
Century Studies* 25/1 (2002), 1–17; and Jon Stobart, 'Culture Versus Commerce: Societies
and Spaces for Elites in Eighteenth-Century Liverpool', *Journal of Historical Geography*
28/4 (2002), 471–85.

[4] Peter Clark (ed.), *The Cambridge Urban History of Britain*, ii. *1540–1840*
(Cambridge, 2000), 23. See also Rosemary Sweet, *The English Town 1680–1840:
Government, Society and Culture* (Harlow, 1999); Joyce Ellis, *The Georgian Town,
1680–1840* (Basingstoke, 2001); Janet Wolff and John Seed (eds.), *The Culture of Capital:
Art, Power and the Nineteenth-Century Middle Class* (Manchester, 1988); R. G. Wilson,
Gentlemen Merchants: the Merchant Community of Leeds, 1700–1830 (Manchester, 1971).

[5] Accounts which describe a 'short' eighteenth century include the pioneering
P. J. Corfield, *The Impact of English Towns 1700–1800* (Oxford, 1982) and Peter Borsay, *The
English Urban Renaissance: Culture and Society in the Provincial Town, 1660–1770* (Oxford,
1989). The nineteenth century has produced an even greater array of texts, many of which
focus specifically on northern and industrial towns: examples are listed in n. 1 above.

There were notable similarities between these towns. Most importantly, they were linked by their recent and rapid expansion and by their
association with manufacturing and industrial development. However,
these urban centres also differed from one another in significant ways:
developing their own forms of social structure, economic organization,
and culture. Perhaps the most obvious area of divergence was industrial
specialism. Each of the towns is traditionally linked with a specific, and
different, type of manufacturing: Manchester with cotton, Leeds with
wool, and Sheffield with metalware, and cutlery in particular. Yet
because of their importance as regional service centres, the towns were
never truly 'industrial' in that they derived all or most of their income
from these sectors; nor were spending patterns dictated by an impoverished class of factory labourers. Manchester was not a mill town in the
way some of its neighbours were.[6] Even in 1815, when employment in
the cotton industry in Lancashire was probably at its height, the estimated number of cotton workers here was less than 12 per cent of the
total population.[7] Despite the importance and fame of the cutlery
trades in Sheffield, Hey notes that the proportion of the workforce
occupied in this area remained constant as the population grew during
the eighteenth century,[8] whilst Morris has shown the preponderance of
shopkeepers and tradesmen (rather than manufacturers) among the
middle classes of both Leeds and Manchester in the early 1830s.[9]

Local government was another obvious area of disparity between
the towns. Manchester was not incorporated until the mid-
nineteenth century. Before that the Court Leet, and latterly the police
commissioners, were responsible for the town's affairs.[10] Sheffield too

---

[6] See J. K. Walton, *Lancashire: A Social History, 1558–1939* (Manchester, 1987);
D. A. Farnie, *The English Cotton Industry and the World Market, 1815–1896* (Oxford,
1979); Lloyd-Jones and Lewis, *Manchester in the Age of the Factory*; Roger Scola, *Feeding the
Victorian City: The Food Supply of Manchester 1770–1870* (Manchester, 1992), 21–3.

[7] Scola, *Feeding the Victorian City*, 22.   [8] Hey, *History of Sheffield*, 63.

[9] R. J. Morris, 'Structure, Culture and Society in British Towns', in Martin Daunton
(ed.), *The Cambridge Urban History of Britain*, iii. *1840–1950* (Cambridge, 2000), 402;
also his *Class, Sect and Party: The Making of the British Middle Class, Leeds 1820–1850*
(Manchester, 1990), ch. 2. See also Richard Trainor, 'The Middle Class', in *Cambridge
Urban History of Britain*, iii. *1840–1950*, 678–9.

[10] Arthur Redford, *The History of Local Government in Manchester*, i. *Manor and
Township* (London, 1939).

was unincorporated, and partially controlled—at least in theory—by the Cutlers' Guild, although by the late eighteenth century the power of the guilds had declined here as elsewhere.[11] Leeds, on the other hand, had long held its Charter, and its administration was dominated by a civic elite.[12] Without similar power structures, places such as Manchester and Sheffield could appear either worryingly chaotic or marvellously free of constraints on enterprise. Contemporaries often associated the absence of a corporation with increased economic freedom and political peace.[13] Yet neither assumption was necessarily true,[14] and in the case of the towns under consideration, it is a generalization which fails to stand up to much scrutiny. All three urban centres demonstrated rapid and impressive economic growth during the late eighteenth and early nineteenth centuries, with little evidence that Leeds was held back by its system of government.

Moreover, Manchester, Leeds, and Sheffield each produced highly divided, lively, and individual brands of politics, frequently associated with religious rivalries: sometimes joining in with fierce national debates—such as those surrounding the American Revolution, the anti-slavery movement, and the Queen Caroline Affair—but often occupied with more local divisions, and frequently blurring the line between the two.[15] Although towns that lacked parliamentary representation were often thought to be more peaceful by contemporaries,[16] Manchester, Leeds, and Sheffield all witnessed highly partisan

[11] J. R. Kellett, 'The Breakdown of Gild and Corporation Control over the Handicraft and Retail Trade in London', *Economic History Review*, ns 10/3 (1958), 381–94; M. J. Walker, 'The Extent of Guild Control in Trades in England, c. 1660–1820: A Study Based on a Sample of Provincial Towns and London Companies', Ph.D. thesis (Cambridge, 1986).   [12] Wilson, *Gentlemen Merchants*, ch. 8.
[13] Joseph Aston, *A Picture of Manchester* (Manchester, 1819), 31; Alexis de Tocqueville, *Journeys to England and Ireland*, trans. George Lawrence and K. P. Mayer, ed. J. P. Mayer (London, 1958), 105; Lloyd-Jones and Lewis, *Manchester and the Age of the Factory*, 32–7; Scola, *Feeding the Victorian City*, 158–9; F. Vigier, *Change and Apathy: Liverpool and Manchester During the Industrial Revolution* (Cambridge, Mass., 1970), 98.
[14] Ellis, *The Georgian Town*, 36.
[15] Hannah Barker, *Newspapers, Politics and English Society, 1695–1855* (Harlow, 2000), 159, 166, 172–4.
[16] See e.g. 'A Native of the Town', *A Description of Manchester* (Manchester, 1783), 93; Edward Goodwin in *Gentleman's Magazine* (1764), 160.

political behaviour. Manchester was divided between high and low church parties from the first half of the eighteenth century.[17] James Wheeler's account of Manchester politics also notes factional rivalries in the early 1760s,[18] which were to continue during the following decades,[19] and resurfaced again between dissenting manufacturers and more established Tories at the start of the nineteenth century.[20] In Leeds, the long-standing relationship between the local gentry and manufacturers was challenged in the late eighteenth century by rival manufacturing and merchant families who had a Whig dissenting, rather than a Tory Anglican, background.[21] In Sheffield, a unique brand of radical politics was evident from before the French Revolution, whilst the *Sheffield Register*, under the editorship of Joseph Gales, was one of the most famous radical provincial newspapers during the 1790s.[22] Indeed, as unenfranchised towns, lacking direct representation at Westminster, all three centres provided fertile ground for local variations of radical and loyalist political activity during the wars with Revolutionary and Napoleonic France, and subsequent reformist activity after 1815.[23] This was to prove the basis for later assaults on the cultural and political dominance of the capital

[17] Paul Langford, *Public Life and the Propertied Englishman* (Oxford, 1990), 120; Craig Andrew Horner, ' "Proper Persons to Deal With": Identification and Attitudes of Middling Society in Manchester, c1730–c1760', Ph.D. thesis (Manchester, 2001).

[18] James Wheeler, *Manchester: Its Political, Social and Commercial History* (London, 1836).

[19] Edward Baines, *History of the County Palatine and Duchy of Lancaster*, 4 vols. (London, 1836), ii; Archibald Prentice, *Historical Sketches and Personal Recollections of Manchester*, 2nd edn. (London, 1851); J. V. Pickstone and S. V. F. Butler, 'The Politics of Medicine in Manchester, 1788–1792: Hospital Reform and Public Health Services in the Early Industrial City', *Medical History* 28 (1984), 227–49.

[20] Sweet, *English Town*, 124.

[21] Wilson, *Gentlemen Merchants*; R. J. Morris, *Class, Sect and Party: The Making of the British Middle Class, Leeds 1820–1850* (Manchester, 1990).

[22] M. J. Smith, 'English Radical Newspapers in the French Revolutionary Era, 1790–1803', Ph.D. thesis (London, 1979); Barker, *Newspapers, Politics and English Society*, 177–9; M. E. Happs, 'The Sheffield Newspaper Press and Parliamentary Reform, 1787–1831,' B.Litt. thesis (Oxford, 1973); E. P. Thompson, *The Making of the English Working Class* (London, 1963), 113.

[23] Donald Read, *Press and People, 1790–1850: Opinion in Three English Cities* (Aldershot, 1993); H. T. Dickinson, *The Politics of the People in Eighteenth-Century Britain* (Basingstoke, 1995), ch. 8.

itself: a history with which we are more familiar, but which was rooted in earlier developments that have remained relatively obscure.

Despite their similarities then, Manchester, Leeds, and Sheffield developed distinct and differing forms of urban life in the period under study. As Joyce Ellis has noted, 'neither the opening up of a national market, nor the creation of a national society, were incompatible with the emergence of strong regional identities, based on dynamic urban centres'.[24] Dror Wahrman has also presented eighteenth-century provincial consciousness as subject to great regional diversity, describing a 'polymorphous communal-provincial culture'.[25] This chapter does not seek to deny differences between Manchester, Leeds, and Sheffield, although it does acknowledge important shared characteristics. In terms of urban development on a national scale, arguably such towns belong to a second wave of 'urban renaissance'—but one that was very different to that described by Peter Borsay for places such as Warwick, Bath, and Winchester.[26] Rather than being elite-led and leisure-orientated, the 'northern urban renaissance' was the product of middling, consumerist cultures, firmly rooted in their localities and subject—at least in theory—to the sobering influences of hard work and religion. As this chapter will demonstrate, the behaviour and outlook of the inhabitants of industrial towns challenges simplistic understandings of metropolitan cultural dominance and questions the utility of national models of consumerism and 'politeness' that ignore the importance of regional variation and provincialism. In this respect,

[24] Ellis, *Georgian Town*, 140. See also Jonathan Barry, 'Provincial Town Culture, 1640–1780: Urbane or Civic?', in Joan H. Pittock and Andrew Wear (eds.), *Interpretation and Cultural History* (Basingstoke, 1991).

[25] Although he states that this provincial culture was increasingly 'plebeian' in character, whereas middling sorts and local elites were more likely to participate in a 'national society' focused on London: Dror Wahrman, 'National Society, Communal Culture: An Argument about the Recent Historiography of Eighteenth-Century Britain', *Social History*, 17/1 (1992), 43–72, p. 43; Hannah Barker, *Newspapers, Politics and Public Opinion in Late Eighteenth-Century England* (Oxford, 1998); and *Newspapers, Politics and English Society*.

[26] Borsay, *English Urban Renaissance*. Although Borsay does not ignore industrial and commercial towns, noting various developments in building and leisure provision that took place there earlier on in the eighteenth century, they do not provide the focus for his description of urban change between 1660 and 1770.

Jonathan Barry's contention that the social and political cultures of provincial towns were to a large extent indigenous, is important.[27] The acknowledgement of distinct civic consciousnesses in northern towns is key to identifying their distinctiveness compared with other provincial centres and with London. It is also important to understand the marked divergences between Manchester, Leeds, and Sheffield themselves. This point is further emphasized by Estabrook's reminder of the influence of 'topographical setting', localism, and the cultural affinity of individuals with their place of provenance.[28] The importance of place and of civic pride are crucial elements in the discussion of urban cultural identity that follows.

URBAN GROWTH

Although many provincial towns experienced huge change during the late eighteenth and early nineteenth centuries, perhaps nowhere in Georgian Britain witnessed more dramatic upheaval than the industrial and manufacturing towns of northern England. Certainly, few places can have attracted more comments on the nature and pace of change from contemporaries at once excited and horrified by them. Manchester, Leeds, and Sheffield were among the fastest growing towns in late Hanoverian England. Between the last quarter of the eighteenth century and the first three decades of the nineteenth, the populations of these urban centres increased at least threefold.[29]

[27] Barry, 'Provincial Town Culture, 1640–1780: Urbane or Civic?'
[28] Carl Estabrook, *Urbane and Rustic England: Cultural Ties and Social Spheres in the Provinces, 1660–1760* (Stanford, Calif., 1999).
[29] Corfield, *Impact of English Towns*, 9; C. M. Law, 'Some Notes on the Urban Population of England and Wales in the Eighteenth Century', *Local Historian* 10 (1972), 13–26; John Langton, 'Urban Growth and Economic Change: From the Late Seventeenth Century to 1841', in Clark (ed.), *The Cambridge Urban History of Britain*, ii. *1540–1840*, 474, 484–5; W. H. Chaloner, 'Manchester in the Latter Half of the Eighteenth Century', *Bulletin of the John Rylands Library* 42/1(1959), 40–60, p. 42; C. J. Morgan, 'Demographic Change, 1771–1911', in Fraser (ed.), *History of Modern Leeds*, 46–7; Sidney Pollard, 'The Growth of Population', in D. L. Linton (ed.), *Sheffield and its Region* (Sheffield, 1956), 172–4; J. Stobart, 'An Eighteenth-Century

By 1801, all were ranked amongst the eight largest provincial towns in England.[30] After visiting Manchester in 1784, the industrial spy, de Givry, reported to his masters in Paris that Manchester was not only 'large and superb', but that it 'has been built almost entirely in the past 20 to 25 years'.[31] His view is supported by population estimates. A survey conducted between 1773 and 1774 of 'the houses and inhabitants of the town and parish of Manchester' by 'a person employed for the purpose . . . at the joint expense of a few gentlemen in the town' counted 24,386 inhabitants in 5,678 families.[32] More modern estimates have suggested that in 1775 the population was closer to 30,000.[33] By 1788, the town's population had increased further to almost 43,000.[34] When the first nationwide census was taken in 1801, numbers had risen to 70,000. This climbed further to almost 80,000 in 1811, over 108,000 in 1821, and more than 140,000 in 1831.[35]

Before the first census of the Leeds population was taken in 1801, two earlier counts of the town's inhabitants were carried out in 1771 and 1775. The first, conducted by Joseph Priestley on behalf of Richard Price, arrived at a figure of 16,380 for the Leeds township. Four years later, Dr Price's friends carried out another canvass and recorded a population of 17,121:[36] a figure that Law suggests should have been closer to 24,000.[37] The population grew rapidly during subsequent years: reaching over 30,000 by 1801, more than 48,000

Revolution? Investigating Urban Growth in North-West England 1664–1801', *Urban History* 23 (1996), 26–47.

[30] Joyce Ellis, 'Regional and County Centres, 1700–1840', in Clark (ed.), *Cambridge Urban History of Britain*, ii. *1540–1840*, 679.

[31] Chaloner, 'Manchester in the Latter Half of the Eighteenth Century', 42. See Thomas Percival, 'Observations on the State of Population in Manchester', in *Essays Medical, Philosophical, and Experimental*, 4th edn., 2 vols. (Warrington, 1788), ii. 1–16; 'Further Observations on the State of the Population in Manchester', ibid. 17–37; 'Observations on the State of the Population in Manchester Concluded', ibid. 38–67.

[32] Thomas Henry, 'Observations on the Bills of Mortality of the Towns of Manchester and Salford', *Memoirs of the Literary and Philosophical Society of Manchester*, iii (1795), 160–2.

[33] Law, 'Some Notes on the Urban Population of England and Wales', 24.

[34] Henry, 'Observations on the Bills of Mortality of the Towns of Manchester and Salford', 160–2.   [35] Vigier, *Change and Apathy*, 139.

[36] Morgan, 'Demographic Change, 1771–1911', 46–7. See also *A Walk Through Leeds, or, Stranger's Guide . . .* (Leeds, 1806), 3–4.

[37] Law, 'Some Notes on the Urban Population of England and Wales', 26.

in 1821, and leaping to over 71,000 by 1831.[38] Sheffield also grew markedly during the later eighteenth century. In 1750, the inhabitants of the town numbered some 12,000 with the parish as a whole standing at 20,000. By 1775 the population was probably 27,000.[39] During the second half of the century, prior to the first census in 1801, this figure more than doubled with almost 46,000 inhabitants in the parish, of whom perhaps as many as 35,000 lived in the built-up urban centre. The town's population continued to grow in the nineteenth century, reaching 65,000 by 1821.[40]

As Sheffield grew in terms of its population, it also expanded physically, as building encroached on former countryside.[41] During the 1770s, Manchester was also said to have 'extended on every side, and such was the influx of inhabitants, that though a great number of houses were built, they were occupied even before they were finished'.[42] The press of commercial activity further resulted in the demolition of large parts of Manchester's medieval centre. The density of Manchester's population rose considerably: from 14.3 persons per acre in 1774, to 44.6 in 1801, 50.4 in 1811, and 68.5 in 1821.[43] Approximately two and a half thousand houses were constructed between 1774 and 1788, 4,000 more in the period 1788 to 1801, and a further 6,000 between 1801 and 1821.[44] Maurice Beresford has pointed out that half of the houses standing in Leeds township in 1801 had been built since 1780.[45] Here too the growth of housing was dramatic: in 1772 there were 3,347 houses recorded, by 1793 this had jumped to 6,691. This figure had reached 11,191 by 1811 and 19,986 by 1841.[46] The effect of piecemeal development in Sheffield caused one commentator to remark that 'as its commerce was extended, and population increased, streets were

---

[38] Wilson, *Gentlemen Merchants*, 202; M. Yasumoto, 'Urbanization and Population in an English Town', *Keio Economic Studies* 10 (1973), 61–94, pp. 70–1.

[39] Law, 'Some Notes on the Urban Population of England and Wales', 26.

[40] Pollard, 'The Growth of Population', 172–4; Hey, *History of Sheffield*, 91.

[41] Hey, *History of Sheffield*, 92.

[42] Thomas Henry, cited in Chaloner, 'Manchester in the Latter Half of the Eighteenth Century', 41.   [43] Vigier, *Change and Apathy*, 130.

[44] Ibid. 132. See also C. W. Chalkin, *The Provincial Towns of Georgian England: A Study in the Building Process 1740–1820* (London, 1974).

[45] Maurice Beresford, 'The Face of Leeds, 1780–1914', in Fraser (ed.), *History of Modern Leeds*, 72–4.   [46] Ibid. 73.

lengthened, and new ones added in every direction, without the least attention to uniformity and order'.[47] Another observer noted, in the *Leeds Mercury* in 1852, that the street plan of Leeds 'looked as if the town had used an earthquake as an architect'.[48]

Other commentators were less critical of urban expansion and celebrated instead the alacrity with which the inhabitants of industrial towns added to their stock of public buildings and invested in cultural space. Joseph Aston remarked in 1819 that 'during the last fifty years, perhaps no town in the United Kingdom, has made such rapid improvements as Manchester. Every year has witnessed an increase of buildings. Churches, Chapels, places of amusement and streets, have started into existence with a rapidity which has constantly afforded matter of astonishment in the minds of occasional visitors.'[49] Spurred on by a combination of commercial motives and cultural aspirations, the residents of northern manufacturing towns were busy transforming the urban landscape.[50] Grady's survey of Leeds and Sheffield during the eighteenth and nineteenth centuries shows a steep rise in public building after 1760: in Leeds this was marked by the erection of the Concert Hall, the General Infirmary, the Leeds Library, and the town's first theatre between 1767 and 1771; in Sheffield the same period witnessed the opening of the Assembly Rooms and Theatre, the town library, and three new places of worship.[51] For its part, Manchester saw its first infirmary built in 1752 with a lunatic asylum added in 1766.[52] The Theatre Royal was opened in 1775, followed by a Concert Hall in 1777; a Literary and

---

[47] Joseph Hunter, *Hallamshire: The History and Topography of the Parish of Sheffield . . .* (London, 1819), 125.

[48] Cited in Maurice Beresford, 'The Making of a Townscape: Richard Paley in the East End of Leeds, 1771–1803', in C. W. Chalkin and M. A. Havender (eds.), *Rural Change and Urban Growth 1500–1800* (London, 1974), 287.

[49] J. Aston, *Picture of Manchester* (Manchester, 1816), 19. See also John Holmes, *A Sketch of the History of Leeds* (Leeds, 1872).

[50] On this process in Leeds see Morris, *Class, Sect and Party*, ch. 2.

[51] Kevin Grady, *The Georgian Public Buildings of Leeds and the West Riding*, Publications of the Thoresby Society 62 (Leeds, 1989), 162–3, 174–5; James Raven, *Judging New Wealth: Popular Publishing and Responses to Commerce in England, 1750–1800* (Oxford, 1992), 113. See also M. Beresford, 'East End, West End: The Face of Leeds during Urbanisation 1684–1842', *Transactions of the Thoresby Society*, 60/1 (1988).

[52] W. E. A. Axon, *The Annals of Manchester* (Manchester, 1886), 91, 97.

Philosophical Society was started in 1781, and the Assembly Rooms opened in 1792.[53]

The later eighteenth century witnessed a rash of library openings in the north of England. According to Kelly, a subscription library was founded in Manchester in 1765, with Leeds following suit in 1768 and Sheffield in 1771.[54] More impressive yet was Manchester's Portico Library, which was erected between 1802 and 1805 for around £7,000 and boasted a library and a newsroom.[55] The Leeds Subscription Library, opened in 1808, itself cost some £5,000.[56] Both the Leeds Philosophical Hall and the town's Public Baths were built between 1819 and 1821: the latter offering bathers premises that were both 'lavish and commodious'.[57] The Sheffield Music Hall opened in 1825 and Manchester's grand Concert Hall in 1831.[58] In addition to leisure facilities, the early nineteenth century also witnessed the building of infirmaries and medical schools, established in Leeds and Sheffield in 1828 and 1831 respectively.[59]

At the same time that this frenzied building was taking place, increasing amounts of parliamentary time were taken up with 'improving' measures for industrial northern towns, as local agencies and interest groups petitioned parliament for better water supply, sewerage, streets, pavements, street lighting, and retailing facilities, and the provision of turnpike roads, canals, and—in the nineteenth century—railways.[60] While in the 1760s, only a handful

[53] C. W. Chalkin, 'Capital Expenditure on Building for Cultural Purposes in Provincial England, 1730–1830', *Business History* 20 (1980), 51–70, p. 54; Axon, *Annals of Manchester*, 103; Aston, *Picture of Manchester*, 187, 189.

[54] Thomas Kelly, *Early Public Libraries* (London, 1966), 126. There is some suggestion that a smaller-scale subscription library was founded at a slightly earlier date in Manchester.

[55] Ann Brooks, 'The Portico Library and Newsroom', MA thesis (Manchester, 1992).

[56] Chalkin, 'Capital Expenditure', 60; Grady, *Georgian Public Buildings*, 22.

[57] Grady, *Georgian Public Buildings*, 33.

[58] Ibid.; Axon, *Annals of Manchester*, 99, 104, 184; Aston, *Picture of Manchester*, 189.

[59] Grady, *Georgian Public Buildings*, 20.

[60] This section is based on an examination of a database of the legislation of the Westminster parliament, 1660–1830, by Julian Hoppit and Andrew Hann. I am very grateful to Joanna Innes and Julian Hoppit, under whose direction it was compiled, for access to their data. For a discussion of their project and its wider findings, see Hoppit,

of these measures had emanated from Manchester, Leeds, and Sheffield, by the 1820s the number had grown sevenfold.[61] This was a rate of increase more than three times the national average. In addition, as their populations rose and the towns' positions as regional commercial centres grew, pressure on existing retailing provision increased and new and more specialized markets and shops were established.[62] Moreover, as shopping became reconceptualized—at least by the middling orders and elites—as a leisure activity in the eighteenth century, retailing districts became one of the main beneficiaries of improvement:[63] streets were widened, paving and lighting provided, and buildings improved in central shopping areas such

Innes, and John Styles, 'Towards a History of Parliamentary Legislation, 1660–1800', *Parliamentary History* 13/3 (1994), 312–21; Joanna Innes, 'The Local Acts of a National Parliament: Parliament's Role in Sanctioning Local Action in Eighteenth-Century Britain', *Parliamentary History* 17/1 (1998), 23–47.

[61] In contrast to towns in the south of England which saw much earlier programmes of improvement: E. L. Jones and M. E. Falkus, 'Urban Improvement and the English Economy in the Seventeenth and Eighteenth Centuries', *Research in Economic History* iv, ed. P. J. Uselding (Greenwich, Conn., 1979), repr. in Peter Borsay (ed.), *The Eighteenth-Century Town: A Reader in English Urban History 1688–1820* (London, 1990). See also Joanna Innes and Nicholas Rogers, 'Politics and Government 1700–1840', in Clark (ed.), *Cambridge Urban History of Britain*, ii. 1540–1840.

[62] Scola, *Feeding the Victorian City*, 150; James Ogden, *Manchester a Hundred Years Ago* (Manchester, 1887; repr. of 1783 publication), 69–71; K. Grady, 'Profit, Property Interests, and Public Spirit: The Provision of Markets and Commercial Amenities in Leeds, 1822–29', *Transactions of the Thoresby Society* 54/3 (1979), 165–95, pp. 165–6; Hey, *History of Sheffield*, 48–9; John Reilly, *The History of Manchester*, 1 vol. only (Manchester, 1861), i. 260. On similar developments in the Midlands, see Andrew Hann, 'Industrialisation and the Service Economy' in *Towns, Regions and Industries: Urban and Industrial Change, 1700–1840*, ed. Jon Stobart and Neil Raven (Manchester, 2005); and Jon Stobart and Andrew Hann, 'Retailing Revolution in the Eighteenth Century: Evidence from North-West England', *Business History* 46/2 (2004), 171–94. I am grateful to Andrew Hann and John Stobart for allowing me to read these pieces prior to publication.

[63] Helen Berry, 'Polite Consumption: Shopping in Eighteenth-Century England', *Transactions of the Royal Historical Society* 12 (2002), 375–94; Andrew Hann, 'The Production of Leisure Space in the 18th Century Town', unpublished paper: I am grateful to the author for a copy of this. In 'Urban Improvement in the Nottinghamshire Market Town, 1770–1840', *Midland History* 25 (2000), 98–114, Catherine Smith argues that improvements were largely concerned with aesthetics and providing spaces for polite members of society, whereas Manchester, Leeds, and Sheffield appear to have been improved for more obviously economic reasons.

as Sheffield's Norfolk Street, Market Street in Manchester, and Briggate in Leeds. Here, the 'consumer revolution' and 'convulsion of getting and spending' that McKendrick and others have described were much in evidence.[64]

As Manchester grew as a regional centre, it developed specialist and luxury trades and crafts such as silversmiths and jewellers, coachmakers, wine and spirit merchants, barometer and looking-glass makers—all of which nearby towns such as Bolton and Bury lacked.[65] Similarly, Wilson has noted that economic growth in Georgian Leeds was marked by an increasing diversification of craft industries as it became 'a centre for entertainment and wholesale distribution, for books and newspapers, wallpapers, chinaware, bricks, tailoring, and the best wigs, medical treatment and furniture'.[66] Indeed, Jon Stobart has claimed that industrial centres offered their residents a greater range of luxury trades and services than most county and resort towns during this period.[67] An examination of trade directories for the three towns has confirmed such a finding.[68] They reveal a marked growth in the number and range of trades listed in Manchester, Leeds, and Sheffield: in each case increases are shown of over 300 per cent between 1773/4 (1797 in the case of Leeds) and 1826/8.[69]

---

[64] Neil Mckendrick, John Brewer, and J. H. Plumb, *The Birth of a Consumer Society: The Commercialisation of Eighteenth-Century England* (London, 1982); B. Fine and E. Leopold, *The World of Consumption* (London, 1993); John Brewer and Roy Porter (eds.), *Consumption and the World of Goods* (London, 1993); Beverly Lemire, *Fashion's Favourite: The Cotton Trade and the Consumer in Britain, 1660–1800* (Oxford, 1991).

[65] Chalkin, *Provincial Towns of Georgian England*, 38.

[66] Wilson, *Gentlemen Merchants*; W. G. Rimmer, 'The Industrial Profile of Leeds, 1740–1840', *Transactions of the Thoresby Society* 14/2 (1967), 130–57; Yasumoto, 'Urbanization and Population in an English Town'. See also Ellis, 'Regional and Country Centres', 684–90.

[67] J. Stobart, 'In Search of a Leisure Hierarchy: English Spa Towns and their Place in the Urban System', in P. Borsay, G. Hirschfelder, and R. Mohrmann (eds.), *New Directions in Urban History* (Munster, 2000).   [68] See Ch. 2 on use of commercial directories.

[69] Directories used for this survey: Griffith Wright, *A History of Leeds . . . to which are added . . . a Leeds Directory* (Leeds, 1797); *General and Commercial Directory of Leeds* (Leeds, 1826); *Manchester Directory* (Manchester, 1773); *The Manchester and Salford Directory* (Manchester, 1828); *Sketchley's Sheffield Directory* (Sheffield, 1774); *Sheffield Directory and Guide* (1828).

THE DEVELOPMENT OF URBAN CULTURE

Economic prosperity and diversity, the increase in overseas trade, and a concomitant rise in the middling sorts, lent Manchester, Leeds, and Sheffield a new degree of sophistication during the second half of the eighteenth century that the authors of local histories and guides were eager to describe. The strong continental trading links which Manchester was forming in the eighteenth century prompted the town's historian, John Aikin, to remark in 1795 that

Within the last twenty or thirty years the vast increase of foreign trade has caused many of the Manchester manufacturers to travel abroad, and agents or partners to be fixed for a considerable time on the Continent, as well as foreigners to reside in Manchester. And the town has now in every respect assumed the style and manners of one of the commercial capitals of Europe.[70]

Improvements in Sheffield were also said to have coincided with the early years of George III's reign, when, according to Joseph Hunter,

the town soon began to experience the benefit of a direct commerce with distant countries, in the erection of warehouses on a scale that had never before been witnessed; in the projection and formation of new streets; in the villas which were seen arising in the vicinity of the town; and in the introduction of some of the refinements and elegancies of social life . . . A subscription library was opened on the plan of one formed a short time before at Leeds; and in 1762 a handsome suite of rooms was prepared for balls and assemblies, to which was soon after annexed a theatre, with scenery and decorations not inferior to those of any provincial theatre.[71]

In Leeds, the author of *Loidis and Elmete* also described significant developments in the West Riding of Yorkshire from around 1760 when he noted the emergence of a 'public spirit' for improvement. The general desire for a higher quality of life resulted, he asserted, in the erection in 1775 of the new Leeds Assembly Rooms, forming part of a 'rising spirit of elegance in the town'.[72]

---

[70] John Aikin, *A Description of the Country from Thirty to Forty Miles Round Manchester* (London, 1795), 184.   [71] Hunter, *Hallamshire*, 125.

[72] Thomas Dunham Whitaker, *Loidis and Elmete* (Leeds, 1816), 82–3. See also Helen Berry, 'Creating Polite Space: The Organisation and Social Function of the Newcastle

Aimed at inhabitants and visitors alike, local histories, guides, and topographies celebrated both the dynamic and civilized qualities of urban culture in 'industrial' centres such as Manchester, Leeds, and Sheffield. Discussions of manufacturing and commerce generally assumed a prominent place in these works, but most devoted far more space to outlining urban expansion, and to detailed descriptions of places of worship, charitable institutions, learned societies, places of amusement, and shopping venues. The *History of Leeds* published around 1797 is typical in this respect, promising to give 'as complete an account of the antiquaries, remarkable buildings, and other matters of note, in and about this town' as was possible, and going on to provide a long list of the major sites of interest such as St John's Church, the General Infirmary, Fleet Market, and the Mixed Cloth Hall.[73] Publications such as these usually contained sections on the history of towns—often stretching back to Anglo-Saxon times—in order to impress upon readers the significance of their subjects long before recent transformations had taken place.[74] However, in the case of centres such as Manchester, Leeds, and Sheffield, it was their current fortunes that received most attention, with the stress on improvement being marked. William White's *History, Guide, and Description, of the Borough of Sheffield* claimed that the town 'seemed to rise with renovated strength' after the American War of Independence, and illustrated this point with a description of how the market place—increasingly unable to meet the demands of the growing town—was replaced in 1784 with a larger site, while slaughterhouses and a cattle market were moved out of the town centre.[75] Joseph Aston's *Manchester Guide*, published in 1804, contained a town plan that illustrated not only the sites of the town's major cultural, religious, and

Assembly Rooms', in Helen Berry and Jeremy Gregory (eds.), *Creating and Consuming Culture in North-East England 1660–1830* (Aldershot, 2004). I am grateful to the author for a copy of this piece prior to publication.

[73] *A History of Leeds* (Leeds, 1797?), 1.

[74] Rosemary Sweet, *The Writing of Urban Histories in Eighteenth-Century England* (Oxford, 1997).

[75] William White, *History, Guide, and Description, of the Borough of Sheffield* (Sheffield, 1833).

charitable institutions, but also the extent to which Manchester had grown during the last thirty years: with newer areas being printed in a different shade to that of the more established town centre.[76] Eleven years later, the *New Manchester Guide* proudly boasted that

Wealth, the natural result and just reward of commercial enterprise and industry, has not only been employed in Manchester for the enlargement of the town, but with a spirit equally creditable to the taste and honest pride of its possessors, has likewise been used to patronise genius, to unite the ornamental with the useful, to furnish conveniences for the purposes of religion and charity, business and pleasure, and at the same time to give an air of respectability and splendour to the town in the number, style, and adjustment of its public edifices.[77]

The emphasis placed on cultural attainments in such works was echoed in private correspondence. A report on the state of Leeds in 1819 noted that 'There is an evident alteration taking place in the character of the people of Leeds. They are putting off in some degree that rudeness which is peculiar to them, enlightened pursuits are more cultivated, and the elegancies and comforts of life are more sought after.'[78] But according to at least one observer, the behaviour of the Leeds residents differed from the showiness associated with other areas of the country. Edward Baines claimed that inhabitants 'are distinguished by simplicity of manners, quick perception, and frank dispositions. They are ingenious, laborious and frugal, and as a natural consequence, they have become an opulent community—more anxious to acquire riches, than ostentatiously to display them.'[79] His comments present a more positive attitude than that of visitors who

[76] Joseph Aston, *The Manchester Guide* (Manchester, 1804).
[77] *New Manchester Guide* (Manchester, 1815), 172.
[78] Report of the surveyors to Earl Cowper on his Leeds estates, 1819, Hertfordshire County Record Office, T4951, cited in Grady, *Georgian Public Buildings*, 94.
[79] Edward Baines, *History, Directory and Gazetteer of the Country of York*, 2 vols. (1822), i. p. xii. On regional diversity, see J. Langton, 'The Industrial Revolution and the Regional Geography of England', *Transactions of the Institute of British Geography*, NS 9 (1984), 145–67.

complained that the inhabitants of industrial towns were interested only in work and money.[80]

In common with Baines, newspaper advertisements also painted pictures of urban cultural refinement of a suitably measured sort: 'fashionable and cheap' being a common refrain.[81] The newspaper was arguably the most prominent form of publishing in northern towns in the late eighteenth and early nineteenth centuries. By 1760 most provincial centres had at least one weekly paper, with Manchester, Leeds, and Sheffield each supporting two titles by the 1790s.[82] These local papers were usually operated by printers who were primarily motivated by profit. In order to attract high sales, newspaper publishers sought to reproduce material that would appeal to a specifically local audience.[83] Such newspapers are therefore a particularly rich source of information about provincial opinion, whilst the advertisements they contain offer a unique insight into the cultural life of towns. Advertising—which was in itself an attraction for readers—was an important source of newspaper profits and dominated the papers themselves: constituting anything from one-quarter to one-third of all printed space between 1760 and 1830.[84]

Newspaper advertisements in Manchester, Leeds, and Sheffield suggest that the press catered for a readership that—at least in part—saw itself as refined and sophisticated.[85] Inns promised to receive 'Ladies, Gentlemen, Travellers &c. in the most Elegant manner',[86] and shops offered up-to-the-minute fashions and top-quality goods.

---

[80] See e.g. Joshua E. White, *Letters on England*, 2 vols. (Philadelphia, 1815), i. 46–7; [R. Southey], *Letters from England* (1807), new edn., ed. Jack Simmons (Gloucester, 1984), 213.

[81] See e.g. *Manchester Mercury*, 18 November 1788, 11 December 1804, 20 September 1828; *Sheffield Iris*, 6 January 1797; *Leeds Mercury*, 9 August 1817.

[82] Barker, *Newspapers, Politics and Public Opinion*, 110–12; Barker, 'Press, Politics and Reform: 1779–1785', D.Phil. thesis (Oxford, 1994), 289–91.

[83] Hannah Barker, 'Catering for Provincial Tastes: Newspapers, Readership and Profit in Late Eighteenth-Century England', *Historical Research* (1996), 42–61.

[84] Barker, *Newspapers, Politics and English Society*, 97–8.

[85] For a discussion of the readership of the provincial press in this period, see Barker, *Newspapers, Politics and English Society*, ch. 3.

[86] *Manchester Mercury*, 12 October 1773.

This vision of good taste and fashionable consumption can be confirmed by other sources. For example, we know that the number of tea licences held by northern shopkeepers in the mid-1790s was impressive compared with the size of the population, and could rival that of towns such as Norwich, Bristol, and Bath.[87] John Seed has shown that Manchester also had a thriving market in art—in the form of both original paintings and prints.[88] In addition to shopping, the press also revealed that the inhabitants of northern towns pursued a variety of 'polite' pastimes. Residents could attend card assemblies, balls, plays, concerts, and the meetings of various clubs. They were encouraged to add to their accomplishments by learning to paint, speak foreign languages, play musical instruments, and perform up-to-date dances.[89] Such skills could enable individuals to show off their social refinement to maximum effect, particularly in spaces dedicated to 'polite' sociability. Thus Miss Gordon reminded her Leeds patrons on 20 December 1828 that there was still time to learn 'the present fashionable style of dancing' in time for the Annual Ball at the Assembly Rooms at the end of the month.[90]

In the midst of such modish activities, it is clear that in Manchester, Leeds, and Sheffield, as elsewhere, there was a specific kudos associated with something from London, and that the middling orders of northern towns were subject to the pervasive spread of metropolitan manners and fashions.[91] This was particularly evident where women's

[87] Based on figures for distribution of tea licences 1795–6 in Hoh-Cheung and Lorna Mui, *Shops and Shopkeeping in Eighteenth-Century England* (London, 1989), 301–3, and 1801 census figures in B. R. Mitchell, *British Historical Statistics* (Cambridge, 1988), 26–7. Cf. David Alexander, *Retailing in England During the Industrial Revolution* (London, 1970), 93.

[88] John Seed, ' "Commerce and the Liberal Arts": The Political Economy of Art in Manchester, 1775–1860', in Wolff and Seed (eds.), *The Culture of Capital*.

[89] See e.g. *Manchester Mercury*, 25 March 1788; *Sheffield Iris*, 3 November 1797; *Leeds Intelligencer*, 21 December 1826 and 19 January 1828. On painting instruction see also Seed, ' "Commerce and the Liberal Arts" ', 48–9.

[90] *Leeds Intelligencer*, 20 December 1828. It is worth noting, however, that while the dancing may have been fashionable, the venue was not. I am grateful to Helen Berry for the suggestion that the fashion for assemblies was waning by the 1780s, and would have seemed extremely dated to many by 1828.

[91] Peter Borsay, 'The London Connection: Cultural Diffusion and the Eighteenth-Century Provincial Town', *London Journal* 19 (1994), 21–35, p. 27; Berry, 'Promoting Taste in the Provincial Press', 6–8.

fashions were concerned, and the newspapers of northern towns bore witness to the cultural capital put on London goods and connections. So, for example, in 1804, Miss Jackson, Straw Hat Manufacturer, advertised in the *Manchester Mercury* that 'she has just returned from London, with a most elegant variety of patterns . . . of the most fashionable shapes now worn in the metropolis'.[92] In 1817 Mrs Sharrow informed the ladies of Sheffield that her daughter was in London selecting 'an elegant and fashionable assortment of MILLINERY'.[93] Later on that year, and following the death of Princess Charlotte, Leeds's Mrs Bickerdike announced her receipt from London of 'a large selection of BLACK CHIP HATS' in view of the 'general mourning'.[94] Leeds ladies were thus being encouraged not only to join in a national expression of grief by virtue of their attire, but to follow metropolitan fashion in doing so.

Yet we also know that while metropolitan fashions were attractive, other provincial towns often supplied more practical models for emulation.[95] As John Money has demonstrated in the case of Birmingham, the development of a musical and theatrical life in the town relied only in part on London models, and also followed the lead of the more 'genteel' town of Lichfield.[96] Indeed, in Manchester, Leeds, and Sheffield, advertisements for theatrical performances, concerts, and assemblies were common, though very rarely was the capital mentioned as a point of reference.[97] The inspiration that one provincial town might provide for another is evident also in other areas. The founders of the Leeds Infirmary sought advice from the trustees of a Manchester institution, whilst the Sheffield Subscription Library was started in 1771 based on one recently completed in Leeds.[98] Manchester's Lit and Phil Society was copied in Newcastle-upon-Tyne,[99] while the idea for the

[92] *Manchester Mercury*, 8 May 1804.   [93] *Sheffield Mercury*, 24 May 1817.
[94] *Leeds Mercury*, 15 November 1817. See also *Manchester Mercury*, 18 November 1817; *Leeds Intelligencer*, 22 November 1828.
[95] Borsay, 'London Connection', 27–8; Ellis, *Georgian Town*, 137–41.
[96] John Money, *Experience and Identity. Birmingham and the West Midlands 1760–1800* (Manchester, 1977), 80–97. See also Barry on Bristol: 'Provincial Town Culture, 1640–1780: Urbane or Civic?'   [97] See survey below.
[98] Grady, *Profit, Property Interests, and Public Spirit*, 96–9; Hunter, *Hallamshire*, 125.
[99] Stephen Harbottle, *The Reverend William Turner: Dissent and Reform in Georgian Newcastle upon Tyne* (Leeds, 1997), 35–6, 53–66.

Royal Institution founded in Manchester in 1823 came from a similar project in Liverpool nine years earlier.[100] While civic pride was clearly an important element in the formulation of such projects, there is little sense that these institutions were the result of intense inter-town rivalry. At least for those individuals most immediately concerned with their inceptions, the relationship between such bodies tended to be one of co-operation, so that 'cultural borrowing' was based on admiration and emulation rather than competition.[101] One might suppose that this process would have led to a certain homogeneity in provincial cultural life; however, as each town borrowed only those elements that suited its individual requirements and specific ambitions, and variation and mod-ification of schemes was commonplace, this was not the case.

In common with building, advertisements for various goods and ser-vices reveal links that seem to underline the interconnectedness of provincial towns and do not suggest a sense of metropolitan superiority. Mrs Owen of Manchester, for example, promised corsets 'far superior' to those found in London.[102] Provincial confidence is also apparent in advertisements for medicine and medical services, where a London provenance was often mentioned, but did not appear necessary to inspire trust. Indeed, there is evidence that a regional pattern of advert-ising was emerging in the late eighteenth century, in which nearby towns were used as points of reference and indicators of trustworthiness. Thus in Leeds and Sheffield adverts appeared for Elliot's Family Cordial from Huddersfield, Lignum's Healing Tincture and Antiscorbutic Drops from Manchester, 'Moxon's effervescent magnesian aperient' from Hull, and 'cordial balm of gilead' produced by Samuel Solomon of Liverpool.[103] 'Molineux's smelling medicine' was advertised in Leeds with a testimonial by John Brewer, the gaoler at York castle,[104] whilst

---

[100] Chalkin, 'Capital Expenditure', 57.

[101] Paul Elliot, 'The Origins of the "Creative Class": Provincial Urban Society, Scientific Culture and Socio-political Marginality in Britain in the Eighteenth and Nineteenth Centuries', *Social History* 28/3 (2003), 361–87.

[102] *Manchester Mercury*, 22 May 1804. On newspaper advertisements and 'taste' in the north-east of England, see Berry, 'Promoting Taste in the Provincial Press'.

[103] *Leeds Mercury*, 3 November 1810; *Sheffield Iris*, 2 and 9 November 1800; *Sheffield Mercury*, 6 November 1820; *Sheffield Iris*, 28 July 1797.

[104] *Leeds Intelligencer*, 20 November 1770.

Ward's Ormskirk medicine positively shouted its regional and provincial credentials, as did Eccles remedy for sheep rot.[105] Mr Oliver, a dentist working in Sheffield in 1788, had, he boasted, worked in Liverpool and Manchester,[106] while the 'surgeon dentist', Mr Humby, who visited the town in 1817, claimed to be 'highly recommended by eminent men of the faculty, and by the nobility and Gentry of York and Hull, whom he has had the honour of attending'.[107] In 1817, Mr W. Dickinson, a surgeon from Doncaster, advertised his cure for ruptures in the *Manchester Mercury*. 'Mr D.' it was noted, had 'served his apprenticeship with Mr. John Dickinson, Surgeon, High-street, Doncaster'.[108] Clearly no greater endorsement was needed.

Foreign influences also loomed large. Manchester, Leeds, and Sheffield newspapers contained advertisements for Johnson and Williams's American soothing syrup,[109] Dr Brodum's botanical syrup from Denmark,[110] Venetian blinds, French corsets and brocades, Genoa silks, Indian muslin, Persian carpets, Italian crapes, French bonnets, Tuscan hats, and Oriental ointment and cordial.[111] Although the grocer, Robert Turner, sold 'London Oysters', he also supplied Manchester's residents with Jordan almonds, Turkey figs, French plums, and Spanish nuts.[112] Elsewhere one could purchase 'hot French dinners', Abyssinian and Swedish soap, Dutch hyacinths, Seville and China oranges, American flour, Teneriffe wines, West India sweetmeats, India Soy, fine 'souchong' tea, and exotic spices.[113] Moreover, residents of the three towns were promised the chance to see elephants

[105] *Manchester Mercury*, 16 March 1773; *Sheffield Mercury*, 27 November 1830.
[106] *Sheffield Register*, 5 January 1788.   [107] *Sheffield Mercury*, 25 October 1817.
[108] *Manchester Mercury*, 11 November 1817.
[109] *Manchester Mercury*, 18 February 1817; *Leeds Intelligencer*, 1 June 1826.
[110] *Leeds Mercury*, 1 November 1800.
[111] *Manchester Mercury*, 30 November 1790; 22 May 1804; 3 and 25 March 1817; 20 November 1830; *Leeds Mercury*, 11 November 1809; 4 January 1817; *Sheffield Mercury*, 22 November 1828.
[112] *Manchester Mercury*, 30 November 1790. See also ibid. 6 May and 18 December 1804; *Sheffield Iris*, 17 February 1791.
[113] *Manchester Mercury*, 22 November 1764; 28 May; 12 November 1771; 30 November 1790; 4 November 1800; 28 February; 8 May; 13 November; 18 December 1804; 20 November 1810; *Leeds Intelligencer*, 6 November 1770; *Leeds Mercury*, 16 November 1790; *Sheffield Mercury*, 27 November 1830.

from Ceylon, lions from Senegal, kangaroos from Botany Bay, and panthers from South America, as well as Siamese twins and a 'Turkish exhibition' of miniatures, which had toured both France and Germany.[114] In addition, and to add to their polite refinements, the inhabitants of Manchester, Leeds, and Sheffield could learn to speak and read French, Italian, Latin, and Spanish,[115] and in Manchester, they could also be tutored in 'Spanish guitar' and 'Italian singing'.[116] As the contemporary historian, John Aikin, has shown, trading interests with continental Europe, the Americas, and other parts of the Empire could make London appear relatively insignificant in many regards.[117] Clearly, dismissing the capital altogether would present a very distorted picture of provincial urban life, but so too would a failure to acknowledge the cultural cross-currents between London and the provinces, between different provincial towns and regions, and between the provinces, continental Europe, and the Americas.[118]

A survey of advertisements in Manchester, Leeds, and Sheffield newspapers between 1760 and 1830 supports this pluralist approach.[119] Adverts for goods and services often included provenance as a selling

[114] *Manchester Mercury*, 13 November 1810; *Sheffield Iris*, 4 November 1820; *Sheffield Mercury*, 20 November 1830.

[115] *Manchester Mercury*, 7 January 1809, 30 December 1817; *Sheffield Register*, 20 October 1787; *Leeds Intelligencer*, 21 December 1826; *Leeds Mercury*, 7 January 1807.

[116] *Manchester Mercury*, 5 January 1828.

[117] Aikin, *A Description of . . . Manchester*, 147–206. See also Hunter, *Hallamshire*, 125; and Kathleen Wilson, 'Citizenship, Empire, and Modernity in the English Provinces, c.1720–1790', *Eighteenth-Century Studies* 29/1(1996), 69–96; and her *The Sense of the People: Politics, Culture and Imperialism in England, 1715–1785* (Cambridge, 1995).

[118] Borsay, 'London Connection'; John Brewer, *The Pleasures of the Imagination* (London, 1997), 493–8; Sweet, *The Writing of Urban Histories in Eighteenth-Century England*, 240; Holger Hoock, *The King's Artists: The Royal Academy of Arts and the Politics of British Culture, 1760–1840* (Oxford, 2004), ch. 3. I am grateful to the author for a copy of this piece prior to publication.

[119] Papers were sampled for November at ten-yearly intervals starting in 1760, except in the case of Sheffield, where very few copies were extant for 1770 and 1780, so alternative months and surviving papers from 1776 were also examined. Newspapers used in this survey were: *Manchester Mercury*, 1760–1820; *Wheeler's Manchester Chronicle*, 1830; *Leeds Intelligencer*, 1760–80; *Leeds Mercury*, 1790–1830; *Public Advertiser* [Sheffield], 1760, 1770 [May], 1776 [April]; *Sheffield Register*, 1790; *Sheffield Iris*, 1800, 1810; *Sheffield Mercury*, 1820, 1830. Advertisements for property sales, lottery tickets, legal notices, and political advertisements were not included in this study.

point, or gave prominence to a particular location. During this period the number of advertisements appearing in provincial newspapers increased at a rapid rate, whilst the ratio between metropolitan, provincial, and foreign references fluctuated significantly. In Leeds and Manchester there were far more adverts for locally produced products in 1760 and 1770, and this provincial dominance was also evident in Leeds and Sheffield in 1800. Conversely, London appeared more prominent in all three towns at various points between 1810 and 1830, with Leeds and Sheffield showing a more marked metropolitan bias than that of Manchester throughout the period examined. These fluctuations were due to changes in three of the most common types of advertisement: for print, medicines, and clothing. The prominence of provincial advertisements for much of the eighteenth century stemmed from the preponderance of advertisements for print and medicine that stressed a local link, many of which were placed by the printer of the newspaper. The apparent popularity of locally produced medicines never declined, but medical advertisements decreased as a proportion of all newspaper advertising after 1800. Judging from the number of advertisements, the provincial print trade in books and pamphlets also remained buoyant, but it was accompanied by a somewhat steeper growth in the proportion of advertisements for printed material from London, which in part explains the additional metropolitan influence in early nineteenth-century newspapers produced in Leeds and Sheffield. Even more important in explaining the change in emphasis here was the steep rise in advertisements for women's clothing, which frequently used the capital as a point of reference. This was a relatively new area of advertising and produced a notable skew in results. However, the trend towards greater metropolitan prominence was by no means clear-cut: in Leeds, after a sharp incline in 1810, London-influenced advertisements were in decline thereafter; in Sheffield a peak in 1820 was reversing by 1830; and in Manchester, no surge in metropolitan advertisements was ever apparent. Not surprisingly, as the town with the most extensive overseas trading connections, Manchester's newspapers published most advertisements with foreign references throughout the late eighteenth and early nineteenth centuries.

Despite fluctuations within towns, the ratios between local, metropolitan, and foreign influences in advertisements seem remarkably balanced over the period 1760–1830 as a whole: with foreign influences recorded at 10 per cent or under, and London and the provinces appearing at roughly equal levels.[120] The emphasis placed on a London provenance in the print and clothing sectors was not repeated elsewhere, and is far more muted—if apparent at all—in other advertisements, for example for food and drink, cosmetics and perfume, medicines and medical practitioners, china and glass, musical instruments, banks, classes, and concerts. Historians who have stressed the metropolitan influence on provincial life have tended to rely on books and other printed sources. Yet whilst it is clear from the findings of this survey that London dominated the print trade, the same could not be said of the consumer market as a whole, and while 'high' fashion and luxury goods may have been more likely to betray a London bias (although this was clearly not always the case), more everyday goods, by and large, did not. However, these sorts of items, and their associations, have been generally overlooked in the debate over metropolitan influence and provincial identity.[121]

The picture of middling culture, economic diversity, and provincial self-confidence presented so far sits uneasily with many of the more familiar contemporary commentaries on industrial towns. Accounts of tours undertaken by the landed elite in this period have become well known. They dominate our picture of northern urban life, while obscuring local observation and sentiment. During one such tour of the north of England in 1792, the particularly irascible John Byng proclaimed that, 'In places, where wealth is procured, it is ignorantly spent; for the upstart man of riches knows no better: the inns therefore are bad, dear, and presumptuous . . .' A man clearly used to more refined surroundings, he described the hostelry used on the

---

[120] Ratio of London : provincial : foreign = Manchester 41 : 48 : 10; Leeds 46 : 47 : 6; Sheffield 48 : 46 : 4.

[121] R. Porter, 'Science, Provincial Culture and Public Opinion in Enlightenment England', *British Journal for Eighteenth-Century Studies* 3 (1980), 20–46; Brewer, *Pleasures of the Imagination*. Cf. Stana Nenadic, 'Middle-Rank Consumers and Domestic Culture in Edinburgh and Glasgow, 1720–1840', *Past and Present* 145 (1994), 122–45.

Mancunian leg of his journey as dirty and noisy and the food served as inedible, and concluded 'Oh! What a dog hole is Manchester!'[122] As anyone familiar with eighteenth-century travel literature can attest, such comments were not unusual.[123] One visitor to Leeds in 1768 noted that the town was 'exceedingly dirty, ill-built and as badly paved'.[124] Little seems to have improved by the nineteenth century, when Barclay Fox's journal entry from the 1830s recorded that

[Leeds] amongst all others of its species is the vilest of the vile. At a mile distant from the town we came under a vast dingy canopy formed by the impure exhalation of a hundred furnaces. It sits on the town like an everlasting incubus, shutting out the light of heaven & the breath of summer . . . Our inn was consistent with its locality; one doesn't look for a clean floor in a colliery or a decent hotel in Leeds.[125]

Horace Walpole described Sheffield as 'one of the foulest towns in England, in the most charming situation' in 1760.[126] In 1798, a London visitor noted: 'shops all shut, place extremely dull and not a person to be seen of a tolerable, decent appearance'. Moreover, he complained that the town was 'completely dirty, and strewed with Nutshells from one end to the other, as if all the inhabitants had been eating them the whole day'.[127] Around the same period, and after a somewhat abortive shopping trip there, Lady Caroline Stuart-Wortley wrote that 'I never was in so stinking, dirty and savage a place.'[128]

The residents of Manchester, Leeds, and Sheffield were condemned by elite visitors as irredeemably vulgar: supposedly excluded from 'polite', fashionable society as they lacked the taste to distinguish what

[122] *The Torrington Diaries*, C. B. Andrews (ed.), 4 vols. (London, 1934–8), iii. 116–17. See also White, *Letters on England*, i. 46–7.
[123] See also Verulam MS, HMC (London, 1906), 239; R. L. Brett (ed.), *Barclay Fox's Journal* (London, 1979), 110; W. S. Lewis (ed.), *Horace Walpole's Correspondence*, 48 vols. (London, 1937–83), ix. 295.
[124] Comments of the third Viscount, diary entry 16 September 1768: Verulam MS, HMC (London, 1906), 239.   [125] *Barclay Fox's Journal*, 110: entry for 9 August 1837.
[126] *Horace Walpole's Correspondence*, ix. 295.
[127] 'Extracts from the Diary of a Tour from London to Yorkshire, Lancashire, Cheshire and Derbyshire—August 3rd—September 22nd 1798', *Transactions of the Hunter Archaeological Society* 5 (1937–43), 191–6, p. 191.
[128] Hey, *History of Sheffield*, 101–2.

was bad from what was good and living in conditions which did not allow a well-mannered, urbane lifestyle. In short, they inhabited cities dominated by factories, workshops, and the pursuit of money and their characters were shaped accordingly. Yet travel literature in this period tended to judge towns according to elite metropolitan norms and—as an extremely derivative form of writing—it was predisposed to find provincial towns lacking in comparison with London.[129] In spite of this, such views were echoed in many other printed sources. As Rosemary Sweet has noted, although some eighteenth-century observers were keen to defend industrial towns for their contribution to the national wealth, another strain of literature ridiculed the cultural pretensions of the manufacturer, merchant, and tradesmen and—as we have seen—derided such towns for lacking the cultural refinements of metropolitan society.[130] As part of a long tradition of complaints against the city, other critiques associated towns with poverty and squalor—the results of a corrupt and luxurious society,[131] and increasingly in the nineteenth century such urban shortcomings were linked to capitalism and the formation of a polarized and class-based society.[132]

Despite damning comments by contemporary visitors though, there is little evidence that northerners felt abashed or embarrassed by their supposed vulgarity, on the contrary, the burgeoning sense of confidence, vigour, and civic pride that was apparent gives us the opportunity to judge provincial culture on its own terms. It is clear that the residents of Manchester, Leeds, and Sheffield felt very differently about the places in which they lived: no doubt agreeing with William

---

[129] Borsay, 'London Connection', 24, 27; R. H. Sweet, 'Topographies of Politeness', *Transactions of the Royal Historical Society* 12 (2002), 355–74, pp. 358–66; Brewer, *Pleasures of the Imagination*, 494.   [130] Sweet, *Writing of Urban Histories*, 131–41.
  [131] Raymond Williams, *The Country and the City* (London, 1973).
  [132] de Tocqueville, *Journeys to England and Ireland*; Frederick Engels, *The Condition of the Working Class in England*, trans. W. O. Henderson and W. H. Chaloner, 2nd edn. (Oxford, 1971; first pub. 1844); P. E. Razell and R. W. Wainwright (eds.), *The Victorian Working Class: Selections from Letters to the Morning Chronicle* (London, 1973); Sir George Head, *Home Tour Through the Manufacturing Districts of England in the Summer of 1835* (London, 1836).

Hutton, who claimed in 1781 that 'a barbarous and commercial people is a contradiction,' or with the author of the *Description of Manchester*, published in 1783, who asserted that 'in places where the immediate dependence of the inhabitants is not upon trade, the health and morals of the people are ruined'.[133] Not only were north-erners proud to stress the importance of their towns as centres of trade and industry, but it also seems they believed them to be places of culture and sophistication. This might lead us to form an alternative vision of 'politeness' in this period that allows for more regional variation.[134] In the case of industrial towns, it may be one where economy, morality, and straightforwardness were as important as conspicuous consumption and more rigid and socially exclusive forms of etiquette.[135] Northern manners, then, might have been more sober than those of a polished national elite, and closer to the 'respectability' or self-governance which historians have identified marking social relations for a later period.[136]

The self-confidence exhibited by the inhabitants of northern towns, and the distinct civic consciousnesses that emerged there, have become apparent. So too has the rising importance of fashionable forms of behaviour. These aspects of northern urban culture were clearly linked

[133] William Hutton, *History of Birmingham* (1781), cited in Sweet, *The English Town*, 221; *A Description of Manchester*, 93. See also Ellis, *Georgian Town*, 20–1; R. Ayton, *A Voyage Round Great Britain Undertaken in the Summer of 1813* (London, 1814), 70. Contemporary artists and writers could also present a far more upbeat representation of life in industrial towns: Caroline Arscott and Griselda Pollock with Janet Wolff, 'The Partial View: The Visual Representation of the Early Nineteenth-Century Industrial City', in Wolff and Seed (eds.), *The Culture of Capital*; Stephen Daniels, 'The Implications of Industry: Turner and Leeds', in Simon Pugh (ed.), *Reading Landscape: Country-City-Capital* (Manchester, 1990); Maxine Berg, 'Representations of Early Industrial Towns: Turner and his Contemporaries', in Michael Rosenthal, Christina Payne, and Scott Wilcox (eds.), *Prospects for the Nation: Recent Essays in British Landscape, 1750–1880* (London, 1997); James Raven, ' "Defending Trade in the Provinces", the Gentleman Merchant and Mrs Gomerall of Leeds', in his *Judging New Wealth* (Oxford, 1992).

[134] See Sweet, 'Topographies of Politeness', on non-metropolitan views of politeness.

[135] See e.g. White, *Letters on England*, i. 46–7; also Stobart, 'Culture versus Commerce'.

[136] Most notably, F. M. L. Thompson called his social history of Victorian Britain, *The Rise of Respectable Society* (London, 1988). See also more recent work on 'governmentality', e.g. Michel Foucault, 'Governmentality', in Graham Burchell, Colin Gordon, and Peter Miller (eds.), *The Foucault Effect: Studies in Governmentality* (London, 1991); Patrick Joyce, *The Rule of Freedom: Liberalism and the Modern City* (London, 2003).

to the experience of particularly dynamic forms of growth. In such bustling centres of commercial activity as Manchester, Leeds, and Sheffield, the middling sorts were becoming increasingly numerous and prominent, and small-scale manufacturers, traders, and retailers both benefited from the developments taking place, and acted as motors for change. Within this type of environment, lower middle-class women might have been uniquely positioned to take part in the world of business, as changing patterns of fashionable consumption would have boosted many of the areas of the economy in which they were most active. As we shall see, they were certainly a common feature of urban commercial life: in evidence not just as consumers, but also as the producers and suppliers of goods and services.

2

Women's Work and Urban Development

ALTHOUGH the presence of lower middling women in urban economies has not gone completely unnoticed, historians of women's work during the eighteenth and nineteenth centuries have tended to concentrate predominantly on those at the lower end of the social scale. Until very recently, research on the middling sorts has been rare, and much of what has been written describes female labour outside the 'domestic sphere' as increasingly restricted under the growing influence of 'separate spheres' ideology.[1] The work of Leonore Davidoff and Catherine Hall has been particularly influential in this respect. In *Family Fortunes*, they argue that middle-class women were progressively excluded from the world of work during the early nineteenth century, as a combination of economic change, religious evangelism, and political upheaval formulated new ideologies of class and gender that did not advocate female activity beyond the home and family.[2] The model of social, economic, and cultural change on which *Family Fortunes* is based has been more widely used by historians of labouring

---

[1] Alice Clark noted this development in the seventeenth century: *Working Life of Women in the Seventeenth Century* (London, 1919). For a discussion of this trend in the eighteenth century see Leonore Davidoff and Catherine Hall, *Family Fortunes: Men and Women of the English Middle Class, 1780–1850* (London, 1987), ch. 6; Stana Nenadic, 'The Rise of the Urban Middle Class', in T. Devine and R. Mitchison (eds.), *People and Society in Scotland, 1760–1830* (Edinburgh, 1988), 110–11; Peter Earle, 'The Female Labour Market in London in the Late Seventeenth and Early Eighteenth Centuries', *Economic History Review*, 2nd ser., 42 (1989), 328–53, p. 337; Catherine Hall, 'Strains in the "firm of wife, children and friends"? Middle-Class Women and Employment in Early Nineteenth-Century England', in Pat Hudson and W. R. Lee (eds.), *Women's Work and the Family Economy in Historical Perspective* (Manchester, 1990).

[2] Davidoff and Hall, *Family Fortunes*.

women, in order to both describe and explain the marginalization of female labour during the eighteenth and nineteenth centuries.[3]

Yet arguments that the eighteenth century witnessed the demise of a 'golden age' of female employment—for women of all social classes—have been the object of vigorous criticism. As Amanda Vickery has pointed out, there is little evidence that early modern capitalism robbed women of the work opportunities and public liberties formerly enjoyed under a 'wholesome family economy'. Such a model of decline and fall, she states, 'rests on the dubious assumption of a lost egalitarian Eden, which has proved elusive to empirical research'.[4] Vickery's emphasis on continuity echoes that of some economic historians, who maintain that industrialization was a gradual process with diverse impacts between regions and industries and over time.[5] The 'gradualist' approach has not been embraced by all historians, however. Maxine Berg and Pat Hudson have argued convincingly that such a view can underplay the economic and social transformations that were apparent in certain sectors of the economy and in particular regions,[6] and regional diversity is now a key theme in studies of the industrial revolution.[7] The need to recognize the diversity of women's experiences, over time, and between different regions, industries, and social groups is particularly relevant to this study, focusing, as it does,

[3] See e.g. Bridget Hill, *Women, Work and Sexual Politics in Eighteenth-Century England* (Oxford, 1989); Deborah Valenze, *The First Industrial Woman* (Oxford, 1995).

[4] Amanda Vickery, 'Golden Age to Separate Spheres? A Review of the Categories and Chronology of English Women's History', *Historical Journal* 36/2 (1993), 383–414, p. 402. See also Judith Bennett, 'History that Stands Still: Women's Work in the European Past', *Feminist Studies* 14/2 (1988), 269–83; Louise A. Tilly and Joan W. Scott, *Women, Work and Family*, 2nd edn. (New York, 1987); and Janet Thomas, 'Women and Capitalism: Oppression or Emancipation?', *Comparative Studies in Society and History* 30 (1988).

[5] See N. F. R. Crafts, *British Industrial Growth During the Industrial Revolution* (Oxford, 1985); E. A. Wrigley, *Continuity, Chance and Change: The Character of the Industrial Revolution in England* (Cambridge, 1989); Pat Hudson, *The Industrial Revolution* (London, 1992); Patrick O'Brien and Roland Quinault (eds.), *The Industrial Revolution and British Society* (Cambridge, 1993); Maxine Berg, *The Age of Manufactures, 1700–1820*, 2nd edn. (London, 1994).

[6] Maxine Berg and Pat Hudson, 'Rehabilitating the Industrial Revolution', *Economic History Review* 155/1 (1992), 24–50.

[7] Steven King and Geoff Timmins, *Making Sense of the Industrial Revolution: English Economy and Society 1700–1850* (Manchester, 2001), ch. 2.

on a particular stratum of society—the lower middle classes—in urban centres that experienced unusual levels of economic growth.

In her study of the English middling sorts between 1680 and 1780, Margaret Hunt suggests that middling women appear to have been pushed aside in growing towns by larger, male-dominated networks linked to the development of a national and international market economy. Local systems—in which women featured more predominantly—were often small-scale and appeared increasingly obsolete, she argues, so that the meaning, if not the reality, of middling women's work changed significantly during the period.[8] This argument is based largely on late eighteenth-century directories, and it is certainly true that some sections of these publications, particularly those describing general urban developments, depicted the world of business as increasingly large-scale and global in nature. However, it is not clear that this sense of cosmopolitanism necessarily marginalized women in business—either in terms of the work they did, or the ways in which it was perceived.

Although major business ventures in the late eighteenth and early nineteenth centuries were unlikely to have been under the control of women,[9] such enterprises, though influential and important, were easily outnumbered—and outweighed—by the sort of small-scale operations that this book examines.[10] It was not until the 1820s that small businesses—in the form of the independent producer or artisan—began to suffer by the actions of merchants and middlemen who drove down prices.[11] As we shall see in this chapter, directory lists bore witness to the continued importance to urban economies, throughout our

[8] M. Hunt, *The Middling Sort: Commerce, Gender and the Family in England, 1680–1780* (Berkeley and Los Angeles, 1996), 131–2.

[9] Davidoff and Hall, *Family Fortunes*, ch. 6; though see Jill Liddington's account of Ann Lister's coalmining business in 'Gender, Authority and Mining in an Industrial Landscape: Anne Lister 1791–1840', *History Workshop Journal* 42 (1996), 59–86.

[10] See Maxine Berg's examination of small businesses in Birmingham and Sheffield: 'Small Producer Capitalism in Eighteenth-Century England', *Business History* 35/1 (1993), 17–39. She demonstrates that while the nineteenth century might have witnessed tougher times for small-producer capitalists, in the preceding period, small businesses could thrive and were especially dynamic. See also Stana Nenadic 'The Small Family Firm in Victorian Britain', *Business History* 35/4 (1993), 86–114.

[11] Clive Behagg, *Politics and Production in the Early Nineteenth Century* (London, 1990), 54–5.

period, of armies of small-scale traders and manufacturers: amongst whose ranks women featured prominently and consistently. In the following chapter it will also become apparent how public and seemingly central to urban economic life such female activity was, and how little controversy it aroused. Although it may have been the case that more wealthy women withdrew from economic life, the evidence that this happened further down the middling social scale is limited. Indeed, more recent work by Nicola Pullin, Penelope Lane, and Christine Wiskin has described middling women fully engaged in business throughout the late eighteenth and early nineteenth centuries.[12] In line with this new approach, this chapter will argue that in Manchester, Leeds, and Sheffield, lower middling women did not draw back into the economic shadows as urbanization and industrialization surged forward. On the contrary, we find businesswomen seemingly at the heart of commercial developments in northern towns.

SOURCES AND APPROACHES

Studies of women's work during the eighteenth and early nineteenth centuries have been hampered by a lack of reliable statistical material. Prior to the 1841 census, there are few sources which present systematic and long-term surveys of the population in terms of occupation,[13] and those that do—such as the poll books of populous boroughs—do not include women.[14] Yet without an abundance of sources, much important and innovative research on women's work has still been

[12] Nicola Pullin, ' "Business is Just Life": The Practice, Prescription and Legal Position of Women in Business, 1700–1850', Ph.D. thesis (London, 2001), ch. 6; Penelope Lane, 'Women in the Regional Economy, the East Midlands 1700–1830', Ph.D. thesis (Warwick, 1999); Christine Wiskin, 'Women, Finance and Credit in England, c. 1780–1826', Ph.D. thesis (Warwick, 2000). See also Deborah Simonton, 'Gender, Identity and Independence: Eighteenth-Century Women in the Commercial World', *Women's History Magazine* 42 (2002), 4–13.

[13] Nineteenth-century census information is, of course, itself a flawed source, particularly concerning female work, as is discussed below.

[14] See Charles Harvey, Edmund Green, and Penelope Corfield, *The Westminster Historical Database: Voters, Social Structure and Electoral Behaviour* (Bristol, 1998).

done. Settlement examinations have been used by those exploring rural employment,[15] while probate inventories, court records, bankruptcy documents, apprenticeship papers, trade directories, and newspaper advertisements have also proved extremely valuable indicators of broad chronological developments.[16]

For those examining middling women's work, fire insurance policies have provided particularly rich evidence.[17] Peter Earle found that between 1726 and 1729, 317, or 9 per cent, of London policies were taken out by women, and that 202 contained evidence of female employment.[18] Other historians have also made profitable use of insurance policies, and the records of the Sun Fire Insurance Office in particular. Leonard Schwarz examined London policies between 1775 and 1787, locating 628 that were taken out by women.[19] Margaret Hunt has completed this exercise on a countrywide basis, by looking at both London and provincial policies issued by Sun Fire (although it should be noted that London policies dominate this collection). Her survey also covers the period 1775–87, where she found 575 women listed in those businesses in which over 4 per cent of the total were owned by women.[20] Unfortunately, all these studies of insurance policies reveal patterns of women's work at a particular moment in time, and do not

[15] Ann Kussmaul, *Servants in Husbandry in Early Modern England* (Cambridge, 1981); and K. D. M. Snell, *Annals of the Labouring Poor: Social Change and Agrarian England, 1600–1900* (Cambridge, 1985).

[16] Snell, *Annals of the Labouring Poor*, ch. 6; Peter Earle, *The Making of the English Middling Class: Business, Society and Family Life in London, 1660–1730* (London, 1989); L. D. Schwarz, *London in the Age of Industrialisation: Entrepreneurs, Labour Force and Living Conditions, 1700–1850* (Cambridge, 1992); Maxine Berg, 'Women's Property and the Industrial Revolution', *Journal of Interdisciplinary History* 24/2 (1993), 233–50; also her 'Women's Consumption and the Industrial Classes of Eighteenth-Century England', *Journal of Social History* 30/2(1996), 415–34; Lane, 'Women in the Regional Economy'; Wiskin, 'Women, Finance and Credit'; Viktoria Louise Masten, 'Women's Work in Eighteenth-Century Bath and Ipswich', Ph.D. thesis (Cambridge, 2000); Pullin, 'Business is Just Life', ch. 6.

[17] Insurance records are detailed and provide information about business partnerships, where women operated their businesses in relation to their homes, who they lived with (often not men), and what possessions they owned: Hunt, *The Middling Sort*, 134. See also Pullin, 'Business is Just Life', 6.

[18] Earle, *The Making of the English Middling Class*, 168–71.

[19] Schwarz, *London in the Age of Industrialisation*, 21–2.

[20] Hunt, *The Middling Sort*, 132–4.

compare their findings with like sources for significantly earlier or later dates. In an attempt to overcome this shortcoming, both Earle and Schwarz compared the evidence they collected from insurance records with the 1851 census. As a result, both have concluded that women's work remained broadly concentrated in the same economic sectors throughout the eighteenth and early nineteenth centuries.[21]

Earle argues that there was little alteration in women's employment between 1700 and 1851 and that women were already clustered in 'feminine' trades by the late seventeenth century.[22] He suggests that women in business were predominantly located in the areas of food and drink, textiles and clothing, pawnbroking and retailing: 'the typical business for a woman was exactly what might be expected: running a catering establishment selling food and drink, or running a shop selling food, textiles, clothing or such fancy goods as toys, glass, china or perfumes . . .'.[23] In addition, he suggests an increase in economic inactivity on the part of women during the eighteenth century. His research on court records indicate that only 28 per cent of women in late seventeenth- and early eighteenth-century London were not in any paid employment, compared with 57 per cent of women aged 20 or over listed in the 1851 census. Although Earle acknowledges that the 1851 census 'seriously undernumerated the employment of wives', he contends that his findings 'give some substance to Richards's hypothesis of a U-shaped curve of women's employment in Britain— high in 1700 and today, low in Victorian times'.[24] Schwarz concurs with Earle's picture of female economic clustering. He argues that employment patterns for women, unlike those for men, did not change much between 1700 and 1850: 'their opportunities for employment were limited at the beginning of this period, and they were limited at the end'.[25] Although she did not subscribe to a model

[21] Earle, *The Making of the English Middling Class*, 166–74; Earle, 'The Female Labour Market in London'; Schwarz, *London in the Age of Industrialisation*, 14–22.
[22] Earle, *The Making of the English Middling Class*, 166–74; Earle, 'The Female Labour Market in London'.   [23] Earle, *The Making of the English Middling Class*, 170.
[24] Earle, 'The Female Labour Market in London', 337; Eric Richards, 'Women in the British Economy since about 1700: An Interpretation', *History* 59 (1974), 337–47.
[25] Schwarz, *London in the Age of Industrialisation*, 14.

of continuity in women's work, Margaret Hunt similarly described women clustered in 'feminine' trades: in clothing, retailing, pawn-broking, and innkeeping.[26] It is no doubt dangerous for historians of towns and regions outside the capital automatically to extrapolate from the London experience described by Earle, Schwarz, and Hunt. However, detailed empirical research by Wiskin on Birmingham and Sanderson on Edinburgh has described broadly similar patterns of female economic clustering.[27]

In terms of presenting a long-term view, both Earle and Schwarz concede that the census is not particularly reliable. Schwarz notes that as insurance records and census returns are very different types of source, they are not especially comparable. The census, he acknow-ledges, dealt with the entire labourforce, while insurance was taken out by those who could afford it.[28] It has been well established that the census is particularly problematic in the case of women's work, as female labour often went unnoticed. As Higgs reminds us, census returns were completed by male heads of household who tended to describe their womenfolk as dependants rather than workers.[29] By contrast, insurance policies were usually taken out by the individual concerned.[30] Using the census to examine women's work is further complicated by the fact that it was more likely to be seasonal than

[26] Hunt, *The Middling Sort*, 132–4. Elizabeth Sanderson's examination of women's work in eighteenth-century Edinburgh also focuses on retailing and on the 'feminine' 'community care' jobs of letting rooms, nursing, and gravesclothes-making: Elizabeth Sanderson, *Women and Work in Eighteenth-Century Edinburgh* (Basingstoke, 1996).

[27] Wiskin, 'Women, Finance and Credit', 105–7; Sanderson, *Women and Work in Eighteenth-Century Edinburgh*. See also R. J. Morris, *Men, Women and Property in England, 1780–1870: A Social and Economic History of Family Strategies Amongst the Leeds Middle Classes* (Cambridge, 2005), 72, on the 1834 Leeds directory.

[28] Earle, 'The Female Labour Market in London', 341; Schwarz, *London in the Age of Industrialisation*, 22.

[29] Edward Higgs, 'Women, Occupations and Work in the Nineteenth-Century Censuses', *History Workshop Journal* 23 (1987), 59–80. See also M. Anderson, 'What Can the Mid-Victorian Censuses Tell Us about Variations in Married Women's Employment?', *Local Population Studies* 62 (1999), 9–30.

[30] Though as Nicola Pullin has noted, insurance clerks could also be selective concern-ing what personal information was recorded, Pullin, 'Business is Just Life', 136. See also Christine Wiskin, 'Urban Businesswomen in Eighteenth-Century England', in Rosemary Sweet and Penelope Lane (eds.), *'On the town': Women and Urban Life in Eighteenth-Century England* (Aldershot, 2003), 91.

men's and to involve more than one occupation.[31] Census enumerators failed to enquire systematically into the field of employment for
both men and women, which, as Schwarz points out, is more serious
the further one descends down the social scale.[32] Moreover, as
Anderson has noted, the accuracy of enumerators varied significantly
between different localities.[33] We must therefore be cautious about
attempts to use the 1851 census as a marker with which to compare
earlier developments,[34] not least when the sources used vary so greatly.

Although the shortcomings of 'snapshot' approaches and the use of
the census for comparison are clear, these studies provided the best quantitative information we had about middling women's work until recently.
A challenge to existing accounts has since been made by Nicola Pullin.
She has also examined the Sun Fire Office insurance policies, but has
scrutinized them for sample years over a 110-year period. Her study of
policies taken out by women between 1735 and 1845 uncovered 1,490
belonging to women (in a sample covering England between 1735 and
1780, but thereafter only London).[35] This research has allowed her to
take issue with some of the arguments put forward by Earle and Schwarz.
Her investigation has led her to conclude that 'broad sectoral continuities
cannot obscure the fact that, particularly within the metropolitan economy, businesswomen became involved in increasingly diverse and
specialized trades'. Pullin found over 40 per cent of her insured businesswomen spread, albeit thinly, over a wide variety of trades other than those
associated with food and drink, dress, and education.[36]

[31] Sally Alexander, 'Women's Work in Nineteenth-Century London: A Study of the
Years 1820–1850', in A. Oakley and J. Mitchell (eds.), *The Rights and Wrongs of Women*
(Harmondsworth, 1976).

[32] Schwarz, *London in the Age of Industrialisation*, 248–9.

[33] Anderson, 'What Can the Mid-Victorian Censuses Tell Us about Variations in
Married Women's Employment?'

[34] This approach is also pursued by Richards, 'Women in the British Economy since
about 1700'.

[35] The London bias of her samples mean that 72 per cent of the policies she examined
relate to the capital: Pullin, 'Business is Just Life', ch. 6.

[36] Pullin, 'Business is Just Life', 151, 148. Indeed, Leonard Schwarz's own examination
of London between the late eighteenth and mid-nineteenth centuries suggests that this
period witnessed increasing numbers of women trading as butchers, cabinetmakers,
upholsterers, chandlers, grocers, drapers, tailors, and shoemakers: Schwarz, *London in the
Age of Industrialisation*, 21.

Given the preponderance of London or south of England policies,[37] and the relatively small number of women (and men) from
northern provincial towns represented, fire insurance records do not
offer a particularly useful source for a study of places such as
Manchester, Leeds, and Sheffield. Far more rewarding are the locally
produced town directories, which began to appear generally in the
English provinces from the last three decades of the eighteenth century.[38] Like all the sources for quantitative studies of women's work
discussed, directories have their limitations. They provide much less
information than do insurance and court records about individual
businessmen and women: usually no more than their name, address,
and occupation. Female entries suffer particularly, with many
women's entries lacking first names (often appearing with the epithet
'Mrs' or 'Widow', or with an initial or surname only, and thus appearing hidden to those searching for evidence of female activity).[39]
Moreover, it is clear that directories listed far fewer women than men
working in trade, services, and small-scale manufacturing.

Margaret Hunt noted that Elizabeth Raffald—who produced the
1773 Manchester directory—did not acknowledge her own grocer's
shop in this work, but recorded it instead under her husband's name.[40]
Yet other women do seem to have been listed separately from their

[37] See L. D. Schwarz and L. J. Jones, 'Wealth, Occupations, and Insurance in the Late
Eighteenth Century: The Policy Registers of the Sun Fire Office', *Economic History
Review*, 2nd ser., 36/3 (1983), 365–73, p. 367. They note that in 1780, the 'only counties
with policies covering more than 2% of the target population [for new policies] are south
of a line from the Wash to the Severn'. London had by far the highest percentage of new
policies, at 10%.

[38] Gareth Shaw, *British Directories as Sources in Historical Geography* (Norwich, 1982),
25–8; P. J. Corfield, with Serena Kelly, ' "Giving Directions to the Town": The Early Town
Directories', *Urban History Yearbook* (1984), 22–35, pp. 27–31. For studies of women's
work that make use of trade directories, see Penelope Lane, 'Women in the Regional
Economy', 70–2; Wiskin, 'Women, Finance and Credit'; Masten, 'Women's Work in
Eighteenth-Century Bath and Ipswich'.

[39] The title given to women is not much help in discerning their marital status, since
most entries in the 1773 directory appeared without an epithet, as did almost 87% of all
working women listed in the directories sampled for this study. In addition, women who
were widowed might also appear with this title, whilst spinsters of mature years might have
used it as well: Davidoff and Hall, *Family Fortunes*, 273. See Ch. 4 for more discussion of
women working separately from their husbands.

[40] Hunt, *The Middling Sort*, 130.

husbands in trade directories.[41] The 1773 Raffald directory contained entries for several women who traded independently of male members of their family. Mrs Priestnall, a grocer, worked on Deansgate where the whitesmith, John Preistnall, also operated. Jane Cotes traded as a milliner at Smithy Door alongside Luke Cotes, a linen draper, whilst Mary Prestwood ran a toyselling business also at Smithy Door, alongside John Prestwood, a confectioner.[42] Yet Elizabeth Raffald's exclusion from her own directory reminds us of the potential pitfalls of using this source.[43] It seems most likely that only women trading independently would appear: widows, single women, and those married women who carried on their own businesses, separate from those of their husband. This means that—in common with most sources for middling women's work—directories often exclude the labours of large numbers of married women, daughters, and sisters who worked within family businesses headed by men. However, as we shall see, this does not mean that women were absent from the historical record, and directories still offer us arguably the best insight into the activities of independent women of business.

Despite the partial coverage of working women, locally produced directories, particularly those which appeared as part of a series, were likely to be reasonably reliable, since, as Jane Norton argues, the

[41] See Ch. 4 for a more detailed discussion of this phenomenon.

[42] None of these individuals appears to have left more of a mark on the historical record. However, a will for a John Priestnall, a Manchester grocer, survives, dated 14 March 1772: Lancashire Record Office, Wills. This document suggests that Ann Priestnall, John's widow and administratrix, was left his grocery business. There is no mention of a John Priestnall, although Thomas Priestnall, a weaver, was a witness.

[43] On the use of directories for historical research in this period see: Jane E. Norton, *Guide to the National and Provincial Directories of England and Wales, Excluding London, Published Before 1856* (London, 1950); W. G. Rimmer, 'The Industrial Profile of Leeds, 1740–1840', *Transactions of the Thoresby Society* 113 (1967), 130–59; W. K. D. Davies, J. A. Giggs, and D. T. Herbert, 'Directories, Rate Books and the Commercial Structure of Towns', *Geography* 53 (1968), 41–54; series of articles in *Local Historian*, 1974–9; C. G. Pooley, 'Residential Mobility in a Victorian City', *Transactions of the Institute of British Geography*, ns 4/2 (1979), 258–77; Shaw, *British Directories as Sources in Historical Geography*; Corfield, 'Giving Directions to the Town'; Gareth Shaw, 'Directories as Sources in Urban History: A Review of British and Canadian Material', in *Urban History Yearbook* (1984), 36–44; Neil Raven, 'The Trade Directory: A Source for the Study of Early Nineteenth-Century Economies', *Business Archives Sources and History* 74 (1997), 13–30; and his 'Chelmsford during the Industrial Revolution, c. 1790–1840', *Urban History* 30/1 (2003), 44–62.

compiler needed to maintain his or her reputation for accuracy in order to ensure sales.[44] The degree of reliability depended on the way in which directories were compiled. Although national directories might plagiarize the work of others, local directories were often produced by compilers or their agents visiting in person the shops and houses they listed.[45] Thus in May 1773, Elizabeth Raffald advertised that she intended:

in order to make such a useful Work as correct as possible, to send proper and intelligent Persons round the Town, to take down the Name, Business, and Place of Abode of every Gentleman, Tradesman, and Shop-keeper, as well as of others whose Business or Employment has any tendency to public Notice; the Proprietor therefore humbly requests, that every one will please to give the necessary Information to the Persons appointed, that she may be enabled to give an accurate Edition of a Work so advantageous to such a large, populous, and trading Town as this is; in the Completion of which, she can assure the Public, that no Labour or Expense shall be spared to make it worthy of their Approbation, as an easy and sufficient Directory, not only to Strangers, but likewise to the Inhabitants of this Town.[46]

William Parson made similar claims in the first of his Leeds directories, published in 1817. In the preface, he described spending 'some months, assisted by a person resident in the town, in visiting the houses of the inhabitants and every building occupied in trade'.[47]

This process of visiting could take several weeks, even months, to complete. Often a list of additions and corrections was either added at the last minute or circulated a few weeks later.[48] This act of including addenda suggests not only that compilers made mistakes and left people out, but also that they strove to correct such errors. The authors of the 1787 *Directory of Sheffield* noted that 'Errors and Deficiencies must unavoidably appear in every Work of this Kind, from the extreme

[44] Norton, *Guide to the National and Provincial Directories of England and Wales*, 16. See also Shaw, *British Directories as Sources in Historical Geography*, 9–10, 29–43.

[45] Norton, *Guide to the National and Provincial Directories of England and Wales*, 16.

[46] *Manchester Mercury*, 6 May 1773.

[47] W. Parson, *Directory, General and Commercial, of the Town & Borough of Leeds* (Leeds, 1817), p. iv.

[48] Norton, *Guide to the National and Provincial Directories of England and Wales*, 20–1.

Difficulty of procuring Information in some Things, and the fluctuat-
ing Variety of Others.'[49] This sort of caveat was commonplace, but so
too was the desire to put right any mistakes.[50] One of the compilers of
the *Sheffield Directory*, Joseph Gales, announced that a register would
be kept open at his shop for entering additions and corrections.[51]
Mrs Raffald promised to insert any person omitted from the first edition
in the next 'on proper notice', and the second edition in 1773 had 380
more entries than the first.[52] Yet despite such efforts, clearly not everyone
involved in trade, manufacturing, and service industries was listed in
the directories. In the 1817 *Sheffield General Directory*, compiled by
W. Brownell, it was implied that an earlier publication, probably *The
Commercial Directory* for 1816–17, included only those names considered important by his rival. By contrast, Brownell, believing, he claimed,
that a guide to unimportant people was more necessary than one to the
well-known, had published a larger list of names and occupations than
any Sheffield directory had included before.[53] 'Every person is interested
in having a directory as complete as possible,' claimed G. Bancks, the
compiler of a Manchester directory in 1800 which promised more frequent publication and an appendix of alterations based on notes left at
his print shop at the corner of St Ann's Square.[54] The rapid rate of change
in towns was clearly a problem for the compilers of directories though,
and the editors of the next Manchester directory, in 1804, noted that
they had taken great expense and trouble to update the publication as so
much had changed since 1800 that the last edition had 'grown almost
useless'.[55] Although it is not surprising that the producers of the new
edition claimed that it was far more valuable that the old, it is likely—
given what we know about the rapidity of urban growth in this
period—that the town had also changed a great deal in the interim.

Certainly, the rate of change in the size of directories themselves
would seem to support such a claim, as Table 2.1 suggests. Although

---

[49] Cited in Corfield, 'Giving Directions to the Town', 22.   [50] Ibid.
[51] *A Directory of Sheffield* (Sheffield, 1787), p. iv.
[52] 'Collectanea Relating to Manchester', *Chetham Society Publications* 68 (1866),
119–66, p. 131.   [53] *Sheffield General Directory* (Sheffield, 1817), p. v.
[54] G. Bancks, *Manchester & Salford Directory* (Manchester, 1800).
[55] *Deans and Co.'s Manchester and Salford Directory* (Manchester, 1804), p. iii.

Table 2.1. Numbers of businessmen and women in town directories as a proportion of the total population

Directory	Entries of individuals with listed occupations	Estimated population[a]	Estimated population in directory (%)
Manchester			
1773	1,198	30,000	4.0
1788	2,024	43,000	4.7
1804	6,506	75,000	8.6
1817	10,292	107,000	9.6
1828	14,215	162,000	8.8
Sheffield			
1774	555	27,000	2.0
1787	1,058	30,000	3.5
1797	1,510	32,000	4.7
1817	1,933	59,000	3.3
1828	3,248	78,000	4.2
Leeds			
1797	871	45,000	1.9
1809	6,215	60,000	10.4
1817	9,946	75,000	13.3
1826	5,323	105,000	5.1

Note: [a]Figures drawn, or estimated, from: C. M. Law, 'Some Notes on the Urban Population of England and Wales in the Eighteenth Century', *Local Historian* 10 (1972), 13–26; B. R. Mitchell, *British Historical Statistics* (Cambridge, 1988); P. J. Corfield, *The Impact of English Towns, 1700–1800* (Oxford, 1982), 9; John Langton, 'Urban Growth and Economic Change: From the Late Seventeenth Century to 1841', in Peter Clark (ed.), *The Cambridge Urban History of Britain*, ii. *1540–1840* (Cambridge, 2000), 474, 484–5; W. H. Chaloner, 'Manchester in the Latter Half of the Eighteenth Century', *Bulletin of the John Rylands Library* 42/1 (1959), 40–60, p. 42; C. J. Morgan, 'Demographic Change, 1771–1911', in Derek Fraser (ed.), *A History of Modern Leeds* (Manchester, 1980), 46–7; M. Yasumoto, 'Urbanization and Population in an English Town', *Keio Economic Studies* 10 (1973), 61–94, pp. 70–1; Sidney Pollard, 'The Growth of Population', in D. L. Linton (ed.), *Sheffield and its Region* (Sheffield, 1956), 172–4; J. Stobart, 'An Eighteenth-Century Revolution? Investigating Urban Growth in North-West England 1664–1801', *Urban History* 23 (1996), 26–47.

the first editions of directories sometimes had a faltering start, and Sheffield's figures are noticeably smaller than those of Manchester or Leeds, the proportions of the populations included in the directories are not unimpressive. This is especially true when compared to the coverage given of the business community by insurance policies.

Schwarz has estimated that even in 1801, the market for *potential* insurance was only 6 per cent of the total population, based on the calculation that insurance was predominantly bought by upper- and middle-class men or their widows, who formed an estimated 20 per cent of the population.[56] Even in London, his figures show that 10 per cent of the target 6 per cent took out policies in 1780 with Sun Fire (or 0.6 per cent of the city's inhabitants). This means that for any one year, Sun Fire policies represent a much narrower section of the population than are included in directories. Nicola Pullin's figures for London insurance policies also indicate that her samples covered less than 1 per cent of the city's population.[57] Other studies of women's work using the Sun Fire policies suggest similar proportions.[58]

Penelope Corfield has claimed that directories were intended as immediate handbooks and research tools for those visiting or living in towns. Their aim, she argues, was to render a town 'intelligible, decipherable and finite, however mysterious, inchoate and vast it might outwardly appear', rather than to form censuses of final record.[59] But in performing their function of demystification, directories do reveal more than most sources about a large proportion of local businesses, and allow for direct comparisons over a number of years. Unlike insurance records, which, as Schwarz reminds us, are only indicative of the

[56] Schwarz and Jones, 'Wealth, Occupations, and Insurance in the Late Eighteenth Century', 366.

[57] This figure was calculated using Pullin's figures ('Business is Just Life', 141) for women's policies and multiplying them by 20 (since she calculated that women's policies constituted 5–9% of all policies) and comparing them with population figures from C. M. Law, 'Some Notes on the Urban Population of England and Wales in the Eighteenth Century', *Local Historian* 10 (1972), 13–26, p. 24; and Leonard Schwarz, 'London, 1700–1840', in Peter Clark (ed.), *The Cambridge Urban History of Britain*, ii. *1540–1840* (Cambridge, 2000), 650. This method produced the following results: 1735 = 0.29%; 1755 = 0.4%; 1780 = 0.8%; 1809 = 0.47%; 1845 = 0.3%.

[58] Earle found that 317, or 9%, of the policies he examined from the 1720s were taken out by women. This suggests 0.6% of the total London population were covered: Earle, *The Making of the English Middling Class*, 168–71. Leonard Schwarz and Margaret Hunt both examined the period 1775–87: Schwarz's figures suggest up to 1.57% of the London population were covered, Hunt, who looked at businesses where more than 4% of the total were owned by women, gives figures which suggest 1.44% of the population: Schwarz, *London in the Age of Industrialisation*, 21–2; Hunt, *The Middling Sort*, 132–4. These figures are higher than those given by Pullin as they cover a period of several years.

[59] Corfield, 'Giving Directions to the Town', 22.

bourgeoisie,[60] directories at least attempted to provide surveys of urban business communities, even if these were only partial: focusing on the more wealthy and socially important, on certain trades,[61] or accompanied by, and indeed part of, an idealized description of a town and its inhabitants.[62]

It is also worth questioning assumptions about the purpose of directories, at least for towns such as Manchester, Leeds, and Sheffield during the late eighteenth and early nineteenth centuries. Although general descriptive sections on industry, commerce, charities, or places of worship were clearly aimed at visitors or attempted to boost the pride of knowing inhabitants, the lists of tradesmen, manufacturers, and professionals would have been far less amenable to such use. Between 1770 and 1828, most directory lists were organized alphabetically by surname, rather than by trade or address, and seem a poor finding tool for both strangers and locals unfamiliar with their surroundings.[63] All directories naturally claimed to be useful to everyone, but the organization of many of these early directories suggests that they were intended to serve a more knowledgeable audience, one likely to demand high levels of accuracy and comprehensiveness, who would use directory lists in order to check or confirm information, rather than to find out about the business community in general. Thus in 1794, the London businesswoman Charlotte Matthews, who was investigating an individual's creditworthiness on behalf of the Birmingham manufacturer Matthew Boulton, consulted her own local directory. She reported, unimpressed, that he 'is not in the directory . . . and only <u>lodges</u> [*sic*]'.[64]

---

[60] Schwarz, *London in the Age of Industrialisation*, 247. On the benefits and limitations of using insurance records to examine female employment, see Pullin, 'Business is Just Life'. See also D. T. Jenkins, 'The Practice of Insurance against Fire, 1750–1840, and Historical Research', in Oliver M. Westall (ed.), *The Historian and the Business of Insurance* (Manchester, 1984).

[61] Shaw makes the point that a comparison of a late eighteenth-century Liverpool directory with parish records shows the directory was biased towards merchants and professional people at the expense of labourers: *British Directories as Sources in Historical Geography*, 43.

[62] Hunt, *The Middling Sort*, 131.

[63] Notable exceptions are the 1826 *General & Commercial Directory of . . . Leeds*, which organized entries by both address and occupation, and the 1787 *Directory of Sheffield*, which listed entries by trade.

[64] Cited in Wiskin, 'Women, Finance and Credit', 40.

While they are not complete censuses then, directories may well have attempted to record the urban business community, or at least that part of it that was deemed important, in its entirety. They therefore provide better coverage of the urban middling sort than most other sources examined by historians for this period. They may also be more representative of the less wealthy middle classes. It seems reasonable to suggest that directories, perhaps more than any other source with significant chronological coverage before 1841 that included women, allow us to map the urban business community with some degree of accuracy. Moreover, as Gareth Shaw suggests that the larger the settlement, the greater the proportion of households that were included in directories, they provide a particularly good source for examining urban centres.[65]

MANCHESTER, LEEDS, AND SHEFFIELD: THE PICTURE FROM DIRECTORIES

For this study, directories produced for Manchester, Leeds, and Sheffield were sampled at approximately ten-yearly intervals between 1770 and 1830. The dates of publication for individual directories meant that it was often not possible to sample the same year in each of the towns. However, where directories were available, proximate years were sampled to provide broadly comparable surveys.[66]

The fourteen directories examined contained 6,450 women's entries, 2,083 of which were excluded from the sample because they

[65] Shaw, *British Directories as Sources in Historical Geography*, 32. Although Wilson notes the inaccuracy of Leeds trades directories from the 1790s: R. G. Wilson, *Gentlemen Merchants: The Merchant Community in Leeds 1700–1830* (Manchester, 1971), 18. Scola also notes that trade directories were very variable in their coverage, and that the categories used and the numbers listed fluctuated a good deal: 'In Manchester's case, it was not until 1840 that these problems were overcome; before then, small shopkeepers and market traders were particularly prone to disappearing from view', Roger Scola, *Feeding the Victorian City: The Food Supply of Manchester, 1770–1870*, W. A. Armstrong and Pauline Scola (eds.) (Manchester, 1992), 11.

[66] In Manchester, directories were examined for the following years: 1773, 1788, 1804, 1817, and 1828: E. Raffald, *The Manchester and Salford Directory* (Manchester, 1773); Edmond Holme, *A Directory for the Towns of Manchester and Salford* (Manchester, 1788); *Deans & Co.'s Manchester and Salford Directory* (Manchester, 1804); *Pigot and Dean's Manchester & Salford Directory* (Manchester, 1817); *The Manchester and Salford Director* [*sic*] *and Memorandum Book* (Manchester, 1828). In Sheffield, directories were sampled

were listed without an occupation. These apparently unemployed women appeared almost entirely in the Manchester and Leeds directories before 1820.[67] This suggests that the directories in each town served differing functions, at least in their earlier incarnations, since Manchester and Leeds directories listed both those who worked for a living and prominent members of society who appear not to have done so. Sheffield directories, in contrast, were clearly *trade* or *business* directories first and foremost throughout the period. Yet of those women listed without an obvious occupation who were excluded from analysis (and who constitute almost one-third of the total number of women listed in directories), not all were gentlewomen. One suspects that at least some may have been active in the commercial life of their towns. Miss Grace Clough of Red Cross Street, for example, was listed in the 1788 Manchester directory without a trade, although newspaper advertising suggests that she was a property agent of some sort.[68]

Those entries one can be more certain described working women appeared in steadily rising numbers in each town between 1770 and 1830. The rate of increase in all cases was significantly higher than that of the population growth. This trend amongst women was, however, generally proportionate to the rise in the number of working men listed in directories, suggesting both that the middling sorts who constituted the bulk of directory entries was growing at a faster rate than the general population, and that directory compilers were providing more comprehensive lists. Throughout the period, women

from 1774, 1787, 1797, 1817, and 1828 (no locally produced directory appeared in Sheffield between 1797 and 1817): *Sketchley's Sheffield Directory* (Bristol, 1774); *A Directory of Sheffield* (Sheffield, 1787); *A Directory of Sheffield* (Sheffield, 1797); *Sheffield General Directory* (Sheffield, 1817); *The Sheffield Directory and Guide* (Sheffield, 1828). The first Leeds directory was not published until 1797. This was used for the study along with directories from 1809, 1817, and 1826: *A History of . . . Leeds . . . & a Leeds Directory* (Leeds, 1797); *The Leeds Directory for 1809* (Leeds, 1809); *Directory, General and Commercial, of the Town & Borough of Leeds* (Leeds, 1817); *General & Commercial Directory of the Borough of Leeds* (Leeds, 1826).

[67] Between 1773 and 1817, only 40–53% of women's entries in Manchester directories and 42–62% of those in Leeds directories included occupational labels. In the 1826 and 1828 directories, 93% of women's entries in Manchester and 99% in Leeds appeared with an occupation. In Sheffield, almost all women were listed with a trade throughout the period (92–100%).

[68] Holme, *A Directory for the Towns of Manchester and Salford*, 30, and *Manchester Mercury*, 12 February 1788.

constituted between 4.3 and 8.9 per cent of employed individuals listed in directories (Table 2.2).

While the proportion of working women listed fluctuated between towns and over time, directories reveal no clear trend towards greater or lesser female involvement in the commercial life of Manchester, Leeds, and Sheffield between the late eighteenth and early nineteenth centuries. These findings contrast forcibly with the model of female economic marginalization described earlier. Moreover it is worth noting that the directories of all three towns from the late 1820s show a rise in the percentage of women listed compared to the previous decade. Not only is there no evidence of a downturn in lower middling women's involvement in the economic life of northern towns then, but it seems that female activity was—if anything—on the rise in the early decades of the nineteenth century. Thus we find women such as Ann Johnson, who manufactured knives and razors with her sons at Furnival Street in Sheffield, the butcher, Ellen Sidley, who ran a shop at 15 Bridge Street Market, Manchester, and Ann Addeman, a flour dealer in Hunslet

Table 2.2. Percentage of women and men in directories

Directory	Women	Men	Total	Women as % of total
Manchester				
1773	70	1,128	1,198	5.8
1788	181	1,843	2,024	8.9
1804	395	6,111	6,506	6.0
1817	621	9,671	10,292	6.0
1828	1,084	13,131	14,215	7.6
Sheffield				
1774	28	527	555	5.0
1787	70	988	1,058	6.6
1797	80	1,430	1,510	5.3
1817	83	1,850	1,933	4.3
1828	265	2,983	3,248	9.0
Leeds				
1797	41	830	871	4.7
1809	104	6,111	6,215	6.0
1817	275	9,671	9,946	5.7
1826	390	4,934	5,323	7.3
TOTALS	3,687	61,208	64,895	6.3 (mean)

Lane, Leeds, appearing for the first time in trade directories in 1826 and 1828.[69] Far from retiring from economic life during the early decades of the nineteenth century, women such as these openly assumed their places in the commercial sphere.

Just as the number of women who appeared in directories grew during the period 1770–1830, so too did the range of occupational labels ascribed to them. We need to be cautious about how we view the sort of occupational descriptions that appear in directories. As R. W. Malcolmson has warned, occupational categories used in this period tended to 'obscure the complexities and intricacies of the real world of labour as it was experienced by individuals and families',[70] whilst Penelope Corfield has noted that occupational descriptions such as those found in directories often confined themselves to the generic business, rather than describing actual work experience and status.[71] Without more information than is given in a directory entry, one cannot be sure, for example, whether Grace Render and Elizabeth Barber, who are both listed in the 1809 Leeds directory as 'milliners and fancy dress makers',[72] ran broadly comparable businesses, or if one confined herself mainly to cheap dresses which she made herself whilst the other operated a grand warehouse selling the latest fashions and employing several needlewomen. In this case, we know from the directory, and from a newspaper advertisement which also appeared in 1809, that Grace Render operated as a linen draper with her son at the same address she ran her millinery business from in Meadow Lane. Moreover, the advertisement noted that Grace's daughter worked with her in her millinery and fancy dressmaking business and that 'several' apprentices

[69] *Sheffield Directory and Guide* (1828); *The Manchester and Salford Director* (1828); *General & Commercial Directory of the Borough of Leeds* (1826).

[70] R. W. Malcolmson, *Life and Labour in England 1700–1780* (London, 1918), 23.

[71] Penelope J. Corfield, 'Defining Urban Work', in Corfield and D. Keene (eds.), *Work in Towns, 850–1850* (Leicester, 1990), 217–18. A similar point was made by Stanley Chapman, *Merchant Enterprise in Britain: From the Industrial Revolution to World War I* (Cambridge, 1992), 59. See also John Patten, 'Urban Occupations in Pre-industrial England', *Transactions of the Institute of British Geographers* NS 2 (1977), 296–313, pp. 301–5; P. Lindert, 'English Occupations, 1670–1811', *Journal of Economic History*, 40 (1980), 685–712, esp. pp. 690–5; M. B. Katz, 'Occupational Classification in History', *Journal of Interdisciplinary History* 3 (1972), 70–80; Pullin, 'Business is Just Life', 138–41; Joyce Ellis, *The Georgian Town 1680–1840* (Basingstoke, 2001), 48–57.

[72] *Leeds Directory for 1809.*

were required.[73] Grace's daughter was presumably either Ann or Mary Render, both of whom appeared as milliners and dressmakers in the 1817 and 1826 Leeds directories, after Grace had disappeared from view.[74] With her son and daughters in tow, Grace Render appears to have been at the centre of a thriving network of family businesses. Elizabeth Barber, by contrast, seems to have acted alone. However, Barber's shop on Briggate was in a much more prominent spot than Render's operation on Meadow Lane. Briggate was at the centre of the fashionable shopping district of Leeds, whilst Meadow Lane was so relatively inconsequential that it was listed in the directory merely as 'near the bridge'.[75] Barber appeared in Leeds directories in 1797 and 1809, both times operating from the same Briggate premises. She originally took over the business of Thomas Upton, who ran a staymaking and millinery business at the same address. The change of ownership was publicized in the *Leeds Mercury* on 3 June 1797, when Barber also advertised for an apprentice. By 1809 she was describing herself both in the town directory and in newspaper advertisements as a 'milliner and dressmaker', with fashionable London stock to sell.[76]

The term 'shopkeeper', which described 11 per cent of working women listed in directories, suggested an even greater variety of occupations than did 'milliner' or 'dressmaker'. This point is illustrated by comparing the sale of stock of two unnamed shopkeepers described in auction advertisements in the *Manchester Mercury* in 1773. In one, it was noted that 'part of the stock of a shopkeeper' included 'a Quantity of Jeweller's Goods, plated Buckles, Toys, Hardware, Silver Buckles, Boxed, and Watches'. In contrast, the other advertisement described the 'stock in trade of a shop-keeper' as consisting of 'Camblets, Ribbons, Stockings, Callimancos, Shalloons, Printed Cottons, broad and narrow Woollen cloth, Cloaks, Silks, Ruffels, Stuffs, Hanging Papers, and a Variety of other Goods'.[77] The way in which specific

[73] *Leeds Mercury*, 6 May 1809.

[74] Though Ann Render and Mary Render operated from different addresses: Ann moving from Commercial Street to Coronation Street in these years, Mary from Simpson's Fold to Kendal Street: *Directory, General and Commercial, of the Town & Borough of Leeds* (1817); *General & Commercial Directory of the Borough of Leeds* (1826).

[75] *Leeds Directory for 1809.*   [76] *Leeds Mercury*, 20 May 1809.

[77] *Manchester Mercury*, 26 January and 23 November 1773.

employments were described also changed over time,[78] and may also have varied according to region. It is also possible that individuals altered their titles in order to keep up with changes in their profession and status: thus in 1809, Hannah Stonehouse was listed in the Leeds directory as a 'pastry cook', whilst in 1817 and 1826 she appeared as a 'confectioner'. Throughout the period, Stonehouse operated from the same premises at Bramley's yard in Leeds, only ending her business upon her death at the age of 72 in 1826.[79]

Despite the degree of variety and the potential for imprecision, the occupational labels used in directories do have the advantage of being largely self-descriptive, since the practice of gathering entries by compilers or their agents visiting businesses in person suggests a degree of input on the part of those listed. The occupational descriptions in directories support this argument both by virtue of their variety and their detail: neither of which suggests that individuals were merely assigned general trade labels by a third party. The Leeds *Directory* for 1826, for example, listed the occupations of the inhabitants of Boar Lane with an impressive degree of precision. There were three confectioners on the street, but while Sarah Lilley was listed simply as 'confectioner', John Wilson was described as a 'confectioner, fruiterer and manufacturer of soda water', and Ann Broster appeared as a 'confectioner, cork dealer, pastry cook and fruiterer'. This suggests three very different operations, which the directory descriptions acknowledged.[80]

A comparison between directory entries and newspaper advertisements also reveals a close correlation between occupational labels in both forms of publication.[81] In the majority of cases, either the occupational description in the advertisement, or the range of goods and services offered, was the same, or very nearly the same, as the directory listing. In 1809, for example, Jane Plint was listed as a 'milliner

[78] Pullin, 'Business is Just Life', 139.

[79] *The Leeds Directory for 1809; Directory, General and Commercial, of the Town & Borough of Leeds* (1817); *General & Commercial Directory of the Borough of Leeds* (1826); *Leeds Mercury*, 28 December 1826.

[80] Parson, *General & Commercial Directory of . . . Leeds* (1826). Further discussion of the inhabitants of Boar Lane is provided in the following chapter.

[81] In the case of newspaper advertisements, it is very likely that individual businessmen and women outlined their occupations themselves, and although they might have suggested that their businesses were grander than they actually were, it is unlikely that they

and fancy dressmaker' in the Leeds directory, and advertised under the same title; by the 1817 edition of the directory she appeared as a 'haberdasher, milliner and dress maker' and adverts from this year reflected this change.[82] In around a third of cases, advertisements suggested a broader range of activities to those described in directories, although never a completely different one. Mary Wilkinson, for example, was a 'tailor' in the 1817 Sheffield directory and a 'tailor and draper' in the 1828 edition, but advertised as a 'habit-maker and tailor' in 1817 and a 'woollen draper, tailor and habit-maker' in 1828.[83] Elizabeth Moseley was listed as a 'carver and gilder' in the 1817 Leeds directory, but described herself as a 'carver, gilder and print seller' in an advertisement in the *Leeds Mercury* of 22 December 1817. Finally, Mary Jozeph was described as 'confectioner and fruiterer' in the 1804 Manchester directory, but her newspaper adverts in that year also revealed that she sold various grocery products in addition to confectionery and fruit.[84] We can, therefore, have a certain degree of confidence in the accuracy of occupational descriptions in directories, whilst acknowledging that they were unlikely to be always precise.

Throughout the period 1773 to 1828, over 600 different women's occupations were identified in the directories. The number of occupations rose in each town during each decade, and—on the whole—increasing numbers of women were described as engaged in each occupation as time went on (Table 2.3). The increase in the number

would have exaggerated too much for fear of deterring or confusing potential customers. Newspapers were surveyed in Manchester, Leeds, and Sheffield in the same years as directories: *Manchester Mercury*, 1773, 1788, 1804, 1817; *Manchester Courier* 1828; *Sheffield Advertiser*, 1774 [only copies for January and February, no proximate years extant], 1787; *Sheffield Register* [later the *Iris, or Sheffield Register*], 1787, 1788 [no extant papers for first nine months of 1787, instead June 1787–May 1788 were examined], 1797; *Sheffield Mercury*, 1817, 1828; *Leeds Mercury*, 1797, 1809, 1817; *Leeds Intelligencer*, 1826. This sample revealed 2,042 advertisements that were placed by, or contained reference to, women in trade. Excluding adverts concerning bankruptcy, deaths, and other instances where the subject of the advertisement was clearly described by others, thirty-one individuals could be positively identified from both a first and second name match as both advertising their businesses in the press and being listed in a directory. In twenty cases, either the occupational description in the advertisement, or the range of goods and services offered, was the same or very nearly the same as the directory listing. In the other eleven cases, advertisements suggested a broader range of activities than those described in directories, although never a completely different one.

[82]   *Leeds Mercury*, 18 March 1809 and 22 November 1817.
[83]   *Sheffield Mercury*, 31 May 1817 and 13 December 1828.
[84]   *Manchester Mercury*, 28 February, 8 May, and 18 December 1804.

Table 2.3. Women's occupations in directories

Directory	No. of occupations	No. of women per label
Manchester		
1773	36	1.94
1788	74	2.44
1804	96	4.12
1817	137	4.53
1828	193	5.61
Sheffield		
1774	17	1.65
1787	20	3.5
1797	40	2.0
1817	50	1.66
1828	75	3.53
Leeds		
1797	18	2.28
1809	39	2.67
1817	86	3.2
1826	113	3.45

of occupations undertaken by women suggests a significant broadening of female economic activity. This diversity is most marked in Manchester—the largest of the three towns studied. A similar picture of diversification was evident in those newspaper advertisements sampled, which are discussed in more detail in the following chapter. In the local press, the variety of women traders advertising increased almost fourfold between 1773 and 1828 in Manchester, threefold in Sheffield between 1787 and 1828, and almost as much in Leeds between 1797 and 1826. Such diversification was not unique to the manufacturing towns in the north of England—although the process might have been more marked in places experiencing greater change—nor was it a development limited to women. The multiplication of urban occupations was a nationwide phenomenon during this period: the result of increased specialization and the subdivision of labour, and the creation of new trades, industries, and services.[85] Yet the growing diversity of women's occupations in Manchester, Leeds, and Sheffield, as we shall see, remains significant.

[85] Corfield, 'Defining Urban Work', 221. See also Rimmer, 'The Industrial Profile of Leeds, 1740–1840'. As has been noted, Nicola Pullin also found businesswomen in

As was the case in the capital and elsewhere, and in line with the findings of other historians, women were still predominantly found in traditionally 'feminine' sectors: as bakers and confectioners, grocers and butchers, milliners, dressmakers, hatmakers, staymakers, and as various types of shopkeeper and dealer. The degree of clustering in operation becomes apparent if women's employment is organized into sectors decided predominantly by type of product (rather than type of work) (Table 2.4).[86] What is most striking is the predominance of women in three areas: clothing, food and drink, and shopkeeping and dealing. In almost all the directories examined, these constituted the three largest sectors of female economic activity: ranging from 61 to 77 per cent of those listed throughout the period under discussion.[87] When the other largely 'feminine' sectors of nursing and medicine, teaching, and accommodation are added to these calculations, the bias in female employment towards 'women's work' in directory lists during the period is more striking still: between 70 and 88 per cent.[88]

In Manchester and Leeds, whilst the three main areas of clothing, food and drink, and shopkeeping and dealing retained their dominance,

London participating in an increasing range of occupations between 1735 and 1845: Pullin, 'Business is Just Life', 144.

[86] Working women were organized into the following sectors: Shopkeepers and dealers (excluding those listed under food and drink, medicines, and clothing); Agents, auctioneers, and pawnbrokers; Food and drink; Clothing; Gardening and livestock; Transport; Accommodation; Building and furnishing; Manufacturing; Teaching; Nursing and medicine; and Other trades. See appendix for a breakdown of employments in each sector and notes on the methodology used for handling occupational data from the directories.

[87] The Sheffield directory for 1774 was the only exception, here these three sectors accounted for only 36% of women. Clothing, food and drink, and shopkeeping and dealing as a percentage of all women: Manchester 1773 = 77%; Manchester 1788 = 72%; Manchester 1804 = 66%; Manchester 1817 = 65%; Manchester 1828 = 69%; Leeds 1797 = 73%; Leeds 1809 = 72%; Leeds 1817 = 74%; Leeds 1826 = 63%; Sheffield 1774 = 36%; Sheffield 1787 = 61%; Sheffield 1797 = 69%; Sheffield 1817 = 63%; Sheffield 1828 = 77%.

[88] Again the exception is the Sheffield directory for 1774, where the figure for all 'female' trades is 39%. Clothing, food and drink, shopkeeping and dealing, teaching, nursing and medicine, and accommodation as a percentage of all women: Manchester 1773 = 84%; Manchester 1788 = 80%; Manchester 1804 = 78%; Manchester 1817 = 76%; Manchester 1828 = 84%; Leeds 1797 = 88%; Leeds 1809 = 84%; Leeds 1817 = 86%; Leeds 1826 = 87%; Sheffield 1774 = 39%; Sheffield 1787 = 63%; Sheffield 1797 = 70%; Sheffield 1817 = 64%; Sheffield 1828 = 88%.

Table 2.4. Women in directories organized by economic sector (in %)

Manchester	1773	1788	1804	1817	1828
Shopkeepers and dealers	21.4	20.4	22	20.1	19.8
	(15)	(37)	(87)	(125)	(215)
Agents, auctioneers, and pawnbrokers	0	1.1	1.3	2.1	2.8
	(0)	(2)	(5)	(13)	(30)
Food and drink	30	23.2	20	16.9	19.3
	(21)	(42)	(79)	(105)	(209)
Clothing	25.7	28.7	26.3	28	29.9
	(18)	(52)	(96)	(174)	(324)
Gardening and livestock	0	0	0	0	0.2
	(0)	(0)	(0)	(0)	(2)
Transport	1.4	3.3	0.76	1.3	0.6
	(1)	(6)	(3)	(8)	(6)
Accommodation	0	1.1	0	0.3	3.6
	(0)	(2)	(0)	(2)	(39)
Building and furnishing	1.4	1.6	2	1.9	0.8
	(1)	(3)	(8)	(12)	(9)
Manufacturing	11.4	14.4	16.7	17.7	10.4
	(8)	(26)	(66)	(110)	(113)
Teaching	4.3	5	8.6	8.4	9.1
	(3)	(9)	(34)	(52)	(99)
Nursing	2.8	1.1	3	2.1	2.8
	(2)	(2)	(12)	(13)	(30)
Other trades	1.4	0	1.3	1.1	0.6
	(1)	(0)	(5)	(7)	(7)
TOTAL	(70)	(181)	(395)	(621)	(1,084)

Leeds	1797	1809	1817	1826
Shopkeepers and dealers	12.2	12.5	18.2	17.4
	(5)	(13)	(50)	(68)
Agents, auctioneers, and pawnbrokers	2.4	1	0.7	1
	(1)	(1)	(2)	(4)
Food and drink	36.6	41.3	27.3	22.3
	(15)	(43)	(75)	(87)
Clothing	24.4	18.3	28.7	23.6
	(10)	(19)	(79)	(92)
Gardening and livestock	0	1	1.1	1
	(0)	(1)	(3)	(4)
Transport	0	1.9	0.4	0.8
	(0)	(2)	(1)	(3)
Accommodation	0	0	1.8	12.8

Table 2.4.(*Continued*)

Leeds	1797	1809	1817	1826
	(0)	(0)	(5)	(50)
Building and furnishing	2.4	1.9	4	3.1
	(1)	(2)	(11)	(12)
Manufacturing	4.9	4.8	6.9	5.9
	(2)	(5)	(19)	(23)
Teaching	12.2	10.6	9.1	9.2
	(5)	(11)	(25)	(36)
Nursing	2.4	1	1.4	1.3
	(1)	(1)	(4)	(5)
Other trades	2.4	5.8	0.4	1.5
	(1)	(6)	(1)	(6)
TOTAL	(41)	(104)	(275)	(390)

Sheffield	1774	1787	1797	1817	1828
Shopkeepers and dealers	14.3	2.8	12.5	10.8	5.3
	(4)	(2)	(10)	(9)	(14)
Agents, auctioneers, and pawnbrokers	0	0	2.5	3.6	0.4
	(0)	(0)	(2)	(3)	(1)
Food and drink	14.3	47.1	40	37.3	27.9
	(4)	(33)	(32)	(31)	(74)
Clothing	7.1	11.4	16.25	14.4	44.2
	(2)	(8)	(13)	(12)	(117)
Gardening and livestock	0	0	0	0	0
	(0)	(0)	(0)	(0)	(0)
Transport	0	0	0	0	0.4
	(0)	(0)	(0)	(0)	(1)
Accommodation	0	0	0	0	0.4
	(0)	(0)	(0)	(0)	(1)
Building and furnishing	3.6	0	2.5	0	1.5
	(1)	(0)	(2)	(0)	(4)
Manufacturing	60.7	37.1	21.2	30.1	8.3
	(17)	(26)	(17)	(25)	(22)
Teaching	0	0	0	1.2	9.8
	(0)	(0)	(0)	(1)	(26)
Nursing	3.6	1.4	1.2	0	0.8
	(1)	(1)	(1)	(0)	(2)
Other trades	0	0	1.2	2.4	1.1
	(0)	(0)	(1)	(2)	(3)
TOTAL	(28)	(70)	(80)	(83)	(265)

there was a slow decline in the proportion of middling women involved in these areas between the late eighteenth and early nineteenth centuries: in both cases, this was largely due to a fall in the proportion of women involved in the food and drink sector. However, this fall was partly compensated for by a rise in the number of teachers in Manchester and in those renting accommodation in Leeds: both of which were noted growth areas for middle-class women's employment from the late eighteenth century onwards.[89] Thus teachers such as Ann Bethell and Harriet Hickson, who ran schools in Booth Street and Chorlton Street in Manchester, or landladies such as Hannah Wormald and Margaret Simpson, who rented out rooms at Park Lane and Albion Square in Leeds, became increasingly common in the early decades of the nineteenth century.[90]

In Sheffield the picture is different. After 1774, women involved in the three main sectors varied between 61 and 77 per cent, while manufacturing—although it showed a remarkable decline in 1828— was a consistently large area of female employment throughout the period. Here women such as the filemaker, Alice Corker, the button-mould manufacturer, Ann Allcar, and the razor manufacturer, Hannah Dewsnap,[91] were a constant feature of economic life. The inclusion of women in all 'female' employments in Sheffield in the sample produced figures only slightly higher than those for the three main sectors alone between 1787 and 1817, but there was a significant jump in 1828 (from 77 to 88 per cent): the result of an upsurge in the number of women employed in the clothing and food and drink sectors and in teaching, at the same time that the proportion of women

[89] Susan Skedd, 'Women Teachers and the Expansion of Girls' Schooling in England, c. 1760–1820', in Hannah Barker and Elaine Chalus (eds.), *Gender in Eighteenth-Century England: Roles, Representations and Responsibilities* (Harlow, 1997); Leonore Davidoff, 'The Separation of Home and Work? Landladies and Lodgers in Nineteenth- and Twentieth-Century England', in Sandra Burman (ed.), *Fit Work for Women* (New York, 1979). Christine Wiskin also noted a sharp rise in the number of schoolmistresses in early nineteenth-century Birmingham: Wiskin, 'Women, Finance and Credit', 112–13.

[90] *Manchester and Salford Director* (1828); *General & Commercial Directory of the Borough of Leeds* (1826).

[91] All three women were listed in the 1817 Sheffield directory: *Sheffield General Directory* (1817).

involved in shopkeeping and dealing fell.[92] The importance of manufacturing in Sheffield suggests distinctive modes of production here that allowed for higher levels of female participation. As we shall see, the manufacture of metalwares appeared from the directory lists to be a greater employer of lower middling women in Sheffield than were the cotton trade in Manchester or woollen manufacturing in Leeds. This may well have reflected the relative dominance of the small workshop in the organization of cutlery production, although it may also be the result of a tendency amongst Sheffield directories to focus on the metal trades at the possible expense of other industries.

Taking all three towns together, the highest numbers of women in 'feminine' employments were unspecified shopkeepers (408), dressmakers (339), victuallers or innkeepers (338), milliners (269), grocers (100), straw hat makers (88), butchers (80), and confectioners (78). As this list reveals, not all the trades organized into these various 'feminine' sectors would be described solely, or even generally, as women's work. This is most notable in the shopkeeping and dealing sector, where butchers, grocers, and victuallers are prominent: all trades commonly undertaken by men as well as women. Moreover, there were, it is worth noting, more women butchers than confectioners. This means that individuals such as Elizabeth Falshaw, who worked as a butcher in Leeds between 1809 and 1826, and Elizabeth Adams, who ran a butcher's shop in Manchester between 1817 and 1828,[93] were more commonplace than confectioners such as Sarah Harvey of Church Street in Sheffield.[94]

Conversely, those trades included in the manufacturing, agents, auctioneers and pawnbrokers, gardening and livestock, building and furnishing, transport, and 'other trades' sectors would generally be regarded as 'male', although pawnbroking appeared traditionally open

---

[92] See appendix for a detailed breakdown of the number and proportion of women in each of the economic sectors.

[93] *The Leeds Directory for 1809; Directory, General and Commercial, of the Town & Borough of Leeds* (1817); *General & Commercial Directory of the Borough of Leeds* (1826); *Pigot and Deans' Manchester & Salford Directory* (1817); *The Manchester and Salford Director* (1828).   [94] *Sheffield General Directory* (1817).

to women.[95] Again there are exceptions to such a generalization: in manufacturing, Harriet Kell's profession as an 'artificial flower maker' and Margaret Mills's as a 'lacemaker' would generally be regarded as female trades,[96] but these are in a tiny minority (accounting for a single individual in Manchester and Leeds respectively). In 'other trades', charwoman was a woman's job, and running a circulating library was commonly held to be a respectable female position, although also an occupation followed by men: again, these constituted a fraction of the whole (nine individuals in all). Although the proportion of women involved in 'masculine' employments is much smaller than those engaged in 'women's work', it still constitutes a significant and steady proportion of the middling women listed in directories: 12–24 per cent in Manchester; 12–16 per cent in Leeds; and 12–37 per cent in Sheffield after 1774 (with 61 per cent, almost all in manufacturing, in 1774).[97] In all three towns, the first two decades of the nineteenth century witnessed some of the highest proportions of women engaged in 'non-feminine' trades. Women who worked in these areas have often been described as anomalies by historians,[98] but it is clear from this study that while such work was not typical, neither was it unusual or in decline.[99]

Of these male-dominated sectors, the manufacturing sector was by far the largest in all three towns (with building and furnishing also being particularly important in nineteenth-century Leeds). Not surprisingly, the type of manufacturing women did in Manchester and

[95] Beverly Lemire, 'Petty Pawns and Informal Lending: Gender and the Transformation of Small-Scale Credit in England, c. 1600–1800', in P. K. O'Brien and Kristine Bruland (eds.), *From Family Firms to Corporate Capitalism: Essays in Business and Industrial History in Honour of Peter Mathias* (Oxford, 1997). See also Melanie Tebbutt, *Making Ends Meet: Pawnbroking and Working-Class Credit* (Leicester, 1983).

[96] *The Manchester and Salford Director* (1828); *Directory, General and Commercial, of the Town & Borough of Leeds* (1817).

[97] Earle suggested that less than 5% of women were engaged in such trades in early eighteenth-century London: Earle, 'The Female Labour Market in London', 339, 341.

[98] Earle, 'The Female Labour Market in London', n. 39; Davidoff and Hall, *Family Fortunes*, 311–12; Schwarz, *London in the Age of Industrialisation*, 19; Masten, 'Women's Work in Eighteenth-Century Bath and Ipswich', 46.

[99] Penelope Lane also comments on the range of businesses undertaken by women in the small Leicestershire towns of Ashby de la Zouche and Hinckley both before and after 1800 in her 'Women and the Regional Economy', ch. 2.

Sheffield was influenced by the different industries supported by each town: thus in Manchester one finds more women involved in various employments connected to the production of cotton (125 out of 323 women); while in Sheffield metalwork was particularly important (49 out of 107 women). Yet in Leeds, manufacturing connected to the production of woollen textiles did not feature prominently. Moreover, with only forty-nine women involved in manufacturing listed in Leeds directories, it was a much smaller employer of women here than in Manchester and Sheffield. The majority of women active in manufacturing in all three towns were not involved in cotton, metalwares, and wool, but in a large range of trades connected to the diverse requirements of consumer-orientated urban economies: these were individuals such as the engraver and copperplate printer Mary Buck, of Exchange Street Manchester,[100] the jeweller Sarah Bowman, who ran a shop at Queen Street in Sheffield,[101] and the saddler Lydia Ratcliffe, whose business was based on Lowerhead Row in Leeds.[102] Also in this category were women such as Elizabeth Saynor of High Street, Sheffield, who made umbrellas and parasols,[103] the paper stainer Rachael Plowman, who operated from the back of the Shambles in Leeds,[104] the pipe manufacturer Deborah Millward, who ran a business on Oldham Street in Manchester,[105] the pocket-book maker Ann Paul, of Silver Street in Sheffield,[106] and the rugmaker Hannah Sandiford, who worked at Bramley's Row in Leeds.[107]

What is striking about the manufacturing sector of all three towns is the number of trades it contained in comparison with the number of individuals involved. Manufacturing accounts for 479 directory entries overall, under 209 different occupational labels: 2.3 women to

---

[100] *Pigot and Deans' Manchester & Salford Directory* (1817).
[101] *The Sheffield Directory and Guide* (1828).
[102] *Directory, General and Commercial, of the Town & Borough of Leeds* (1817).
[103] *The Sheffield Directory and Guide* (1828).
[104] *Directory, General and Commercial, of the Town & Borough of Leeds* (1817).
[105] *The Manchester and Salford Director* (1828).
[106] *A Directory of Sheffield* (1797); *Sheffield General Directory* (1817).
[107] *Directory, General and Commercial, of the Town & Borough of Leeds* (1817).

every label. Compare this with shopkeeping and dealing, where 654 entries were listed under 110 labels (5.9 women per label); or clothing, with 1,016 women under 108 labels (9.4 women per label). This suggests that women in manufacturing were spread more thinly over a wider variety of trades. One might speculate why this was the case. Were women discouraged from such work, which thus remained the preserve of the desperate or obstinate? If this was the case, why was the percentage of women involved in manufacturing so constant, even rising in the nineteenth century when one would assume they would be more likely to shy away from such occupations? Women might more commonly have inherited such businesses rather than setting up in them on their own, suggesting that given a choice, they would opt for a 'feminine' trade, but the evidence for this is sketchy. Also lacking is proof that women were not skilled enough to operate in 'male' trades. Both of these issues are discussed in more detail in Chapter 4.

What is clear from the findings discussed in this chapter is that while women might have been far more likely to engage in 'feminine' trades in Manchester, Leeds, and Sheffield, they were not barred from most areas of lower middling economic life.[108] Moreover, as a proportion of total employment in the 'middling trades', women remained a

---

[108] See Pullin, 'Business is Just Life', 148. While it seems reasonable to suggest that trades involving women's clothing and millinery became 'femininized' during the eighteenth century: Pamela Sharpe, *Adapting to Capitalism: Working Women in the English Economy, 1700–1850* (Basingstoke, 1996), 15; Masten, 'Women's Work in Eighteenth-Century Bath and Ipswich', 47; John Styles, 'Clothing the North: The Supply of Non-elite Clothing in the Eighteenth-Century North of England', *Textile History* 25 (1994), 139–66, it is not clear that women's work was restricted to such areas: Hill, *Women, Work and Sexual Politics*, 85; Susan Wright, ' "Holding up Half the Sky": Women and their Occupations in Eighteenth-Century Ludlow', *Midland History* 14 (1989), 53–74, pp. 56–69; Olwen Hufton, *The Prospect Before Her: A History of Women in Western Europe*, i. *1500–1800* (New York, 1996), 239; and her 'Women without Men: Widows and Spinsters in Britain and France in the Eighteenth Century', *Journal of Family History* 9/4 (1984), 355–76, p. 365. The continuity of some types of women's work in Manchester is revealed by Martin Hewitt's analysis of the 1841 census, which suggests that women dominated the retail trades and pub and innkeeping: 7,047 women worked in retail, compared to 5,170 men, whilst 853 women ran pubs and inns compared to 655 men: Martin Hewitt, *The Emergence of Stability in the Industrial City: Manchester, 1832–67* (Aldershot, 1996), 31, 42.

consistent presence during the late eighteenth and early nineteenth centuries. In these respects, Manchester, Leeds, and Sheffield may have been very different from other English towns, particularly those where borough custom did not explicitly allow married women to trade independently of their husbands. Although there is evidence of restrictions on married women's work in older market towns such as Oxford where such a freedom did not exist, and where male guilds and their control of the apprenticeship system might have been particularly strong,[109] more recent research on London and the Midlands does not support a model of middling women's retreat from economic activity.[110] It may well be that in faster-growing and less-regulated urban centres, women were able to exploit commercial opportunities with greater ease and for a longer period than in less dynamic settings. Moreover, since female traders seem to have been particularly associated with certain sectors of the economy, such as clothing, food and drink, and retailing, that are most clearly linked to the emergence of 'polite', fashionable, or consumerist society in Manchester, Leeds, and Sheffield, it can be argued that rather than being swamped or marginalized by changes in urban life, women traders found more opportunities open to them. As we

---

[109] Wendy Thwaites, 'Women in the Marketplace: Oxfordshire c. 1690–1800', *Midland History* 9 (1984), 23–42; Mary Prior, 'Women and the Urban Economy: Oxford 1500–1800', in Prior (ed.), *Women in English Society 1500–1800* (London, 1985). On borough custom and independent trading on the part of married women, see Mary Bateson (ed.), *Borough Customs*, 2 vols. (1904–6), i. 227–8; Prior, 'Women and the Urban Economy', 102–3; Judith Bennett, 'Medieval Women, Modern Women: Across the Great Divide', in David Aers (ed.), *Culture and History, 1350–1600: Essays in English Communities, Identities and Writing* (Hemel Hempstead, 1992), 154–5. Both Prior and Bennett suggest that the custom of allowing married women to trade with 'femme sole' status became increasingly rare, though see Ch. 4. In addition, as was noted in Ch. 1, the power of guilds was in decline on a national scale by the late eighteenth century.

[110] Indeed, the figures for Manchester, Leeds, and Sheffield are comparable with those found by Christine Wiskin in her examination of Birmingham directories: Wiskin, 'Women, Finance and Credit', 103–5. See also Pullin, 'Business is Just Life'; Berg, 'Women's Property and the Industrial Revolution'; Lane, 'Women in the Regional Economy'. The work of Wiskin and Lane, in particular, should be compared with Davidoff and Hall's examination of more wealthy middle-class Midlands families: Davidoff and Hall, *Family Fortunes*, and Hall, 'Gender Divisions and Class Formation in the Birmingham Middle Class, 1780–1850', in her *White, Male and Middle Class: Explorations in Feminism and History* (London, 1992).

shall see in the following chapter, the manner in which women engaged in business was self-confident and apparently uncontroversial: with little suggestion that female labour ought to be hidden or limited to the 'domestic sphere', or indeed that urban developments were damaging to the prospects of women in business.

3

The 'Public' Face of
Female Enterprise

ON 22 November 1817, the readers of the *Sheffield Mercury* were told of a new business in the centre of town:

MISS CRESWICK, AND MRS. LITHERLAND, RESPECTFULLY inform their Friends and the Public, that they have commenced the Hosiery Business, At their house in Bank Street, nearly opposite the Bank, where they have had in a choice assortment of all articles in the above line, and hope to obtain a share of public encouragement and support, which they will always endeavour to merit, by assiduity and attention to their customers.

This advertisement was not remarkable in itself, and indeed was typical of those placed by businessmen and women in the newspapers of Manchester, Leeds, and Sheffield between 1760 and 1830. Little more is known of Creswick and Litherland's venture: it opened too late to be included in the Leeds directory for 1817, and it was not listed in the next directory that appeared nine years later.[1] Moreover, this appears to have been the partners' only newspaper advertisement that year. Whether Creswick and Litherland succeeded in the hosiery business, and in securing the 'public encouragement and support' to which they aspired, is therefore unclear. Yet their advertisement, in common with others like it, does reveal the importance of attracting trade by forming a positive impression on the minds of the consuming public. Creswick

---

[1] William Parson's *Directory, General & Commercial of . . . Leeds for 1817* (Leeds, 1817), had a preface dated 1 October 1817. The next Leeds directory was Parson's *General & Commercial Directory of . . . Leeds* (Leeds, 1826).

and Litherland may have hoped to win over and retain customers by the civility with which they treated them and the quality of their stock, but their use of newspaper advertising suggests that the more 'private' worlds of shop-based interaction and word-of-mouth reputation were thought insufficient to ensure success. Instead, they needed to promote their image and reputation in the most public of arenas, and, moreover, in a manner that differed little from that used by men. Women such as Creswick and Litherland submitted themselves to the public gaze readily and willingly, hoping to further their reputations and their fortunes, not by emphasizing those domestic qualities that we are used to thinking formed the basis of female identity in this period, but by presenting themselves as respectable women of business.

This chapter explores the 'public' face of women's businesses in Manchester, Leeds, and Sheffield, and describes their visibility during the late eighteenth and early nineteenth centuries. Where the previous chapter measured female involvement in the urban business community in terms of numbers and occupations, this chapter will assess women's work differently: by examining the ways in which women sought to present their business activities in public, the place of businesswomen at the centre of business networks, and by exploring the physical presence of women's businesses in town centres. In these ways, this chapter will draw further links between the picture of urban development described in Chapter 1 and the role of businesswomen in promoting commercial and cultural change. It will also suggest the complexity of gender identities in this period amongst the lower middling sort.

THE ROLE OF ADVERTISING

As was noted in Chapter 1, newspapers were probably the most prominent form of publishing in northern towns in the period under study, so that newspaper advertising was arguably one of the most effective ways for businessmen and women to publicize their ventures. Nancy Cox and Claire Walsh have warned historians against assuming that the press was the only, or indeed the most important, way in which retailers appealed to potential customers in eighteenth-century towns. Walsh's study of London suggests that most shopkeepers did not advertise in newspapers, and that domestic goods were marketed more commonly using handbills and trade cards.[2] It is certainly true that many more traders operated in Manchester, Leeds, and Sheffield than appeared in newspaper advertising, which might suggest the use of alternative methods to entice customers.[3] Yet so few handbills and trade cards appear to have survived in these towns, that one is forced to conclude that newspaper advertising was more important outside London,[4] perhaps because of the greater distances into town that many provincial customers travelled, and the far reach of the press.[5] Moreover, there is clear evidence of a move away from more personalized forms of advertising in the early nineteenth century as more and more traders made use of newspapers.[6] Thus in 1809, the milliner and dressmaker Elizabeth Barber announced in the *Leeds Mercury* that: 'E.B. presents her Compliments to the Ladies of Leeds in *particular,*

[2] Claire Walsh, 'The Advertising and Marketing of Consumer Goods in Eighteenth-Century London', in C. Wischermann and E. Shore (eds.), *Advertising and the European City: Historical Perspectives* (2000); Nancy Cox, *The Complete Tradesman: A Study of Retailing, 1550–1820* (Aldershot, 2000), 107–14. Compare with the concentration on newspaper advertising in McKendrick's chapters in Neil McKendrick, John Brewer, and J. H. Plumb, *The Birth of a Consumer Society* (London, 1982) and Lorna Mui and Hoh-cheung Mui, *Shops and Shopkeeping in Eighteenth Century England* (Montreal, 1982), ch. 12.

[3] For those newspapers and directories sampled, the numbers of working women who appeared in advertisements in any one year were generally between 15% and 50% of the numbers of individual working women who appeared in the corresponding directories (Sheffield in 1817 is an exception to this generalization, when the figure was 81%).

[4] See Jon Stobart and Andrew Hann on the popularity of newspaper advertising amongst retailers in the north-west of England: 'Retailing Revolution in the Eighteenth Century? Evidence from North-West England', *Business History* 46/2 (2004), 171–94. Nicola Pullin found only printed trade cards from larger traders in London and Bath amongst the accounts of the Durham gentlewoman, Judith Baker: Pullin, 'Business is Just Life: The Practice, Prescription and Legal Position of Women in Business, 1700–1850', Ph.D. thesis (London, 2001), 101.

[5] See J. Jefferson Looney, 'Advertising and Society in England, 1720–1790: A Statistical Analysis of Yorkshire Newspaper Advertisements', Ph.D. thesis (Princeton, 1983); and Hannah Barker, *Newspapers, Politics, and Public Opinion in Late Eighteenth-Century England* (Oxford, 1998), ch. 4.

[6] The sharp rise in clothing adverts in the nineteenth century, described in Ch. 1, coincided with a spate of announcements that the use of cards had been abandoned.

informs them through this Medium, that from the Multiplicity of Business it has been totally out of her Power to send Cards individually, therefore she solicits the favor of a Call from them, which will be esteemed a great Obligation.'[7] Similarly, J. Plint announced in the same paper in that year that 'she has determined in future . . . to discontinue the Practice of sending Letters, and to Advertise more frequently in both Leeds papers'.[8]

For Manchester, Leeds, and Sheffield then, advertising remains one of the best sources of information about women in trade throughout the late eighteenth and early nineteenth centuries. Although they lend themselves less well than directories to quantitative analysis, advertisements give us far more detail about businesswomen's activities: the goods and services they sold, the manner in which they sold them and the customers they sought to serve. Advertisements also convey, much more than do directory lists, the sophistication of the eighteenth- and early nineteenth-century commercial world during this period. The vividness and persuasiveness of advertising in this period has been described by Neil McKendrick in his exploration of the 'consumer revolution', and particularly in his discussion of the activities of George Packwood.[9] These characteristics were also evident in advertisements placed in the newspapers of northern towns. The distinction between directories and advertisements is clear in the case of Elizabeth Raffald, the Manchester businesswoman who produced the town's first directory in 1773.[10] As Margaret Hunt has noted, Raffald listed her business under her husband's name in her directory, although she kept her own shop at the time.[11] Yet this apparent reluctance to make her commercial activities public is deceptive, since Raffald still advertised her shop widely in the press, and published

[7] *Leeds Mercury*, 20 May 1809.

[8] Ibid. 4 November 1809. A similar announcement was made by Mrs Whitman, a Sheffield milliner, in 1817: *Sheffield Mercury*, 24 May 1817.

[9] See chapters by McKendrick in McKendrick, Brewer, and Plumb, *Birth of a Consumer Society*.

[10] Elizabeth Raffald, *The Manchester Directory for the Year 1773* (Manchester, 1773).

[11] M. Hunt, *The Middling Sort: Commerce, Gender and the Family in England, 1680–1780* (Berkeley and Los Angeles, 1996), 130.

books (including the directory) under her own name. As was shown in the previous chapter, married women were less likely to appear in directories than widows and spinsters, but as we have also seen, they were not barred from doing so. That Raffald chose not to list her shop under her own name in her directory, though she clearly claimed it as her own in her numerous newspaper advertisements, might have more to do with the desire of a directory compiler to appear impartial than with a general trend amongst married women to deny their involvement in commerce. If we explore Elizabeth Raffald's business activities through advertising rather than directories, a clear and contrasting picture emerges of an ambitious and confident business-woman who was eager to push an ever-expanding variety of ventures with an impressive degree of confidence.

Shortly after moving to Manchester with her husband in 1763, Elizabeth Raffald began to advertise her Fennel Street shop in the Manchester press (whilst her husband ran a market gardening business with his brother).[12] By the end of the year, she was promoting a register office for servants, and her grocery business had expanded, and promised customers 'Cold Entertainments, Hot French Dinners, Confectionery &c, and still continues to serve Her Friends with everything in that way in the genteelest Taste and on the easiest terms'.[13] In August 1766, the Raffalds moved to new premises at 12 Market Place. Elizabeth continued to advertise frequently, and soon expanded her stock even further to include confectionery goods such as creams, possetts, jellies, flummery, lemon cheese cakes, and even grander productions such as bride and christening cakes.[14] By May 1771 she had also turned her hand to the supply of cosmetics, and now sold perfumed waters, shaving powder, swan-down puffs, lip salve, and six varieties of wash balls.[15] In addition she rented 'genteel lodgings' and storage space, took on 'the daughters of the principal local families' as cookery

    [12] J. Harland (ed.), *Collectanea Relating to Manchester and its Neighbourhood, at Various Periods*, 2 vols. (Manchester, 1866–7), ii. 144–6; Raffald, *The Manchester Directory for the Year 1773*, p. vi; Roy Shipperbottom (ed.), 'Introduction' to Elizabeth Raffald, *The Experienced English Housekeeper* (Lewes, 1997), pp. vii–ix.
    [13] *Manchester Mercury* 22 November 1763.   [14] Ibid. 19 August 1766.
    [15] Ibid. 28 May 1771.

students,[16] and sold an increasingly exotic array of foods, including anchovies, isinglass, vermicelli, truffles, hartshorn shavings, and drops flavoured with peppermint, lemon, ginger, cinnamon, clove, saffron, barbery, and currant.[17] In June of 1771 she published a cookery book, *The Experienced English Housekeeper*, by subscription (raising more than £800). The book, like her other business activities, was extensively advertised.[18]

Elizabeth Raffald was not alone in her desire to promote her commercial activities through print, and in seeking to diversify and enlarge her business interests.[19] In the late eighteenth century, Manchester newspaper readers would also have been familiar with other businesswomen who advertised extensively, such as the milliner, Elizabeth Lighthazle, the schoolmistress, Mrs Sydney, the grocer and auctioneer, Mary Berry and the coffee-house keeper, Mary Crompton.[20] Elsewhere, other names also rose to prominence through the press. In Sheffield, the Gales sisters, Ann and Elizabeth, advertised their bookselling and stationery business on a weekly basis during much of the 1790s and up to at least 1817.[21] In common with many booksellers in this period, the Gales sold not only books and pamphlets, but also medicines such as Spilsbury's Antiscorbutic drops, Dr Bodrum's nervous cordial, and Dr Arnold's pills for the treatment of venereal complaints.[22]

In Leeds, the names of the milliner, Jane Plint, and the bookseller, Mrs E. Langdale, also appeared frequently in the press.[23] Mrs Plint was a prominent feature of the Leeds millinery scene from at least 1797,

[16] *Manchester Guardian*, 19 May 1852.   [17] *Manchester Mercury*, 12 November 1771.

[18] Ibid. 12, 26 October; 2, 9, 16, 23, 30 November; 7, 14, 21, 28 December 1773.

[19] Christine Wiskin's study of Birmingham businesswomen also shows an eagerness to diversify: Wiskin, 'Women, Finance and Credit in England, c. 1780–1826', Ph.D. thesis (Warwick, 2000), 182–5.

[20] Berry and Crompton are discussed in more detail below. For Lighthazle and Sydney, see *Manchester Mercury*, 26 February; 4 March; 6, 13, 20, 27 May; 1, 8, 22 July; 26 August 1788.

[21] See *Iris, or Sheffield Advertiser*, 1797 and *Sheffield Mercury*, 1817.

[22] *Iris, or Sheffield Advertiser*, 6 January; 3 February 1797.

[23] *Leeds Mercury*, 13 May 1797; 6, 13, 20 May; 4, 11, 18, 25 November; 2, 9, 16 December 1809; 11, 18, 25 January; 15 March; 17, 24, 31 May; 7 June; 9, 22 November 1817; 26 January; 9, 23 February; 16, 30 March; 27 April; 11, 18 May; 8 June; 13, 20 July; 24 August; 2, 16 November 1826.

when she announced her move to 'a HOUSE, near the HOTEL, lately occupied by MISS CLIFTON, Confectioner'. In the same advertisement, Plint thanked her 'FRIENDS and the PUBLIC for the many Favors conferred upon her' and advised them that she was to show a 'genteel Assortment of Fashionable Millinery' on the following Wednesday.[24] Plint continued to publicize her business throughout the early nineteenth century. In March 1809, she advertised for two apprentices,[25] whilst in May of that year she announced that she was presently in London 'and intends returning with an Elegant Assortment of the most fashionable Articles'. This visit was repeated that November,[26] and in 1817 these twice-yearly trips to the capital were still in evidence.[27] By that time she had moved to new premises on Commercial Street, was publicizing a wider stock, including hats and baby linen,[28] and was advertising for four apprentices.[29] Plint's burgeoning business enterprise came to an end with her death in 1826. On 30 March, Mr T. Plint thanked 'those Ladies who so long and so kindly favoured his Wife with their Support' in an advertisement placed in the *Leeds Mercury*. Thomas Plint was a mercer by trade.[30] He was listed as running his wife's millinery and dressmaking shop on Commercial Street in the 1826 Leeds directory, but if he had planned to continue the enterprise, he did not succeed. The sale of her extensive stock—including caps, bonnets, feathers, wreathes, lace, ribbons, 'and numerous other articles too tedious to mention' was announced in May of that year. In November, the shop and dwelling-house 'lately occupied by Mrs Plint in Commercial Street' was put up for sale.[31]

Women such as Jane Plint were prominent amongst advertisers, but were by no means alone in their efforts at self-promotion. As was the case with directories, the numbers of working women who appeared in

---

[24] *Leeds Mercury*, 13 May 1797. This address 'near the Hotel' was probably Mill Hill, where she was listed in the 1809 Leeds Directory.   [25] Ibid. 18 March 1809.

[26] Ibid. 6 May, 4 November 1809.   [27] Ibid. 31 May, 2 November 1817.

[28] Ibid. 31 May 1817.   [29] Ibid. 15 March 1817.

[30] See *A History of . . . Leeds . . . & a Leeds Directory* (Leeds, 1797).

[31] *Leeds Mercury*, 11 May, 2 November 1826.

newspaper advertisements rose significantly between 1770 and 1830.³² Many businesswomen clearly found this a profitable way to promote their enterprises. Grace Render, the milliner and dressmaker discussed in the previous chapter, for example, placed seven advertisements in the *Leeds Mercury* during 1809 alone.³³ Sampling newspapers in a similar manner to directories revealed 2,420 advertisements that were placed by women in trade or contained reference to them. Amongst this group were 843 individual women—470 of whom placed or appeared in only one advertisement during each year surveyed—whilst the remaining 373 women appeared more than once. Not surprisingly, given the relative size of the populations, the highest volume of advertisers appeared in Manchester, with the lowest in Sheffield.³⁴

In common with directories, newspaper advertisements suggest that women in business were concentrated in clothing, food and drink, and shopkeeping and dealing. Also evident in advertisements is the significant growth in teaching during the early nineteenth century. What is markedly different from the directory findings, however, is the number of advertisements for performers and writers: often from out of town, and unlikely to have been listed in directories by virtue of both their occupations and provenance. Thus one can find advertisements for Mrs Cross, playing 'Priscilla Tomboy (the Romp)', in a production of 'Know Your Own Mind' at the Playhouse in Sheffield in 1787,³⁵ and for Miss Paton, 'Of the Theatre-Royal, Drury-Lane and

³² Newspapers were surveyed in Manchester, Leeds, and Sheffield in the same years as directories: *Manchester Mercury*, 1773, 1788, 1804, 1817; *Manchester Courier* 1828; *Sheffield Advertiser*, 1774 [only copies for January and February, no proximate years extant], 1787; *Sheffield Register* [later the *Iris, or Sheffield Register*], 1787, 1788 [no extant papers for first nine months of 1787, so June 1787–May 1788 examined instead], 1797; *Sheffield Mercury*, 1817, 1828; *Leeds Mercury*, 1797, 1809, 1817; *Leeds Intelligencer*, 1826. This sample revealed 2,042 advertisements were placed by, or contained reference to, 2,420 women in trade. Numbers increased from slightly over 200 during the 1770s to almost 400 in the 1790s and just under 900 during the 1820s.

³³ *Leeds Mercury*, 6, 13, 20 May; 11, 18, 25 November; 2 December 1809.

³⁴ In total, 412 women advertised in Manchester newspapers in the sample years, in 1,041 advertisements, 143 (782) in Sheffield and 288 (585) in Leeds. The figures for Sheffield appear skewed largely because of the advertising activities of two women: the printers and newspaper proprietors Ann and Elizabeth Gales, who together placed 288 advertisements between 1797 and 1817.   ³⁵ *Sheffield Register*, 1 December 1787.

Covent Garden' appearing in Manchester's Theatre Royal in 'the new Fairy, Melo-drame, Peter Wilkins!' in 1828.[36]

Despite the preponderance of advertisements for women in 'feminine' occupations, those in 'male' trades, such as most types of manufacturing, building, and furnishing, did not shy away from publicly advertising their businesses. Both Mr *and* Mrs Sedmon publicized their ability to perform 'every useful and ornamental Operation on the Teeth and Gums' in the *Sheffield Register* of 1787.[37] The following year, S. Stevenson of the 'Tobacco and Snuff Manufactury [*sic*]' in Manchester, begged 'Leave to inform her FRIENDS, and the PUBLIC, That She is going to REMOVE to her NEW SHOP, The Top of SALFORD-BRIDGE, MANCHESTER, Where a Continuance of their Favors will be most gratefully received'.[38] Sarah Askin, a plumber and glazier, whose business at the Calls in Leeds was listed in the town's directories from 1809 until 1826,[39] assured readers of the *Leeds Mercury* in 1809 that 'all Commands with which she may be honoured, will be executed with Punctuality and Dispatch'.[40]

Newspaper advertisements represented a variety of businesses, not just in terms of type—giving space to both dentists and plumbers, for example—but also allowing operations of different sizes and rank to appeal to the public. Thus in 1828, one can find advertisements placed by Mary Idle, who had opened a new fish stall in Manchester,[41] as well as the improbably named Madame Paris, who sold winter fashions from her 'show room' in Sheffield.[42] Most advertisements took the form of announcements (of the arrival of new stock, the start of a new term, change of address or ownership) rather than making more direct appeals for custom, and except in the cases of medicines and books, advertisements did not tend to promote particular brands, but rather individual retailers and manufacturers.[43] As was discussed in

[36] *Manchester Courier*, 19 January 1828.   [37] *Sheffield Register*, 21 July 1787.
[38] *Manchester Mercury*, 22 January 1788.
[39] *The Leeds Directory for 1809* (Leeds, 1809); *Directory, General and Commercial, of the Town & Borough of Leeds* (Leeds, 1817); *General & Commercial Directory of the Borough of Leeds* (Leeds, 1826).   [40] *Leeds Mercury*, 7 January 1809.
[41] *Manchester Courier*, 20 December 1828.   [42] *Iris*, 15 November 1828.
[43] Advertisers such as the razor manufacturer George Packwood, the subject of Neil McKendrick's study of eighteenth-century advertising, were unusual in this respect,

the case of the hosiers, Creswick and Litherland, and as Christine Wiskin has stressed in her study of Birmingham businesswomen, establishing a personal reputation was of vital importance to members of urban business communities in this period.[44] Although such reputations—by their very nature—were strongly associated with the person who ran a particular venture, it was also something that new businesses might inherit. Thus when Miss Hassal advertised her Manchester school in 1828, she described herself as 'Successor, and many years Assistant to Mrs. Holt'.[45] Widows who announced their intention to continue a dead husband's business commonly stressed their part in running it prior to his demise, and even employees could bring kudos with them, so that Miss Bray, a Leeds milliner, advertised in 1826 that she had just engaged 'a Young Person as MILLINER, from the Establishment of the late Mrs. Plint'.[46]

The importance of reputation and public approval meant that advertisements were almost always couched in a particular form of polite, deferential language. They generally expressed the hope of attracting 'public patronage', coupled with thanks for 'favours' already received. Mrs Sydney, who announced the opening of her new school near Manchester in 1788, proclaimed in typical style that 'she rests with the Hope of Public Patronage, and a determined Purpose of endeavouring to deserve it'.[47] Other teachers hoped for the 'honour' of looking after people's children,[48] and schoolmistresses, in common with businesswomen in general, usually sought 'to merit . . . future Favours'.[49] Most advertisements described existing customers as

---

although books and patent medicines were also advertised according to their brand: 'The Commercialisation of Shaving', in McKendrick, Brewer, and Plumb (eds.), *Birth of a Consumer Society*.

[44] Wiskin emphasizes creditworthiness and demonstrations of economic substance, as well as conduct and lifestyle, including public displays of moral worth such as philanthropy: Wiskin, 'Women, Finance and Credit', 128–38. See also Craig Muldrew's description of the importance of a 'culture of credit' in Muldrew, *The Economy of Obligation: The Culture of Credit and Social Relations in Early Modern England* (Basingstoke, 1998).

[45] *Manchester Courier*, 12 January 1828.   [46] *Leeds Intelligencer*, 18 May 1826.

[47] *Manchester Mercury*, 1 July 1788.   [48] See e.g. ibid. 1 April 1788.

[49] *Leeds Mercury*, 17 June, 8 July 1797. See also ibid. 24 June 1809.

'Friends', suggesting a familiar and not overtly commercial set-up,[50] as did the frequent encouragements for potential customers to honour shopkeepers with a personal visit or 'call'. E. Johnson, a dressmaker in Leeds, advertised a new collection in 1809 and noted that 'she will be happy to receive a Call from her Friends'.[51] A similar invitation was made to the ladies of Leeds in 1826 when S. Wilcox, advertising winter fashions, announced that 'a favour of a Call from any of her Friends will be greatly esteemed'.[52]

The wording of advertisements can be seen to echo the ways in which shopkeepers dealt with customers in person, flattering and reassuring them under often elaborate codes of polite behaviour.[53] This language of polite social interaction—of deference, favours, gratitude, and obligation—is found in almost every advertisement placed by women between 1760 and 1830, yet there is little sense that the language used in these advertisements was very different from that in adverts for men's businesses.[54] The Leeds linen draper and mercer, Samuel Render, son of the milliner, Grace Render, announced in the *Leeds Mercury* in 1809 that he: 'AVAILS himself of this Opportunity of returning his most grateful Acknowledgements for the liberal Encouragement he has been favoured with since his commencing the above Business, and begs leave to assure [his customers] that no Exertion on his Part shall be wanting to merit their future Patronage.'[55]

[50] See Naomi Tadmor on the use of the term 'friend' in the eighteenth century: ' "Family" and "Friend" in *Pamela*: A Case-Study in the History of Family in Eighteenth-Century England', *Social History* 14/3 (1989), 289–306.

[51] *Leeds Mercury*, 18 November 1809.

[52] *Leeds Intelligencer*, 2 November 1826. See also a series of milliners' adverts in the *Sheffield Mercury*, 17, 24 May, 22 November 1828.

[53] Helen Berry, 'Polite Consumption: Shopping in Eighteenth-Century England', *Transactions of the Royal Historical Society* 12 (2002), 375–94, pp. 388–91. See also Elizabeth Kowaleski-Wallace, *Consuming Subjects: Women, Shopping, and Business in the Eighteenth Century* (New York, 1997), 79–98, on the rituals of shopping.

[54] Deborah Simonton makes a similar point in the case of advertising in Aberdeen newspapers: 'Claiming Their Place in the Corporate Community: Women's Identity in Eighteenth-Century Towns', in Isabelle Baudino, Jacques Carré, and Cécile Révauger (eds.), *The Invisible Woman: Aspects of Women's Work in Eighteenth-Century Britain* (Aldershot, 2005), 108–9.   [55] *Leeds Mercury*, 6 May 1809.

Perhaps what is most striking is not that women used the same language as men in their advertising, but the degree of servility that this form of 'aristocratic discourse' conferred on male traders.[56] This was potentially far more problematic for men's gendered identity than was the public stance taken by businesswomen in terms of their claim to a degree of respectable femininity.

Indeed, women advertisers did not appear more shy of promoting their businesses than men: M. Jackson, for example, advertised her 'Straw, Chip, and Leghorn Hat, and bonnet Manufactury' in 1804, 'which she flatters herself she has now, by her exertions and attention to every branch of the business, brought to that perfection which can scarcely be equalled by any manufactory of the kind in the kingdom'.[57] Certain advertisements were, however, aimed at a specifically female audience. The purveyors of female clothing, for example, were most likely to address their advertisements 'to the ladies'. Miss Banks's advert for painting and drawing classes in Sheffield was also specifically addressed to the town's ladies,[58] Mrs Jones's portrait, figure, and landscape classes in late eighteenth-century Manchester were 'particularly suited to the Sex',[59] whilst Mrs Smith's handwriting lessons offered to teach 'an *Elegant Style of Writing* such as is peculiarly adapted to Ladies' epistolary correspondence'.[60] Similarly, a Leeds hat manufacturer promised 'to gratify all the varied Partialities of Female Taste' in 1809,[61] and female visitors to a Manchester optician, T. Bowen, in 1828, were informed that they could be waited upon by Mrs Bowen.[62]

Yet such specifically female-orientated advertisements were in the minority, and advertisers of both genders sought to appeal to potential customers' polite and fashionable aspirations whatever their sex. Thus, for example, Mrs Clapham announced in 1788 that she had 'taken and fitted up' the Swan-with-two-Necks in Lad Lane, Manchester, 'in a genteel Manner',[63] and Mrs Harvest proclaimed

[56] I am grateful to Matthew McCormack for this point.
[57] *Manchester Mercury*, 8 May 1804.   [58] *Iris, or Sheffield Advertiser*, 3 November 1797.
[59] *Manchester Mercury*, 25 March 1788.   [60] *Leeds Courier*, 30 August 1828.
[61] *Leeds Mercury*, 13 May 1809.   [62] *Manchester Courier*, 12 January 1828.
[63] *Manchester Mercury*, 21 October 1788.

herself a schoolteacher 'many Years accustomed to the Profession in a very genteel Line'.[64] Occasionally, adverts also sought to flatter potential customers by association with existing ones: R. Owen, of Tib Street in Manchester, announced that she was 'impressed with gratitude for the very liberal encouragement she has received in her business, from some noble, and very many ladies of the first rank and distinction, not only in the vicinity of and town of Manchester, but also in many parts of this and the adjacent counties'.[65]

Walsh claims that advertisers in eighteenth-century London tried to appeal to an increasingly wealthy and powerful middle class, who shied away from overt references to commercialism, so that shopkeepers sought instead 'to create images of refinement for their shops and reputations of taste and discernment for themselves, which would draw customers to them without suggesting the pushy selling techniques of the street market or the emotional, repetitive claims of patent product sellers'.[66] Although advertisements in Manchester, Leeds, and Sheffield were worded to convey an impression of politeness and gentility, it is not necessarily true to say that they underplayed references to commercialism, nor that they appealed only to the more wealthy. Indeed, Berry notes a change in shopping culture from the late eighteenth century, as a new form of retailing—based increasingly on fixed prices and cash rather than credit—robbed some types of shopping of its leisurely pace and politeness. New enterprises aimed, Berry argues—contra Walsh—at a less elite class of customers.[67] In

[64] *Manchester Mercury*, 1 April 1788.   [65] Ibid. 22 May 1804.

[66] Walsh, 'The Advertising and Marketing of Consumer Goods in Eighteenth-Century London', 83. On issues of newspaper readership and social class see also K. Schweizer and R. Klein, 'The French Revolution and the Development of the London Daily Press to 1793', *Publishing History* 18 (1985), 85–97; Stephen Botein, Jack R. Censer, and Harriet Ritvo, 'The Periodical Press in Eighteenth-Century English and French Society: A Cross-Cultural Approach', *Comparative Studies in Society and History* 23/3 (1981), 464–90; Bob Harris, *Politics and the Rise of the Press: Britain and France 1620–1800* (London, 1996), 94–6.

[67] Berry, *Polite Consumption*, 392–4. The rise of fixed-price shopping for ready money was noted by McKendrick, 'The Commercialization of Fashion', in McKendrick, Brewer, and Plumb, *Birth of a Consumer Society*, 83. See also Christina Fowler, 'Changes in

Manchester, Leeds, and Sheffield there was little evidence that the language of advertisements changed during this period. Indeed, the adherence to certain linguistic codes and practices is striking. Thus the milliner E. Lighthazle informed Manchester residents in 1788 that she 'takes this Opportunity of returning most grateful Thanks to those Ladies who have honoured her with their Commands, and trusts, by the most assiduous Attention, to merit a Continuance of the same liberal Patronage'.[68] Whilst forty years later, in 1826, Miss Bray, a Leeds milliner, announced that she 'gratefully estimates the numerous Favours she has received, and will make it her utmost Study to merit a Continuance'.[69]

A few adverts were found which promised lower prices for ready money only: Mrs Urquhart, a Leeds linen draper and haberdasher did so in 1817, as did Margaret Eyre, who sold dresses for cash only.[70] Yet Eyre's advertisement is couched in the same language of servility and politeness, and states that she 'would feel herself Wanting in gratitude to her numerous and increasing Friends, were she to let pass the present Opportunity of acknowledging the Favours conferred upon her . . .'.[71] Rather than shy away from questions of money, advertisers in Manchester, Leeds, and Sheffield combined polite language and commercialism, and promised good taste with value for money.[72] Mary Jozeph, the Manchester fruiterer and confectioner, noted that she sold goods 'on the most reasonable terms' whilst assuring 'her friends and the public' that they 'are purchased at the best markets, and of the first quality'.[73] Mrs Iredale of Sheffield offered an 'elegantly

Provincial Retail Practice During the Eighteenth Century, with Particular Reference to Central-Southern England', *Business History* 40/4 (1998), 37–54, pp. 48–9.

[68] *Manchester Mercury*, 6 May 1788.   [69] *Leeds Intelligencer*, 23 November 1826.
[70] *Leeds Mercury*, 24 May, 20 September, 22 November 1817. See also *Leeds Mercury*, 11 January 1817. Mrs Urquhart is listed in the 1817 and 1826 Leeds directories, running a shop at 50 Briggate, while Margaret Eyre appeared in Leeds directories for 1809 and 1817 with a shop in North Street.   [71] *Leeds Mercury*, 24 May 1817.
[72] Compare with Walsh, 'The Advertising and Marketing of Consumer Goods in Eighteenth-Century London', 83, who found that London advertisers rarely provided detailed lists of the goods they sold.
[73] *Manchester Mercury*, 18 December 1804. See also 28 February, 13 November 1804.

assorted stock of MILLINERY DRESSES' at 'prime cost and under',[74] M. Jackson of St Ann's Square in Manchester, also combined promises of low prices—furs 'from twenty to thirty per cent. Cheaper than they were last season', straw hats 'Cheaper than they were three months ago'—whilst still thanking 'the Nobility, Gentry, and others' for 'the very great encouragement and patronage she has received'.[75] Canny shoppers were also offered the chance to exchange old hats for new in Leeds, and to have hats altered and cleaned 'to the prevailing fashion' in Manchester.[76]

Businesswomen in Manchester, Leeds, and Sheffield thus used a variety of devices to appeal to the public in advertisements: they sought to flatter and entice them with their choice of words, to tempt them with fashionable selections of goods and services at low prices, and to instil in them a sense of trust and confidence by promoting their own reputations. Although it may have been the case that women traders were implicitly assumed to differ from their male counterparts in some respects—by being more attuned to changes in women's fashions, or more suited to the education of girls, for example—there is little sense of this in their advertisements. Indeed, it is striking how infrequently the language of advertising appears to have been influenced by gender. Advertisements from Manchester, Leeds, and Sheffield rarely played on the woman trader as somehow victimized or constrained by her femininity, for example. A rare exception is provided by Mrs E. Hardcastle, a widow who opened a tea warehouse at the back of the Shambles in Leeds in 1797. In an advertisement in the *Leeds Mercury*, Mrs Hardcastle expressed her hope that 'the same benevolent Principles' which had encouraged the 'Friends' of her husband 'so generously to assist the *Fatherless* and the *Widow*, will secure their Patronage and Encouragement in her present Undertaking'. Yet Mrs Hardcastle did not rely solely on sympathy, and her advertisement first noted that she had 'formed such Connexions in London, as will enable her to supply her Customers with the best

[74] *Sheffield Mercury*, 16 August 1817.   [75] *Manchester Mercury*, 23 October 1804.
[76] *Leeds Mercury*, 18 March 1809, and *Manchester Mercury*, 4 November 1817.

Articles, on the most reasonable Terms', and ended with the postscript that she could also supply 'a good assortment of IRISH LINEN, on the lowest Terms'.[77] Hardcastle employed a variety of devices to try to ensure commercial success: one of these was to play upon her widowed state and the fate of her children, but in this she was unusual. Moreover, it is clear that she did not see this appeal to sympathy as sufficient in itself, so that she also chose to place greater emphasis on her good business sense.

It is significant that in many of the advertisements from Manchester, Leeds, and Sheffield examined, businesswomen described themselves in terms of their occupation: as milliners, tobacconists, tea dealers, and plumbers.[78] In an advertisement announcing her intention to carry on her husband's business in 1797, Ann Mearbeck described herself as 'PLUMBER AND GLAZIER, Bank Street, SHEFFIELD', and thanked the public for 'the friendship of her deceased husband, JOHN MEARBECK', also 'PLUMBER AND GLAZIER'.[79] In 1804, Elizabeth Baron advertised as 'Cabinet-Maker and Upholster' in the *Manchester Mercury*,[80] and in 1826, 'MARGARET HAY, DRAPER and FURRIER' offered the ladies of Leeds furs at wholesale prices.[81] In all advertisements, women's involvement in business was clear, and their role in supplying goods or services naturally took centre-stage. Of course, directories also published businesswomen's names with occupational badges. However, the way in which information was given in directory lists was more formulaic, and it could be argued that women were described in terms of their occupations here almost by default. This reasoning does not work as well in the case of advertisements,[82] where individual women clearly made conscious choices about how to portray themselves.

[77] *Leeds Mercury*, 10 June 1797.

[78] See also discussion in Ch. 2 on occupational descriptions in directories and advertisements, and Deborah Simonton's discussion of Scottish women's advertising in 'Claiming Their Place in the Corporate Commuity', 108–10. *Iris, or Sheffield Advertiser*, 8 December 1797; *Leeds Intelligencer*, 30 November 1826.

[79] *Iris, or Sheffield Advertiser*, 8 December 1797.

[80] *Manchester Mercury*, 31 July 1804.   [81] *Leeds Intelligencer*, 30 November 1826.

[82] The same is true of cases brought before the Court of Exchequer, described in Ch. 5.

We are used to thinking of occupation as a way in which men could define themselves and were defined by others, particularly in the nineteenth century. Men's work has been linked by historians to independence, masculine self-respect, male authority, and respectability.[83] Such arguments have been connected to the creation of separate-spheres ideology, the rise of the male breadwinner ideal, and female domesticity: thus explicitly linking the rising importance of male work identity with an increasing tendency to associate women with the domestic.[84] Yet it is clear that—for the sorts of working middling women discussed in this book—occupation was also a major determinant of status and identity, alongside those 'domestic' characteristics with which we are more familiar.[85] Lower middle-class women would not have seen themselves as being the same as men, nor would others have seen them in this way (a point made clear in the following chapters). Gender remained, without doubt, a defining concept for lower middling men and women, but gendered identities did not conform to a simple model of separate spheres, where women were defined solely by their roles as wives and mothers. Businesswomen—particularly those who controlled their own enterprises—could clearly carve out a respectable niche for themselves in the public sphere by virtue of their occupation, in addition to more 'private'

[83] See Leonore Davidoff and Catherine Hall, *Family Fortunes: Men and Women of the English Middle Class, 1780–1850* (London, 1987), ch. 5; Keith McClelland, 'Masculinity and the "Representative Artisan" in Britain, 1850–1880', in Michael Roper and John Tosh (eds.), *Manful Assertions: Masculinities in Britain Since 1800* (London, 1991); Sonya O. Rose, *Limited Livelihoods: Gender and Class in Nineteenth-Century England* (London, 1992), ch. 6; Anna Clark, *The Struggle for the Breeches: Gender and the Making of the British Working Class* (London, 1995); John Tosh, *A Man's Place: Masculinity and the Middle-Class Home in Victorian England* (London, 1999), chs. 1–3; M. Cohen and T. Hitchcock (eds.), *English Masculinities 1660–1800* (London, 1999), 234.

[84] Davidoff and Hall, *Family Fortunes*; Wally Seccombe, 'Patriarchy Stabilized: The Construction of the Male Breadwinner Wage Norm in Nineteenth-Century Britain', *Social History* 11 (1986), 53–76; Rose, *Limited Livelihoods*, ch. 6; Clark, *Struggle for the Breeches*.

[85] Anna Clark has also found evidence to support a link between women's work and female social status in the rules of late eighteenth- and early nineteenth-century female friendly societies: *The Struggle for the Breeches*, 36–7. See also Jane Long, *Conversations in Cold Rooms: Women, Work and Poverty in Nineteenth-Century Northumberland* (Woodbridge, 1999); Carole E. Morgan, *Women Workers and Gender Identities, 1835–1913: The Cotton and Metal Industries in England* (London, 2001), ch. 3.

expressions of domestic femininity and moral worth. Thus work
appears to have been potentially crucial for both men and women of the
lower middle sorts: not merely as a way to earn the means to live, but
in helping to define identity and social status.[86] Despite the existence
of a large body of didactic literature in this period which was critical of
women's involvement in non-domestic arenas, including a strain of
writing that specifically attacked women in business,[87] there is little
evidence in Manchester, Leeds, and Sheffield of an ideological abhor-
rence of, or even a growing discomfort about, female employment
amongst lower middling women. Indeed, women's continued and
unabashed activities in the commercial life of these towns suggests that
'domestic ideology' was of limited influence amongst the 'petit bourgeoisie'—certainly this was true in the 'public' arena of work and economic life, where other considerations and ideals held more sway.

THE FEMALE PRESENCE IN THE URBAN BUSINESS COMMUNITY

As the preceding discussion of advertising has suggested, women's
commercial activity in Manchester, Leeds, and Sheffield was highly
visible throughout the period 1760–1830. In addition to women
advertising goods and services, newspaper readers would also have
come across businesswomen acting alongside their male counterparts
in various trading associations: such as Sarah Hulme, Elizabeth Tonge,
and Mary Whitelegg, who signed a petition defending the right of
dyers, dressers, bleachers, whitsters, printers, and calenderers to retain

---

[86] Cf. 'Introduction' in Baudino, Carré, and Révauger (eds.), *The Invisible Woman*, 6,
where it is argued that the female association with the domestic during the eighteenth
century meant that women's 'public' identities as workers in both textual and pictoral form
were 'invisible' in the sense that they were 'unrepresentable'.

[87] Kowaleski-Wallace, *Consuming Subjects*, 111–28; J. G. Tuner, ' "News from the New
Exchange": Commodity, Erotic Fantasy and the Female Entrepreneur', in Ann
Bermingham and John Brewer (eds.), *The Consumption of Culture, 1600–1800: Image,
Object, Text* (London, 1985); Pullin, 'Business is Just Life', ch. 8.

goods until work had been paid for, which was published in the *Manchester Mercury* in 1788,[88] or Dorothy Wilson, whose name was recorded in a report of a maltsters' meeting in Leeds in 1826.[89] Women's prominence in the business life of Manchester, Leeds, and Sheffield is particularly marked when focusing on the central fashionable, trading areas of towns. In Manchester, the area around Market Place was established as a prime spot for trade from the 1780s.[90] In Leeds, Briggate provided a focus for shops and businesses, whilst in Sheffield, activities centred around Church Street and Norfolk Street. Stobbart has noted how shops in leisure towns such as Chester became concentrated in the very centre of cities, with high-status establishments placing themselves along principal walks and near meeting places, such as assembly rooms, in order to attract wealthy visitors engaged in the social round:[91] thus reinforcing the role of shopping as a social or leisure activity.[92] These 'arenas of consumption'[93] are also apparent in Manchester, Leeds, and Sheffield, and although the location of retail establishments might not have been determined by the presence of assembly rooms, it was the case that shops and manufacturer-retailers clustered together in town centres, and that businessmen and women were keen to establish themselves at the heart of such commercial

[88] *Manchester Mercury*, 20 May 1788.

[89] *Leeds Intelligencer*, 2 February 1826. See also *Manchester Mercury*, 21 December 1773, 5 August 1788.

[90] *Manchester Mercury*, 14 February, 27 March 1804. On the fashionable centre of Manchester, see Hannah Barker and Karen Harvey, 'Women Entrepreneurs and Urban Expansion: Manchester, 1780–1820', in Rosemary Sweet and Penny Lane (eds.), *'On the Town': Women and Urban Life in Eighteenth-Century England, c. 1660–1820* (Ashgate, 2003).

[91] Jon Stobbart, 'Shopping Streets as Social Space: Leisure, Consumerism and Improvement in an Eighteenth-Century County Town', *Urban History* 25/1 (1998), 3–21, pp. 13–15. See also Peter Borsay, *The English Urban Renaissance: Culture and Society in the Provincial Town, 1660–1770* (Oxford, 1989), 168–70; Cox, *The Complete Tradesman*, 65–74.

[92] Cox, *The Complete Tradesman*, 139–45; Walsh, 'Advertising and Marketing in Eighteenth-Century London', 91–2; Berry, *Polite Consumption*.

[93] Stobbart, 'Shopping Streets as Social Space'. Stobbart borrows for this concept from J. Towner, *An Historical Geography of Recreation and Tourism in the Western World, 1540–1940* (London, 1996). See also P. Glennie and N. Thrift, 'Consumers, Identities, and Consumption Spaces in Early Modern England', *Environment and Planning* 28 (1996), 25–45.

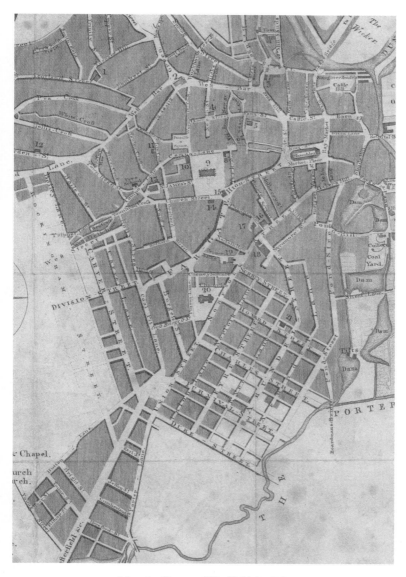

Map 1. Centre of Sheffield (1797)

Source: John Robinson, *A Directory of Sheffield* (1797).

Map 2. Centre of Manchester (1794)

Source: William Green, *A Plan of Manchester and Salford Drawn From an Actual Survey* (Manchester, 1794).

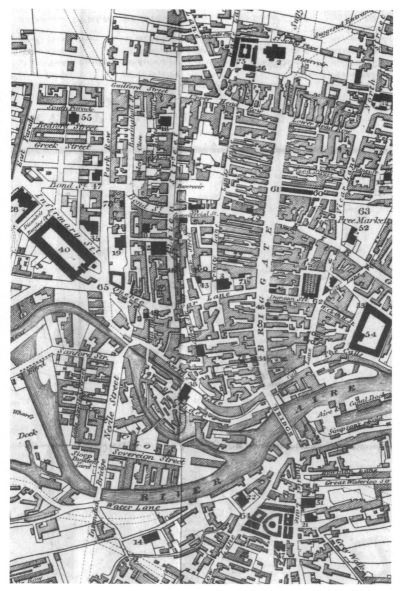

Map 3. Centre of Leeds (1826)

Source: William Parsons, *General & Commercial Directory of the Borough of Leeds* (Leeds, 1826).

activity. Thus in 1788, Miss Lighthazle's millinery shop was described as 'eligibly situated near St. Ann's Square',[94] at the centre of Manchester's fashionable shopping district, whilst in 1828, the confectioner, fruit-dealer, and register office keeper, Mary Dewsnap, advertised that she was moving from the relatively quiet Oldham Street to Piccadilly, which was a major thoroughfare, as 'it is her desire to have her office as to be more convenient for her customers in general'.[95]

In such vibrant places of trade and business, women were conspicu-ous.[96] These town centres were home to many of those businesswomen who helped to promote Manchester, Leeds, and Sheffield's polite and commercial credentials through trade, and who were instrumental in urban growth. This was particularly true of those businesswomen who ran inns, taverns, and coffee houses, providing spaces in which both the leisure and commerce of burgeoning provincial towns could thrive. Such women were fully incorporated into economic life and were emblematic of small-scale economic activity, operating as part of a network of individuals facilitating and exploiting the growth in trade.[97] Throughout the late eighteenth and early nineteenth cen-turies, sites such as inns and coffee houses were crucial to the smooth-running of urban business and cultural life, and appeared time and again in newspaper advertisements for auctions, bankruptcy hearings, political meetings, and local government sessions, as well as being places to purchase tickets for theatre performances and assemblies, and to enquire about property for sale and situations vacant.

During the late eighteenth century, the *Manchester Mercury* depicted several female-run venues as being particularly important.

[94] *Manchester Mercury*, 26 August 1788.   [95] *Manchester Courier*, 23 February 1828.

[96] Similar evidence of the prominence of women traders in the centre of towns has been found by Christine Wiskin in the case of Birmingham (Wiskin, 'Women, Finance and Credit', 107–12); by Shani D'Cruze in Colchester (D'Cruze, ' "To Acquaint the Ladies": Women Traders in Colchester c.1750–c.1800', *Local Historian* 17/3 (1986), 158–62); and by Debborah Simonton in Scottish towns ('Claiming Their Place in the Corporate Community', 109–10).

[97] On women and business networks see Shani D'Cruze, 'The Middling Sort in Eighteenth-Century Colchester: Independence, Social Relations and the Community Broker', in Jonathan Barry and Christopher Brooks (eds.), *The Middling Sort of People: Culture, Society and Politics in England, 1550–1800* (London, 1994); Wiskin, 'Women, Finance and Credit', ch. 4.

In the 1770s, Mary Berry's grocers and auction house and Mary Crompton's coffee house were especially prominent. Berry advertised sales of books, medicines, horses, clothing, and lottery tickets at her establishments in Market Place and Hanging Bridge,[98] and in 1773 her name appeared alongside those of thirty-one male traders in an advertisement placed by some of Manchester's grocers, tea dealers, and tobacconists, proclaiming their determination 'to abolish the oppressive Custom of bestowing Cards, Boxes, Tea, Spice, Tobacco, Snuff, or any other Gratuity whatsoever, upon Customers or their Servants, under the Denomination of *Christmas-Boxes*, or *New-Year's Gifts*, which has, of late, become intolerably expensive . . .'[99] In common with Berry, Mary Crompton was also involved in a variety of businesses. Crompton's coffee house at 29 Market Place hosted card assemblies, commissions of bankrupts, meetings, and auctions of property and business goods, whilst she also sold tickets for theatrical performances. The coffee house also served as a site for sessions of the Court Leet between 1768 and 1775.[100] During the 1780s, Alice Gregson's inn, the Coach and Horses on Deansgate, was hosting many of the bankruptcy commissioners' meetings and property sales advertised in the *Manchester Mercury*.[101] At the start of the year, Gregson's name was listed alongside Mrs Smith of the Sun, in New-Market, Maria Travis of the White Bear, opposite the Infirmary in Lever's Row, and ten other male-run inns, as places where a petition against the slave trade could be signed by members of the public.[102] The White Bear also featured in several newspaper advertisements,[103] and received particular prominence as the setting-off point for the New Commercial Post Coach that left Manchester three times a week for London.[104] By the nineteenth century, Gregson's and Travis's names had disappeared

[98] See e.g. *Manchester Mercury*, 26 January; 23 February; 16 March; 6 April; 17, 24, 31 August; 28 September; 5, 12 October; 2 November; 7 December 1773.

[99] *Manchester Mercury*, 21 December 1773.

[100] *The Court Leet Records of the Manor of Manchester*, 11 vols. (Manchester, 1884–90), viii. 117 ff. See also e.g. *Manchester Mercury*, 23 February; 9 March; 20 April; 18 May; 31 August; 21 September; 19 October; 14, 21 December 1773.

[101] See e.g. 22, 29 April; 6, 13 May; 10 June; 15, 22 July; 4, 11 November 1788.

[102] *Manchester Mercury*, 8 January 1788.

[103] See e.g. ibid. 19 February; 11 November 1788.

[104] Ibid. 15 January; 5 February 1788.

from view, and Manchester's residents were now being called to auctions, meetings, and commissions of bankruptcy at the Unicorn Inn, Smithy Door, run by Mrs Jones, and at Hannah Webb's Commercial Inn on High Street.[105] On 6 March 1804, for example, Mancunians were encouraged to attend the annual general meeting of the Society for the Prosecution of Felons and Receivers of Stolen Goods, which was to be held the following week at the Unicorn where one could also purchase tickets for the dinner.[106] Thirteen years later, the Society was still hosting its annual meetings at the Unicorn, now run by a Mrs Fisher, and described by James Weatherley in his unpublished history of Manchester as 'a Tory house'.[107] Fisher was still in charge in 1828 (although this was to be her last year in business) when the Society met again on 27 March.[108]

In Leeds and Sheffield, a similar pattern to women's involvement in commercial and corporate life is apparent. In late eighteenth-century Leeds, Mrs Tinsdill's Three Legs Inn in Call Lane was host to a number of property auctions and was also the place to buy theatre tickets.[109] In the early nineteenth century, public events in both towns were commonly held at two hotels owned by Mrs Greaves and Mrs Healey. Healey's hotel on Haymarket in Sheffield hosted a meeting of the Commercial Travellers Society and several property auctions in 1817,[110] and the same year saw Mrs Greaves Hotel on Briggate in Leeds also holding a variety of property auctions.[111] Both establishments were clearly local landmarks, since no address was given in advertisements. Indeed, places such as these were often used as points of reference. John Pollitt, who opened up a fashionable hairdressing business in

[105] See e.g. adverts for meetings at the Unicorn: *Manchester Mercury*, 16 October; 20 November; 4 December 1804; and those for meetings at the Commercial Inn on 10, 24, and 31 January; 21 February; 6 March 1804.   [106] Ibid. 6 March 1804.
[107] Ibid. 11 March 1817. Chetham's Libarary, James Weatherley, 'Recollections of Manchester and Manchester Characters and Anecdotes Relating to Manchester and Lancashire Generally from the Year 1800 to 1860', 1860, p. 71.
[108] *Manchester Mercury*, 5 April 1828. An advert in the paper on 26 January 1828 announced that her business was up for sale due to her retirement, and another on 15 November announced that she had sold the Unicorn to a Joseph Challenor.
[109] *Leeds Mercury*, 4 March; 15 and 22 April; 30 September 1797.
[110] *Sheffield Mercury*, 18 January; 16 March; 22, 29 May; 7 June 1817. Auctions were also held at Mrs Lawton's George Inn in Market Place: ibid. 22 March 1817.
[111] *Leeds Mercury*, 4, 25 January; 8, 15, 22 March; 20 September 1817.

Market Place, Manchester in 1773, for example, described it being opposite Mary Crompton's coffee house.[112]

As we have seen, businesswomen were prominent in much of the local print culture of northern towns between 1760 and 1830, and in directories and newspapers in particular. However, women's visibility in commercial life would have been most obvious to contemporaries walking the streets, since the physical appearance of businesswomen in urban centres would have been particularly marked. The evidence from directories has suggested that the proportion of female-run enterprises in towns ranged from 4.3–9 per cent between 1773 and 1828 in our three towns. However, the bias in female businesses towards shopkeeping and dealing, food and drink, and clothing means that they were especially likely to be clustered in urban centres, and would therefore have appeared more prominent in central trading areas than these figures suggest.[113] To illustrate this sense of a female presence, Boar Lane in Leeds was selected as a fairly typical street in terms of the range of goods and services on offer and the proportion of female-owned enterprises found there in 1826. Boar Lane ran between Briggate and Quebec Street. It was home to Trinity Church and the Chief Constable's Office and was close to two banks, one on the aptly named Bank Street and one on Briggate, as well as to the Post Office on Mill Hill, the New Library on Park Row, and the Northern Society of Fine Arts in Albion Street.[114]

Boar Lane provided Leeds's residents with a wide choice of goods and services. One could purchase medicines, stationery, leather products, including saddles and portmanteaus, linen, blankets, tobacco and snuff, watches, and both musical and scientific instruments. Homes could be beautified with oil paintings, engravings, furniture, and china and glass, and bodies could be adorned with hosiery, hats, jewellery, tailored clothes, perfume, and fashionable haircuts. One could seek out the

[112] Barker and Harvey, 'Women Entrepreneurs and Urban Expansion', 124.
[113] Roger Scola notes that in Manchester, most food shops remained centrally located during the eighteenth century, but that there was a gradual move to the suburbs as the nineteenth century progressed: Roger Scola, *Feeding the Victorian City: The Food Supply of Manchester 1770–1870* (Manchester, 1992), ch. 10.
[114] See map in William Parson, *General & Commercial Directory of . . . Leeds* (Leeds, 1826).

Map 4. Traders in Boar Lane, Leeds (1826)

BRIGGATE

Issac Clark, bookseller, stationer, and fire insurance agent	1	21	William Smith, chemist and druggist
Martha Cass, Punch Bowl Inn	2, 3	22	M. A. Davies, leghorn and straw hat warehouse
Mary Dearlove, musical instrument manufacturer	4	23	William Fawcett, carver and gilder, printseller, and dealer in oil paintings
Joseph Cheetham, watch and clock manufacturer, goldsmith, jeweller, and cutler	5	24	Ann Broster, confectioner, cork dealer, pastry cook, and fruiterer
John Wade, surgeon	6	26	J. Rothery, Saracen's Head Inn
Thomas Bill, glass and china warehouse and rag merchant	7	27	Anthony Hutchinson, carver, gilder and dealer in oil paintings, prints, piano fortes, etc. Bowes and Milnes, woolstaplers
James Carlile, tobacco and snuff manufacturer	8	28	Sarah Lilley, confectioner
George Topham, saddler and manufacturer of portmanteaus, trunks, etc.	9, 10	29	Timothy Ingham, butcher
Thomas Topham, engraver John Labron, tailor and draper	11	30	John Dalby, cabinetmaker
			TRINITY CHURCH
John Adams, ladies' and gentlemen's hair cutter, perfumer, and dealer in London hats	12	33	Edward Smeeton, chemist and druggist, manufacturer of soda, magnesia, Cheltenham and Seidlitz waters
William Blackburn, grocer and tobacconist	13	34	Gabriel Davis, manufactuer of optical, mathematical, and philosophical instruments, and barometer, thermometer, sacharometer, and hydrometer maker
T. Turnbull, White Horse Hotel	14	35	William Hargrave, tobacco and snuff manufacturer and hop merchant
John Royce, gem and seal engraver Samuel Topham, historic and writing engraver	15	36	Samuel Holmes, woollen, stuff, and blanket merchant, importer of Irish linen, wholesale and retail linen draper
George Gascoigne, wholesale and retail confectioner	17	37	C. and W. Dove, curriers and leather merchants

Map 4 (*Continued*)

Martha Wilson, sempstress Grace Lazenby, lodgings			Charles Watson, agent
John and Mary Kemplay and daughters, ladies' boarding and day boarding seminary	18	38	John Wilson, confectioner, fruiterer and manufacturer of soda water William Wailes, solicitor
Joseph Gillham, hat manufacturer	19	39	John Ray, solicitor
Joseph Stenson, wholesale and retail linen drapery and hosiery	20	40	William Squire, tea dealer and agent to the French Brandy Distillery co.

QUEBEC STREET

Source: William Parson, *General & Commercial Directory of . . . Leeds* (Leeds, 1826). The organization of the different businesses (though not the ordering) is speculative, and assumes that numbering went up one side of the street and down the other: see Gareth Shaw, *British Directories as Sources in Historical Geography* (Norwich, 1982), 36.

services of a surgeon, solicitor, or schoolteacher, feast on confectionery, fruit, tea, brandy, and meat from the butchers, or choose to eat and drink at either of two inns. Moreover, visitors could stay at the White Horse Hotel, the Punch Bowl Inn or Saracen's Head Inn, or at lodgings in Gascoigne's Yard. As Map 4 shows, to contemporary observers used to walking down streets such as Boar Lane and partaking of the goods and services on offer, female-run businesses would not have appeared at all unusual. In a street of retailers, small-scale manufacturers, and service providers who could have supplied many of the needs of Leeds's middling sorts, one could dine at Martha Cass's Punch Bowl Inn, buy a musical instrument from the manufacturer-retailer Mary Dearlove next door, or obtain confectionery goods from either Ann Broster or Sarah Lilley across the road. Further towards Briggate, one could visit the sempstress, Martha Wilson, rent lodgings from Grace Lazenby or send a daughter to the ladies' seminary run by John and Mary Kemplay with the assistance of their daughters. Of the forty-one businesses operating in Boar Lane, at least seven can be identified as wholly, or partly, run by women: constituting 17 per cent of the total.

Of course, shops and shopkeepers would have attracted particular notice from passers-by because of the pains taken over their appearance. Neil McKendrick notes the delight of foreign visitors at the capital's shops during the eighteenth century, with Sophie von la Roche enthusing that 'Behind the great glass windows absolutely everything one can think of is neatly, attractively displayed, in such abundance of choice as almost to make one greedy.'[115] Claire Walsh has also shown how London shopkeepers' inventories from the early part of the century demonstrate high levels of spending and concern for interior design,[116] while Helen Berry has described the importance of shops' appearance to drawing in prospective purchasers in the capital, and the impact on the shopping experience of improvements to paving, street cleaning, and lighting.[117] Chapter 1 has already described the strong pressure for local Improvement Acts in Manchester, Leeds, and Sheffield: many of them aimed at making town centres more attractive. The desire to entice shoppers was behind the efforts of Manchester traders to prevent obstructions to the easy passage of customers in the late eighteenth century, by threatening to prosecute porters and others for 'The DAILY Inconveniences arising to the Public and the Residents of St. Ann's-Square, by Carts, Benches, &c. obstructing the Way or Passage through the same'.[118] It seems likely that efforts were also taken to entice shoppers into individual establishments, along similar lines to those employed in London. Indeed, when the grocer, George Heywood, visited his home town of Huddersfield in 1815, after several years in Manchester, he noted 'I cannot help noticing how rough and slovenly the shops appear in Huddsfd from what they are in Manr.'[119]

---

[115] McKendrick, 'The Commercialization of Fashion', in McKendrick, Brewer, and Plumb (eds.), *Birth of a Consumer Society*, 79, citing Clare Williams (ed.), *Sophie in London, 1786, Being the Diary of Sophie v. la Roche* (London, 1933), 87.

[116] Claire Walsh, 'Shop Design and the Display of Goods in Eighteenth-Century London', *Journal of Design History* 8/3 (1995), 157–76.

[117] Berry, 'Polite Consumption', 382–5. See also Claire Walsh, 'The Design of London Goldsmith's Shops in the Early Eighteenth Century', in D. Mitchell (ed.), *Goldsmiths, Silversmiths and Bankers: Innovation and the Transfer of Skill, 1550–1750* (Stroud, 1995); Penelope Corfield, 'Walking the City Streets: The Urban Odyssey in Eighteenth-Century England', *Journal of Urban History* 16/2 (1990), 132–74, pp. 142, 149–52; Stobbart, 'Shopping Streets as Social Space'; Nancy Cox and Claire Walsh, ' "Their Shops are Dens, the Buyer is their Prey": Shop Design and Sale Techniques', in Cox (ed.), *The Complete Tradesman.*   [118] *Manchester Mercury*, 5 August 1788.

[119] John Rylands Library, Diary of George Heywood, MS 703 [48].

In addition to their physical presence in towns, women traders also appeared ubiquitous in the financial records of aristocratic and gentry families.[120] The household accounts of Lord and Lady Irwin, who lived at Temple Newsham, near Leeds, detail transactions from the 1760s and 1770s.[121] During this period Lady Irwin was presented with a bill from Mary Shepheard for bedding; paid Ann Upton, Mary Weightman, a Miss Harry, and Louisa Ingram for various items of haberdashery; was supplied by Susannah Greene with thread and buttons; and by Grace Mason and Elizabeth Sheep with clothing.[122] The Irwins also paid Mary Matthews and Jane Blond for the supply of meat,[123] Mary Gillbeard for china,[124] Mary Ogle for paper, pencils, and books,[125] and Mary Luttman for bread, butter, and fruit.[126] The household records of Dunham Massey Hall, the home of the Grey family near Manchester, also show the widespread use of women traders in the 1820s. During this period Mary and Sarah Dean supplied clothing, bedding, fabrics, and paper, Ann Sykes was paid for chimney pots, Sarah Southern provided leather skins, and Mary Allen charged the family to repair a thermometer, and for the sale of tobacco water and silver paper.[127]

It was not only aristocratic and gentry families that recorded their dealings with female traders. The Gotts of Leeds, a family of woollen merchants and manufacturers, received an estimate for painting windows and shutters 'with the Best of Paint & in the Best Manner' in 1792 from Mary Simpson & Sons.[128] Elizabeth Gott also recorded her frequent shopping trips and purchases in her diary. In 1809 and

[120] See Penelope Lane's discussion of the estate accounts of Donnington Park in Leicestershire in her 'Women in the Regional Economy, the East Midlands 1700–1830', Ph.D. thesis (Warwick, 1999), ch. 3. Also Pullin, 'Business is Just Life', ch. 5, on women traders and the Baker family of Durham.

[121] West Yorkshire Archive Service, Leeds District Archives, Temple Newsham Accounts (TN), EA/12/1 (household accounts); EA/12/2 (clothing bills); EA/12/18 (books).

[122] TN/EA/12/2–7.   [123] TN/EA/12/1, bills dated November 1770 and May 1772.

[124] TN/EA/12/1, bill dated 3 June 1773.

[125] TN/EA/12/18, bills dated 1772 and 1774.

[126] TN/EA/12/1, bill dated 21 June 1773.

[127] John Rylands Library, Papers of the Grey family, EGR7/12/1–12.

[128] Brotherton Library, Gott papers, MS 193/33, letter dated 7 May 1792.

1829 she detailed a number of transactions with female traders: all of them in clothing and associated trades. She paid Misses Stevenson and Jackson for gowns, Mrs Plint—the Leeds milliner discussed earlier— for a black and gold cap and a pair of grey gloves, Mrs Goodson for 4 yards of white satin ribbon and for children's shoes, Mrs Hawker for a pair of stays, Mrs James for a white satin bonnet, and Mrs Bean for a muslin petticoat, red satin dress, and a brown silk pelisse.[129] A collection of tradesmen's bills for the family of Thomas Hibbert, a Manchester merchant, shows several payments being made between 1806 and 1810 to Widow Winter and son, wine merchants at 101 Deansgate.[130] Mrs Hibbert also paid a bill of 15s. in September 1810 to Miss Blinkhorn, owner of the circulating library.[131] Lower down on the social scale, John Hughes, a Manchester shoemaker, kept detailed accounts of his purchases between 1798 and 1807. During this period he bought tobacco and snuff at frequent intervals from Sarah Stephenson, whose 'Tobacco and Snuff Manufactury [*sic*]' on Salford Bridge has already been mentioned. Hughes also purchased butter and flour from Mrs Whitby; snuff, candles, soap, and sugar from Mrs Bentley; coffee, starch, mustard, and salt from Ann Chester; and other groceries from his staple list of bread, butter, flour, cheese, and potatoes from Mrs Ripley, Mrs Richardson, Betty Parkinson, and Mrs Smith.[132]

Both locally produced town histories and contemporary commentaries described the presence of women traders matter-of-factly, acknowledging the uncontroversial nature of their existence. In 1816, Joseph Aston's *Picture of Manchester* noted that the present librarian of the Manchester Circulating Library in King Street, which boasted 370 subscribers (including, as we have seen, Mrs Hibbert), was a Miss Blinkhorn 'who, for correctness and attentions to the subscribers, deserves much praise'.[133] An unpublished history by the impoverished

---

[129] Gott papers, MS 193/194/3/8, entries for 1, 18 January; 25 February 1809; 14 January; 29 April; 6 July; 3 August 1829.
[130] John Rylands Library, Hibbert-Ware papers, Eng MS 1024, fos. 67, 85, 92, 119, 143.
[131] Ibid. Eng MS 1024, fo. 157.
[132] Manchester Central Reference Library, John Hughes account book, MISC/258.
[133] Joseph Aston, *A Picture of Manchester* (Manchester, 1816), 175.

bookseller, James Weatherley, entitled 'Recollections of Manchester and Manchester characters', noted that Mrs Basnett ran a draper's shop opposite St Mary's Gate in 1803 and that Mrs Denton operated a circulating library on Shude Hill in 1822.[134] Also recalling Manchester in the early nineteenth century, Josiah Slugg described the working lives of two female druggists—Ann Cooke and Ann Thorp—and recorded the activities of the Binyon sisters, two of whom were tea dealers, whilst the other ran a ready-made linen shop in Piccadilly. In the late 1820s, Slugg noted, Miss Boardman operated a 'well known' confectioner's shop on King Street, whilst Mary Harrison ran an even more successful confectioner's on Deansgate.[135] Harland's *Collectanea Relating to Manchester and its Neighbourhood at Various Periods* included reminiscences of Market Place and neighbouring streets in 1772. Here, it was noted, could be found Mrs Cooke, the druggist, Mrs Budworth's coffee and dining rooms, Mrs Crompton's coffee house and 'an old woman who sold herrings, red and white, also black and white puddings, for which I was sometimes a customer'.[136] In common with many of these Manchester histories, Robert Leader's *Sheffield in the Eighteenth Century* was based on recollections and interviews with elderly residents. A description of the market place in 1784 describes one shop as having belonged to the grocer, Hannah Firth.[137] Leader notes that 'Old Milly Lowther' ran a fish stall in Pudding Lane,[138] that Hannah Haslehurst and Sons started a short-lived bank in the town,[139] and that in 1787, Miss Lister succeeded Samuel Simmons in his stationery, newsagent, and postmaster business.[140]

As this and the previous chapter have made clear, independent businesswomen such as Miss Lister—operating in a wide range of ventures—were fully integrated into the economic life of Manchester,

---

[134] Weatherley, 'Recollections of Manchester and Manchester Characters', 3, 38.
[135] Josiah Thomas Slugg, *Reminiscences of Manchester Fifty Years Ago* (Manchester, 1881), 69, 94, 99, 100.
[136] Harland, *Collectanea Relating to Manchester and its Neighbourhood*, ii. 209–13.
[137] Robert Eadon Leader, *Sheffield in the Eighteenth Century* (Sheffield, 1901), 165.
[138] Ibid., 170.   [139] Ibid., 309.   [140] Ibid., 310.

Leeds, and Sheffield throughout the late eighteenth and early nineteenth centuries. Their presence would have excited neither surprise nor concern and appears in stark contrast with much of what has been written about acceptable female behaviour in this period. Rather than retiring from economic life, or participating only through a 'hidden investment' in family businesses,[141] lower middling women remained firmly enmeshed in the commercial lives of their towns well into the nineteenth century. The same might not be true of wealthier women, or of women in other towns and regions, and significant changes may well have occurred after the 1820s.[142] Yet within the constraints of time, place, and social class of this study, not only were women capable of being independent economic actors, but it seems that their presence in the urban business communities within which they operated gave them a more complex gendered identity than we are used to, and one in which occupation played an important role. Not only were women actively involved in the 'public' world of work, but it seems likely that their inclusion allowed them additional status in a society which was not necessarily embarrassed by overt expressions of female labour and economic power.

[141] Davidoff and Hall, *Family Fortunes*, ch. 6. See also Catherine Hall, 'Strains in the "Firm of Wife, Children and Friends": Middle-Class Women and Employment in Early Nineteenth-Century England', in her *White, Male and Middle Class: Explorations in Feminism and History* (Cambridge, 1992).

[142] Indeed, the 1820s and 1830s appear pivotal to many accounts that describe significant shifts in gender relations. See e.g. Davidoff and Hall, *Family Fortunes*; Clark, *Struggle for the Breeches*.

4

Family Firms, Partnerships, and Independent Traders

MOST female enterprise (like that of the majority of men) took place within family firms, but women can also be found operating alone, or in partnership with non-relatives. The work of middling women in family enterprises has not gone unnoticed by historians, and Leonore Davidoff, Catherine Hall, and Margaret Hunt have described the ways in which female participation could be crucial to ensuring financial stability.[1] Moreover, as Shani D'Cruze and Craig Muldrew have shown, a family's social standing and creditworthiness could also be dependent on the work and conduct of female family members.[2] Such accounts tend to pay less attention to the role of women as more independent economic actors, in partnerships with non-family members or heading their own businesses. These women have been considered at greater length in recent work by Pullin, Wiskin, and Lane.[3] Finding out about the way in which small enterprises were run

---

[1] Leonore Davidoff and Catherine Hall, *Family Fortunes: Men and Women of the English Middle Class, 1780–1850* (1987), ch. 6; Margaret Hunt, *The Middling Sort: Commerce, Gender and the Family in England, 1680–1780* (Berkeley and Los Angeles, 1996).

[2] Shani D'Cruze, 'The Middling Sort in Eighteenth-Century Colchester: Independence, Social Relations and the Community Broker', in Jonathan Barry and Christopher Brooks (eds.), *The Middling Sort of People: Culture, Society and Politics in England 1550–1800* (Basingstoke, 1994); Craig Muldrew, *The Economy of Obligation: The Culture of Credit and Social Relations in Early Modern England* (London, 1998), 148–59.

[3] Nicola Pullin, ' "Business is Just Life": The Practice, Prescription and Legal Position of Women in Business, 1700–1850', Ph.D. thesis (London, 2001); Christine Wiskin, 'Women, Finance and Credit in England, c. 1780–1826', Ph.D. thesis (Warwick, 2000); Penelope Lane, 'Women in the Regional Economy, the East Midlands 1700–1830', Ph.D. thesis (Warwick, 1999).

in the late eighteenth and early nineteenth centuries is not an easy task. However, surviving business records, legal papers, and local histories, coupled with material from advertising and trade directories, have been used to piece together a picture of female business activity both within, and separate from, the family firm. What emerges is a broad picture of middling women's involvement in commercial life: from 'helpmeet' to a husband in a small shop, to the head of a sizeable firm. Also evident are not just instances of success and profitability, but also of the possibility of failure, reflecting individual fallibility and the vicissitudes of economic life in the late eighteenth and early nineteenth centuries that were common to both sexes.

Historians have already noted the predominance of small-scale family businesses in Britain during this period.[4] In Manchester, Leeds, and Sheffield, this pattern of commercial organization was particularly important for middling women, who were less likely than their menfolk to receive a formal apprenticeship.[5] One of the main entries for women into trade was through the family and familial connections. Growing up with a family business meant that girls could become experienced in trade from an early age. Marriage might also offer women the chance to learn new skills, while the death of a husband could present the opportunity to take charge completely. Indeed, widows were commonly left in control of family firms when their husbands died and this was a frequent stipulation in the wills of lower middling men of business.[6] Even if a husband died intestate, ecclesiastical law stated that a widow was legally entitled to administer her deceased husband's estate and was allowed to enjoy one-third of her

---

[4] See Maxine Berg, 'Small Producer Capitalism in Eighteenth-Century England', *Business History* 35/1 (1993), 17–39; Stana Nenadic, 'The Small Family Firm in Victorian Britain', *Business History* 35/4 (1993), 86–114.

[5] Hunt, *The Middling Sort*, 90–2; Deborah Simonton, 'Earning and Learning: Girlhood in Pre-industrial Europe', *Women's History Review* 13 (2004), 363–85.

[6] See ch. 5 for a more detailed discussion of women and inheritance. Also, Alastair Owens, 'Inheritance and the Life-Cycle of Family Firms in the Early Industrial Revolution', *Business History* 44/1 (2002), 21–46, pp. 30–8 (though many of the businesses Owens discusses in this later period were sold up soon after inheritance); and R. J. Morris, *Men, Women and Property in England, 1780–1870: A Social and Economic History of Family Strategies Amongst the Leeds Middle Classes* (Cambridge, 2005), 104–5. Morris notes an

husband's real property during the remainder of her life.[7] In practice, this meant that widows would assume the running of a family firm *at least* until, and often *after*, any sons came of age.

Formal partnerships between family members—such as that between mothers and sons—were extremely common in Manchester, Leeds, and Sheffield between 1760 and 1830. Indeed, 6.3 per cent of working women in the trade directories sampled were listed in partnership with others: almost all (6 per cent) with other family members. It was most common for women to appear alongside female relatives (3.9 per cent), with 2.2 per cent listed next to male relatives and only 0.4 per cent in partnership with non-relatives (or at least individuals with different surnames), all of whom were women.[8] Similar figures emerged from the sample of newspaper advertisements. Here 6 per cent of advertisements concerning businesswomen described them working in partnership with others: 4.8 per cent in family partnerships (2.5 per cent of these with female relatives and 2.3 per cent with male), while 1 per cent concerned partnerships between individuals who did not appear to be related, of whom three-quarters were partnerships between women and the remainder involved men.[9]

Both familial inheritance and partnership were evident in the case of the Gales sisters, Anne and Sarah, who succeeded their brother, Joseph, in a stationery and bookselling business in 1794 after he had been forced to flee to America having been threatened with prosecution over his radical newspaper, the *Sheffield Register*. Perhaps wisely,

increased tendency amongst lower middle-class men, and retailers in particular, to leave their wives greater control of their estate than did those men further up the social scale.

[7] Amy Erickson, *Women and Property in Early Modern England* (London, 1993), 174, 178, 186; Susan Staves, *Married Women's Separate Property in England, 1660–1833* (Cambridge, Mass., 1990), chs. 2 and 3; Alistair Owens, 'Property, Will Making and Estate Disposal in an Industrial Town, 1800–1857', in Jon Stobart and Alistair Owens (eds.), *Urban Fortunes: Property and Inheritance in the Town, 1700–1900* (Aldershot, 2000), 82–3; Morris, *Men, Women and Property in England*, 101–9.

[8] The 3,687 directory entries for women listed with an occupation appear to refer to 3,166 individual women (based on the name, occupation, and address information given). Elizabeth Sanderson noted a similar prevalence of partnerships between female relatives in eighteenth-century Edinburgh: *Women and Work in Eighteenth-Century Edinburgh* (Basingstoke, 1996), 99.   [9] See Ch. 3.

the sisters chose not to continue the paper, leaving their friend, James Montgomery, to set up the *Sheffield Iris* as a successor to the *Register* (which was also prosecuted and attacked by government agents).[10] Although the sisters operated from the same address as had their brother, they altered the nature of the business: keeping on the book-selling and expanding the sale of medicines, and dispensing not only with newspaper publishing, but also with other activities that Joseph had been involved in, namely print selling, auctioneering, and acting as an agent for Royal Exchange Insurance.[11]

Yet as has been noted, the majority of businesses left to family members were inherited not by siblings, but by widows. Some women left businesses by their husbands must have relished the control that widowhood gave them, whilst others would have feared the loss of a partner's protection and his valuable labour, as well as the increased responsibility thrust upon them. Indeed, a husband's death might lead a widow to sell up entirely, and historians of nineteenth-century family firms have noted that businesses frequently died along with their proprietors.[12] In 1797, for example, Sarah Wright advertised her intention to dispose of her late husband's business:

SARAH WRIGHT, (Widow of HENRY WRIGHT, late of Kirkgate, Plumber and Glazier deceased,) RETURNS her Thanks to the FRIENDS and CUSTOMERS of her late Husband, for all Favours; and hereby informs them, That she has declined the said Trades and Businesses in favor of Mr. CHRISTOPHER HEAPS, the Younger, and of Mr. SAMUEL MALTBY, late Apprentice and Journeyman to the Deceased, whom she humbly recommends for a continuance of future Favours from the said Deceased's Friends and Customers.[13]

[10] Hannah Barker, *Newspapers, Politics and English Society, 1695–1855* (Harlow, 2000), 73.

[11] For details of Joseph's businesses see *Sheffield Register*, 16 June and 13 October 1787, 30 June 1797. For the sisters, see *Iris, or Sheffield Advertiser*, 1797, and *Sheffield Mercury*, 1817.

[12] M. J. Daunton, 'Inheritance and Succession in the City of London in the Nineteenth Century', *Business History* 30 (1988), 269–86; M. B. Rose, 'Beyond Buddenbrooks: The Family Firm and the Management of Succession in Nineteenth-Century Britain', in J. B. Brown and M. B. Rose (eds.), *Entrepreneurship and Networks in Modern Business* (Manchester, 1993); Owens, 'Inheritance and the Life-Cycle of Family Firms', 29–31.

[13] *Leeds Mercury*, 22 July 1797.

Similarly, Widow Hemmings advertised her intention to sell her dead husband's business, the Angel Inn in Sheffield, in 1826, 'In consequence of the late Mr Hemmings Decease'.[14] Despite dispensing with their husbands' businesses, such women did not necessarily retire from commercial life. On a visit to Manchester in 1832, the Leeds milliner, Robert Ayrey, visited a 'Sister Abigal [*sic*]', who was just about to set herself up as a greengrocer with money inherited from her late husband. Ayrey noted that she had

been a Widow some time but apears to be in a good State of health at present and is going to remove from her Old place to a more eledgable situation to keep a Small Shop in the Green grosery line Which I hope She Will be able to make a livley hood of along with her Son and She intends to keep a few lodgers . . .[15]

Earle claims that few widows in early eighteenth-century London carried on their husbands' trade after their death.[16] Yet despite the experience of women such as Sarah Wright and Sister Abigail, continuing to run the family business appears to have been a common practice amongst widows in Manchester, Leeds, and Sheffield during the late Georgian period.[17] Phoebe Fletcher, for example, ran the Old Iron Foundry at Red Bank during the 1790s, after her husband, the former owner, died in 1785,[18] and the widow of the buttonmaker, Joseph Cofin, a member of one of the few Jewish families in late eighteenth-century Sheffield, took over his business in the Park

---

[14] *Leeds Intelligencer*, 2 February 1826. Deborah Simonton describes similar advertisements in the Aberdeen press: 'Claiming their Place in the Corporate Community: Women's Identity in Eighteenth-Century Towns', in Isabelle Baudino, Jacques Carré, and Cécile Révauger (eds.), *The Invisible Woman: Aspects of Women's Work in Eighteenth-Century Britain* (Aldershot, 2005), 108–9.

[15] Leeds Central Library, MS letter book of Robert Ayrey, SR826.79 AY 74, fos. 11–12.

[16] Peter Earle, 'The Female Labour Market in London in the Late Seventeenth and Early Eighteenth Centuries', *Economic History Review*, 2nd ser., 42 (1989), 328–53, pp. 338–9. In contrast, Bridget Hill describes widows in Coventry continuing husbands' trades: *Women, Work and Sexual Politics in Eighteenth-Century England* (Oxford, 1989), 245–6.

[17] Todd found a similar tendency in her study of Abingdon widows in the sixteenth and seventeenth centuries: Barbara J. Todd, 'The Remarrying Widow: A Stereotype Reconsidered', in Mary Prior (ed.), *Women in English Society, 1500–1800* (London, 1985), 65 ff.

[18] Richard Wright Proctor, *Memorials of Manchester Streets* (Manchester, 1874), 44.

district of town after he died sometime before 1787.[19] Another
Sheffield button manufacturer, Sarah Holy, inherited her business
from her husband in 1758 and ran it until her own death ten years
later. The surviving Holy family papers show that Thomas Holy's
estate was valued at over one thousand pounds on his death and that
he owned not only a button and casting shop, but also land and
property.[20] Sarah had been a practising Calvinist during her husband's lifetime, but converted to Methodism two years after his
death, no doubt because many other members of her family had also
converted. She was soon enmeshed in the local Methodist community, so much so that she lent money to the Mulberry Street
chapel to pay for new pillars during the 1760s.[21] According to her
son's biographer, Sarah had been 'tenderly attached to her deceased
husband' and wore mourning dress until her death as a result of her
grief.[22] Yet despite her distress, she appears to have run the business
with a degree of competence and seemingly left it profitable,
although—in common with most businesses in the period—owed a
significant amount by various creditors that her son, Thomas, spent
the next few years attempting to collect.[23] Her personal effects spoke
of a comfortable, middling lifestyle: mahogany chairs, a writing
desk, card table, china, silverware, and Delft plates.[24]

Advertisements announcing the intention of newly widowed
women to assume control of a family concern were commonplace in
the newspapers of Manchester, Leeds, and Sheffield. In 1817, for
example, Susannah Linley of Leeds offered

her most grateful Thanks to the numerous Friends of her late Husband, for
their liberal Support, so long enjoyed by him, and begs respectfully to inform

[19] Neville David Ballin, *The Early Days of Sheffield Jewry, 1760–1900* (Sheffield, 1986),
3; *Directory of Sheffield* (1787).

[20] Sheffield Archives, Holy family papers, 5733/2–4.

[21] James Everett, *Historical Sketches of Wesleyan Methodism in Sheffield*, 2 vols.
(Sheffield, 1823), i. 148–69.

[22] Jabez Bunting, *Memoir of the Late Thomas Holy, Esq., of Sheffield* (London, 1832), 4.

[23] Holy papers, 5733/5–12. See Dennis Smith, 'The Buttonmaking Industry in
Sheffield', in Melvyn Jones (ed.), *Aspects of Sheffield* (Barnsley, 1997), 84–101.

[24] Holy family papers, 5733/5.

them, that the Business of HOUSE PAINTING, &c. &c. in all its Branches, will be carried on as usual, under the firm of S. LINLEY & SON, and earnestly solicits a Continuation of their Patronage and Favour, which it will always be their Study to merit.[25]

A similar advertisement was placed by a Mrs Garnett, the widow of Mr Bryce Garnett, who announced in the same year that she intended to continue his hairdressing business in York Street, Sheffield, with the assistance of her son, and hoped 'to merit the indulgence of the public'.[26] Working with other family members, or engaging outside help, appears to have been common amongst widows who carried on the family firm. This is not surprising, considering the loss of labour that a husband's death brought about. Mrs Binns, widow of John Binns, a Leeds bookseller, also kept on his business after his death in 1796 when she was left with two sons to care for. She hired John Heaton as a manager, but did not absent herself from trade since 'being an active capable woman she took a lively interest in all that was passing in the business'. It is her name that appears on the firm's advertisements for books and medicines during 1797, and it was only nine years later, in 1805, that she sold up (to her manager) and moved to London.[27]

Morris has described the eagerness of male middle-class willmakers to ensure business continuity after their deaths, so that family enterprises could continue to maintain those wives and children that were left behind,[28] whilst Hunt has noted how the idealized widow in trade was meant to act as caretaker of a family business, supporting her children before handing it over to her son once he came of age.[29] Yet though the family firm frequently continued in the hands of a widow following her husband's death, its passage from mother to adult son was clearly not automatic, and widows often stayed in control of businesses

[25] *Leeds Mercury*, 11 January 1817.
[26] *Sheffield Mercury*, 22 November 1817. See also *Leeds Mercury*, 22 November 1817; *Manchester Mercury*, 20 November 1804; *Iris*, 22 September; 8 December 1797; *Leeds Mercury*, 27 May; 10 June 1797; 24 June 1809; 20 September 1817.
[27] Wemyss Reid, *A Sketch of Old Leeds* (n.d.), 38–40; *Iris*, 6 January; 19 May; 2 June; 24 November 1797.   [28] Morris, *Men, Women and Property in England*, 119–23.
[29] Hunt, *Middling Sort*, 137.

even after their sons reached the age of majority.[30] Mary Labron and son, for example, were ironmongers on Briggate in Leeds and are listed in the town's directories from 1809 until 1826: long after the son would have come of age.[31] Similarly, the sons of Jane Green, who helped her run the edge tool manufacturing business, 'Jane Green and sons', first at Scotland Street and then at Arundel Street in Sheffield, and who are listed in directories from 1787 to 1817,[32] must have reached their majorities during this period, as would the son of Ann Ford who operated with his mother in a firm of braziers and tinplate workers from Old Bridge Street in Manchester between 1804 and 1828.[33] Examples such as these suggest that patterns of inheritance within family firms could be dictated by relative age and experience, as well as by considerations of gender. Despite the fact that most wills in this period insisted that widows should continue businesses primarily for the benefit of the family, and until their sons came of age, this appears to have been taken as a suggestion, rather than a stipulation.[34] Individual personality no doubt played a part in such decisions, with more indomitable women less likely to hand over the reins to one of their offspring. But when the widow was more experienced and skilled at running a particular enterprise, as must often have been the case, this would also have been a sound commercial decision. Thus Josiah Slugg, in his *Reminiscences of Manchester*, noted that Mary Bealey, widow of Richard Bealey, continued the Methodist family's bleaching business after his death in 1817,

---

[30] Hannah Barker, 'Women, Work and the Industrial Revolution: Female Involvement in the English Printing Trades, c. 1700–1840', in Hannah Barker and Elaine Chalus (eds.), *Gender in Eighteenth-Century England: Roles, Representations and Responsibilities* (London, 1997), 96–8; Christine Wiskin, 'Urban Businesswomen in Eighteenth-Century England', in Rosemary Sweet and Penelope Lane (eds.), *'On the Town': Women and Urban Life in Eighteenth-Century England* (Aldershot, 2003), 97–8.

[31] *Leeds Directory for 1809* (1809); *Directory, General and Commercial, of . . . Leeds* (1817); *General & Commercial Directory of . . . Leeds* (1826).

[32] *Directory of Sheffield* (1787); *Directory of Sheffield* (1797); *Sheffield General Directory* (1817).

[32] *Leeds Directory* (1797); *Leeds Directory for 1809* (1809); *Directory, General and Commercial, of . . . Leeds* (1817); *General & Commercial Directory of . . . Leeds* (1826).

[33] *Manchester and Salford Directory* (1804); *Manchester & Salford Directory* (1817); *Manchester and Salford Director* (1828).   [34] For examples of this practice see Ch. 5.

and ran it for at least ten years.[35] It was only after she died that the firm passed to her son, Richard.[36]

The Ayrey diary describes one widow who was clearly more astute than her offspring:

I believe I told you of the death of Mr Harper I had Mrs Harper 2 Nights at our House very lately & She wished to be Remembered to you She is Very Well of She has £80 a year that her Father left her in Stockport Where She is now Residing with her Children Her son tho I am Sorry to say Went to Rotherham College and got Turned Ought for Some miss Conduct or other but I never Could get properly in to the merits of the Case & he is now preaching up and down any Where near Where they reside on the Sabath days and on the Weeke days he assists his Mother in keeping a School one Boys & the Other Girls . . . and What they make of their School they are Able to Appear very respectably Although She was left With v many Small Children when Mr Harper died.[37]

Far more formidable in her control of both her business and her family was Jane Clowes, a confectioner listed in the 1817 Manchester directory who was described by Harland in his *Collectanea Relating to Manchester*. Mrs Clowes, we are told,

Though at first she was in a humble way of business, she was so industrious, persevering and successful, that she realised a fortune, and bequeathed £18,000 or £20,000 to her relatives, and left a flourishing business to her successor. She had several men and boys (apprentices) in her sugar-bakery; and in the summer of 1812, when several regiments of militia were encamped on Kersal Moor . . . so great was the demand for sweets to vend to the numerous visitors to the Moor, that all her hands worked almost night and day for some time, to meet this extraordinary demand.[38]

Jane Clowes headed the confectionery business she had built up despite the fact that her adult stepson worked for her. She was clearly

[35] *Manchester and Salford Director* (1828).

[36] Josiah Thomas Slugg, *Reminiscences of Manchester Fifty Years Ago* (Manchester, 1881), 42.   [37] Ayrey diary, fos. 101–2.

[38] John Harland, *Collectanea Relating to Manchester and its Neighbourhood at Various Periods*, 2 vols. (Manchester, 1866–7), i. 202; *Pigot and Deans' Manchester & Salford Directory* (Manchester, 1817).

both skilled in the trade of sweetmaking, and used to taking part in the production process. Harland notes that

> She would often herself take an active part in the labour, for severe labour it was, of pulling the boiled sugar into long ropes; and when her step-son, who worked in this part of the business, one day fell exhausted and fainting on the floor, overcome by the severe toil in a necessarily heated atmosphere, while his comrades got him water, she only looked at him and said, 'Thou'rt a poor soft thing'.[39]

Harland remarked, however (and not entirely convincingly), that 'It must not be supposed . . . from this circumstance, that she was hard-hearted or stern', rather that 'She was only so strong, physically, that she could not understand how a man could be more feeble than herself.' In an attempt to bolster her reputation, he recorded that 'She was a kind mistress to her servants' and that once a week 'she gave a good dinner to fourteen old men and women in poor circumstances; and she never tasted until they had all dined, serving them herself'.[40] Yet he also noted that she insisted that her household all attend the local Anglican church with her, and 'kept them at work till the last bell "put in"; and they had to make the necessary change of attire in the very few minutes left before the commencement of service'.[41]

Of the seventy partnerships between men and women listed in the directories, we can be certain that fifty were between mothers and sons. In these cases, sons were not named, emphasizing the superior role that their mothers held. In the advertisements sample, the trend towards mother and son partnerships was less pronounced, and involved nineteen of the forty-seven cases of women working in partnership with men. It was also common for mothers and daughters to work together, and for daughters to be left in control when their mothers died or retired. R.J. Richardson noted that

> My own maternal Grandmother Johanna was born in the year 1745 and resided in the house next to the Old Black a Moors head . . . during the

---

[39] Harland, *Collectanea Relating to Manchester*, i. 202.   [40] Ibid.
[41] Ibid. i. 202–3.

<u>whole</u> of her life. She there kept a register office for servants above 50 years . . . she died in 1819 or 20 the office being afterwards kept by her youngest daughter Mrs Hulme subsequently Mrs Clayton she died 1860 aged 72.[42]

Yet in comparison to mother and son partnerships, very few daughters were listed as working with either mothers or fathers in directories. This reflects a gender bias in the way lists were compiled, and reminds us that whilst age might override considerations of gender in terms of cross-generational relationships, sons were still considered more worthy of public attention than daughters. The entry in the 1826 Leeds directory for 'John and Mary Kemplay and daughters', who ran a school at 18 Boar Lane, is unusual.[43] Newspaper advertisements more commonly described partnerships between mothers and daughters, with ten of the fifty-two advertisements for family partnerships amongst women positively identifiable as being between mothers and their female offspring. Mrs Elizabeth Sharrow, a Sheffield milliner, listed in the 1828 Sheffield directory as running a business from Surrey Street, for example, advertised in 1817 that 'her daughter is presently in London, selecting an elegant and fashionable Assortment of MILLINERY'. Yet despite her daughter's presence in the capital, it was Mrs Sharrow who was described as having 'opened a connexion in London'.[44] We can find evidence that suggests daughters succeeded their mothers in several Manchester directories. Sarah Garside's clear starching business at 73 Hanover Street, for example, listed in the 1804 Manchester directory, was under the control of Mary Garside in the 1817 version.[45] Similarly, Frances Pownall's shop at 13 Marble Street in 1804 had passed to Mary Pownall by 1817,[46] and Hannah Willett's pawnbrokers at 1 Lees Street, Piccadilly in 1817 was run by Elizabeth Willett in 1828.[47] Yet despite such suggestive evidence, it remains the

[42] Chetham's Library, R. J. Richardson, 'Old Manchester', MS notes for a history of Manchester, A.0.2.   [43] *Directory of the Borough of Leeds* (1826).

[44] *Sheffield Mercury*, 24 May 1817.

[45] *Deans & Co.'s Manchester and Salford Directory* (1804); *Pigot and Deans' Manchester & Salford Directory* (Manchester, 1817).   [46] Ibid.

[47] *Manchester & Salford Directory* (1817); *Manchester and Salford Director* (1828).

case that business relationships between mothers and daughters were not as likely to be formalized in published sources as those between mothers (or indeed fathers) and their sons. This might have been because daughters were thought less likely to inherit and run businesses on their own, while sons were mentioned in print in the expectation that they would eventually succeed their mothers—through illness or old age—and so needed to build up some form of personal reputation beforehand.

The manner in which patterns of cross-generational inheritance often appeared to ignore considerations of gender, at the same time that hierarchies within generations were so highly gendered, shows us the importance of both age and sex in the control of family firms. The pattern of inheritance in the Thorp family of Manchester illustrates this well. According to the local historian, Josiah Slugg, Ann Thorp, the Manchester apothecary with a shop in Oldham Street

had a son, Issachar, who acquired a knowledge of the business when a young man and who afterwards became a calico printer, having a warehouse in Fountain Street, and who, on the death of his mother, took her business. For a few years he had both businesses on his hands, and I doubt not that his wife Ellen assisted him at this time in the shop, and so enabled to follow them up after his death . . . Ellen Thorp, on the death of her husband, continued the business, which is still carried on by her successor.[48]

Manchester's directories support Slugg's version of the Thorp family history. Ann Thorp appeared as 'Apothecary, Oldham Street' in an 1811 directory, whilst a subsequent directory for 1817 included her son, Issachar, as a calico printer on Fountain Street.[49] By the time the next directory was published in 1821, however, he appeared as a druggist at his mother's Oldham Street shop.[50] Sometime after that he must have died, since his wife, Ellen, was listed as a druggist with

[48] Slugg, *Reminiscences of Manchester Fifty Years Ago*, 69.
[49] *Deans' Manchester & Salford Directory* (Manchester, 1811); *Pigot and Deans' Manchester & Salford Directory* (Manchester, 1817).
[50] *Pigot and Deans' New Directory of Manchester* (Manchester, 1821).

premises on Oldham Street from 1824 until 1851.[51] After that date, a Thomas Foden appears to have taken over the business.[52] Whilst Foden's relationship to the Throps is unclear, what is apparent is that the valuable apothecary's shop was passed from mother to son to wife (and possibly to a more distant male relative) as part of well-established patterns of inheritance in this period.

Since—as we have seen—parents usually assumed the senior role in any family business, the majority of the women listed in the directories in all female partnerships were likely to have been sisters, or at least female relatives of roughly the same age. Most newspaper advertisements for all-female family partnerships also seem to have involved sisters. The familial relationship was made explicit in the case of 'Sarah Foster & sisters', who ran a hosiery business in Piccadilly in early nineteenth-century Manchester, and were listed in the town's directory.[53] But this is an unusual entry, and suggests that the unnamed sisters were under age. In most female partnerships in the directories, the exact nature of the relationship is not made clear, although it can be inferred with some degree of confidence. Women such as Elizabeth and Sarah Pool, hosiers at 10 Change Alley in Manchester in 1773, Ann and Elizabeth Bailiffe, milliners in Camp Lane, Sheffield in 1817, and Ellen and Charlotte Foster, confectioners and tea dealers of 7 Vicar Lane, Leeds in 1826,[54] were all probably sisters. Also sisters were the 'Misses Rivington', 'glass and china dealers' of Market Street, Sheffield, who were listed in the town's 1817 directory. In December of that year they announced in the press that they were selling off their entire stock 'CONSIDERABLY UNDER PRIME COST'.[55] We know that

[51] *Pigot and Deans' Directory of Manchester* (Manchester, 1824); *Slater's General and Classified Directory . . . of Manchester and Salford* (Manchester, 1858).

[52] *Pigot and Deans' Directory of Manchester* (Manchester, 1824); *Slater's General and Classified Directory . . . of Manchester and Salford* (Manchester, 1861).

[53] *Manchester and Salford Director* (1828).

[54] *Manchester and Salford Directory* (1773); *Manchester and Salford Directory* (1804); *Manchester and Salford Director* (1828); *Sheffield General Directory* (1817); *Sheffield Directory and Guide* (1828); *Directory, General and Commercial, . . . of Leeds* (1817); *General & Commercial Directory of . . . Leeds* (1826).

[55] *Sheffield Mercury*, 27 December 1817.

Hannah and Ann Binyon, tea dealers at 23 Piccadilly and listed in the 1828 Manchester directory were siblings, because of their description in a local history.[56] Slugg's *Reminiscences of Manchester* describes the Binyon family's various concerns, including the sisters' partnership (which dated from the late eighteenth century).[57] The Binyons were a Quaker family,[58] and Hannah and Ann had another sister, Deborah, who ran a ready-made linen shop at 45 Piccadilly, as well as three brothers, Thomas, Edward, and Benjamin. Thomas and Edward were tea dealers with shops in St Ann's Square and Oldham Street,[59] whilst Benjamin, who lodged with Deborah, was a salesman of some sort.[60] Slugg also records the business of the Harrison sisters, who operated as 'Mary Harrison and Co.', and ran a confectioner's shop from 245 Deansgate around 1829, where 'Though the shop was small, the business done in it was large'. He noted that 'the Misses Harrisons came from Buxton, and were known as the "Buxton Bakers" '.[61]

Although most partnerships with a female element listed in the directories were likely to consist entirely of women, one-third of familial partnerships were between men and women, where women were given equal billing alongside their menfolk. In these cases, the relationship between individuals is likely to have been more varied: involving not only siblings, but husbands and wives, parents and children, and perhaps even aunts, uncles, nieces, and nephews.[62] We know that Samuel Goodier worked as a grocer and tea dealer at Fountain Street in Manchester in 1788 with his sister, because, unusually, she was

---

[56] *A Directory of Sheffield* (1797); *Manchester and Salford Director* (1828).

[57] Slugg, *Reminiscences of Manchester Fifty Years Ago*, 93–4.

[58] The activities of Quaker businessmen and women and the particular role of the Meeting House system in governing the business practices of Quakers in this period is discussed in Ann Prior and Maurice Kirby, 'The Society of Friends and the Family Firm, 1700–1830', *Business History* 35/4 (1993), 66–85.

[59] Manchester Central Reference Library, deeds of partnership between Thomas, Edward and Benjamin Binyon, 1827–37, M/C, 751–3.

[60] *Pigot and Son's General Directory of Manchester* (Manchester, 1830).

[61] Slugg, *Reminiscences of Manchester Fifty Years Ago*, 100; *Pigot and Son's General Directory of Manchester* (Manchester, 1830).

[62] See Stana Nenadic, 'The Social Shaping of Business Behaviour in the Nineteenth-Century Women's Garment Trades', *Journal of Social History* (Spring, 1998), 625–45, p. 631, for a detailed description of a partnership between a brother and sister.

described in these terms (though more typically, she was not named individually). In other cases, such as John and Sarah Kent, table-knife cutlers at 13 Brocco Street, Sheffield in 1797, Martha and John Dixon, blacksmiths on Kirkstall in Leeds in 1817, and Sarah and John M'Kinnell, pawnbrokers at 6 Chapel Street, Manchester in 1828, we can be less sure. The equal billing given to men and women involved in the same businesses in these instances makes it most likely that these were partnerships of siblings or mothers and sons, rather than husbands and wives, since we would expect the men in married couples to assume the position of head of the firm. But this was not necessarily the case. We know, for example, that John and Mary Kemplay, who operated a school on Boar Lane in the early nineteenth century, were a married couple since they advertised their business as being run in conjunction with their daughters.[63] Yet we also know, from the memoirs of Mrs Owen's suitor,[64] that Ann and Peter Owen, grocers of 19 Withy Grove in Manchester and listed in the 1828 directory, were a parent–child partnership. Evidence of a similar set-up was offered in July 1804, when the recently widowed Elizabeth Baron informed readers of the *Manchester Mercury* that she would be taking over her late husband's cabinet-making and upholstery business, 'with the advantage of a steady set of workmen'.[65] The business was listed in the 1804 Manchester directory as 'Elizabeth, Peter, and Thomas Baron, cabinet-makers', suggesting that she was also working alongside her children.

In addition to those 6.3 per cent of working women in the directories who were listed in partnership with others, a further 3.3 per cent of women ran businesses at addresses from which another family member conducted an entirely different enterprise. So, for example, in the 1817 Leeds directory, Elizabeth King was listed as a straw hat maker at 14 Hunslet Lane, while John King operated as a watch- and clockmaker from the same address, and Tabitha Blanchard was a linen draper at 98 Briggate, from where William Blanchard ran a plastering business. Of the 103 instances found of individuals with the same

[63] William Parson, *General & Commercial Directory of . . . Leeds* (Leeds, 1826).
[64] John Rylands Library, Diary of George Heywood, MS 703 [63–7]: see Ch. 5 for a detailed discussion of Ann Owen.   [65] *Manchester Mercury*, 31 July 1804.

surname running different businesses from the same address, only six cases were solely female. These included Ann and Elizabeth Ainley, who both ran businesses at 51 Pye Bank, Sheffield in 1828. While Ann was listed as 'rubber, shampooner, and electricioner', Elizabeth appeared as 'dressmaker'.[66] It seems likely that these were incidences of siblings with different skills and experiences living and working together for reasons of security and economy.[67] Yet, as the figures show, it was far more common for men and women to be involved in such set-ups. Although brothers and sisters might also live together, as was the case for a Miss Hammersley, who announced in the *Manchester Courier* of 5 January 1828 that she would be carrying on the business of a stay- and corsetmaker from her brother's house at 2 Police Street, most of these couples were likely to have been husbands and wives.

This is the likely scenario for Ann and Robert Handley, for example. Ann was listed in the 1774 Sheffield directory as a druggist in Market Place, from where Robert operated as a peruke-maker. Ann's business was a long-running one, and she was listed in directories between 1774 and 1797: first at Market Place, and then moving to the adjacent Angel Street by 1787. She seems to have moved at the same point that Robert moved to Hartshead, off Campo Lane, and not far from Angel Street, which was given as his address in the 1787 directory. By 1797, Robert was operating from 76 Campo Lane.[68] This new, separate arrangement, probably reflected an increase in fortunes and the desire for more commercial space, although it might also have resulted from marital separation. In 1797 Ann advertised in the *Iris* that she was selling 'the GOODWILL and STOCK IN TRADE of an Old Established DRUGGIST' at Angel Street. Mrs Handley, it was noted, wished to retire from business due to ill health: 'The House, Shop and Warehouses,

[66] *Sheffield General Directory* (1817); *Sheffield Directory and Guide* (1828).
[67] For examples of such 'spinster clustering' see P. Sharpe, 'Literally Spinsters: A New Interpretation of Local Economy and Demography in Colyton in the Seventeenth and Eighteenth Centuries', *Economic History Review* 44 (1991), 46–65; O. Hufton, 'Women Without Men: Widows and Spinsters in Britain and France in the Eighteenth Century', *Journal of Family History* 9 (1984), 355–76.
[68] John Robinson, *A Directory of Sheffield* (Sheffield, 1797).

are in an excellent situation, and well calculated for carrying on the business to a great extent,' boasted the advertisement.[69]

Similarly, Elizabeth Chorley ran a millinery and fancy dressmaking business in Nile Street, Leeds, at the same address as William Chorley, bookkeeper, in 1809, Martha Mellor ran a 'herring warehouse' at 19 Withy Grove in Manchester, from where Thomas Mellor also operated as a smallware dealer in 1817, and both Sarah and Samuel Alsop ran businesses at 64 Carver Street in Sheffield in 1828: Sarah as a milliner and dressmaker, Samuel as a grocer and flour dealer. In several such cases, women appear to have run businesses from a couple's home, whilst the man conducted his trade from a separate business address. Thus Ann Bewsher is listed as a hatter at 19 Church Street, in the Manchester directories for 1817 and 1828, which was the home address of William Bewsher, a joiner and trunkmaker who had a workshop at 30 Dale Street. Ann Daff was a straw hat maker at Silver Street 'head', Sheffield in 1828, the home address of Robert Daff, a stonemason with commercial premises at 30 Trippet Lane.[70]

The separate commercial operations and distinct public personas of these men and women should not surprise us, since we know from the work of Hunt and D'Cruze that women who were already established in business continued to trade independently when married:[71] thus Mary Fitton, staymaker of Marble Street had '(late Wilson)' after her name in the 1817 Manchester directory, whilst Hannah Hancock was listed as '(late William)' in her entry as optician and beer machine manufacturer in the 1828 Sheffield directory.[72] In 1828, Mrs H. Cave announced her new millinery and fancy dressmaking business in the *Manchester Courier* and reminded readers that she was 'late Miss Platford, St. Ann's-Square'.[73] The same year saw Mrs Horsfall of 17 King Street, and 'late

[69] *Iris*, 24 November 1797.

[70] *Manchester & Salford Directory* (1817); *Manchester and Salford Director* (1828); *Sheffield Directory* (1774); *Sheffield Directory and Guide* (1828); *Leeds Directory for 1809* (1809); *Directory, General and Commercial, of . . . Leeds* (1817).

[71] Hunt, *Middling Sort*, 125; D'Cruze, 'The Middling Sort in Eighteenth-Century Colchester', 188.

[72] *Manchester & Salford Directory* (1817); *Sheffield Directory and Guide* (1828).

[73] *Manchester Courier*, 13 September 1828.

Miss Potter', inform the ladies of Manchester that 'she is just returned from London with a fashionable and elegant assortment of Millinery'.[74] Susanna Franks, a milliner based at 16 Exchange Street in Manchester, advertised on her own in the *Manchester Mercury* of 15 May 1804 and was listed in the 1804 directory as an independent trader. Her marriage to John Taylor was announced in the paper on 23 October of that year, and on 6 November John advertised a 'NEW LINEN DRAPERY' at the Exchange Street address:

J. TAYLOR begs most respectfully to inform the inhabitants of Manchester and its vicinity, that he has just furnish'd the shop, No. 16 Exchange-street, and proposes opening on Wednesday Nov. 7, with an elegant assortment of Linen Drapery, Haberdashery, and Hosiery goods of every description, which he flatters himself will be found worthy of the attention of those who may honor him with their commands. N.B. The Millinery and Dress making business will be carried on as usual by Mrs T. late S. Franks.

Despite this proclamation of their different interests, in the 1809 Manchester directory, John Taylor appeared as 'linen draper and haberdasher' at Exchange Street, with no listing given for his wife.[75]

Women such as Susanna Taylor clearly worked alongside their husbands in the same or allied trades although such labour would rarely appear in sources such as directories. Earle has claimed that it was unusual for a husband and wife to work together in this way,[76] while Hunt also asserted that women were typically involved in entirely different trades from their husbands.[77] These assumptions about married women's work have been questioned by Bailey, whose research into the middling sorts and wage labourers suggests that women commonly worked either alongside their husbands or in servicing the family concern.[78] Similar evidence emerges from late-Georgian Manchester, Leeds, and Sheffield. Slugg, for example, noted that Mrs Varley helped

[74] *Manchester Courier*, 15 November 1828.
[75] *Deans' Manchester & Salford Directory for 1808 & 1809* (1809).
[76] Earle, 'The Female Labour Market in London', 338–9.
[77] Hunt, *Middling Sort*, 125.
[78] Joanne Bailey, *Unquiet Lives: Marriage and Marriage Breakdown in England, 1660–1800* (Cambridge, 2003), 94. See also Davidoff and Hall, *Family Fortunes*, ch. 6.

her husband to run his smallware shop in Manchester's Market Street and 'used to attend to the business as well as her husband'.[79] Ann and James Hopps were another married couple who worked together—at least in principle—running a bookshop in the New Market Buildings in Manchester. Mr Hopps had bought the business from his brother, 'Old John Hopps', another bookseller, after he returned to England from the Napoleonic Wars. James Weatherly described Ann as 'a very good and kind civil woman and very attentive to the business for her Husband would not take any Interest in the shop but left it entirely for her to manage'. James, it is alleged, spent his pension on gin. Not surprisingly, his wife 'survived him many years',[80] and she is listed in the 1828 directory still operating as a bookseller at the same address.

In the advertisement sample for this study, nearly half of all cases where women were found working with men concerned what appear to have been married couples.[81] Thus we find advertisements for the dentists, Mr and Mrs Seddon in the *Sheffield Register* in 1787;[82] the milliners, Mr and Mrs Carr in the *Sheffield Mercury* of 1817;[83] and Mr and Mrs Wilcox advertising their school for young ladies in the *Leeds Intelligencer* in 1826.[84] In an advertisement which appeared in the *Sheffield Mercury* in 1817, D. Ibbertson, a 'Straw and Chip Hat Manufacturer' based on Angel Street, announced to the 'Ladies of Sheffield and its Vicinity' that his wife 'is now in London, selecting a Fashionable Assortment of Split Straw Hats and Bonnets . . . which he intends opening for their inspection on Thursday'.[85] In common with the Taylors' clothing business discussed above, the Ibbertsons clearly divided the labours and responsibilities that their enterprise entailed, although the husband remained the dominant partner.

We can find more evidence that husbands and wives worked together in court records. As we shall see in the following chapter,

[79] Slugg, *Reminiscences of Manchester Fifty Years Ago*, 100.

[80] Chetham's Library, James Weatherley, 'Recollections of Manchester and Manchester Characters and Anecdotes Relating to Manchester and Lancashire Generally from the Year 1800 to 1860 by James Weatherly for nearly half a Century a Bookseller in the locality of the Manchester Exchange', unpublished memoir, 21.

[81] Twenty-one out of forty-seven cases.   [82] *Sheffield Register*, 21 July 1787.

[83] *Sheffield Mercury*, 25 October 1817.   [84] *Leeds Intelligencer*, 20 July 1826.

[85] *Sheffield Mercury*, 17 May 1817.

lower middling women had a complex relationship with the law, and were involved in cases brought before a number of different courts. In 1799, for example, Thomas Briscale, a Manchester gentleman, took Matthew Lofthouse to the Court of Exchequer over a disputed grocery bill. Lofthouse had apparently charged Briscale in another court for owing him money for goods bought on credit, whilst Briscale maintained that this was untrue, and accused Lofthouse of producing a false set of accounts. Briscale's defence depended on Lofthouse's wife. Matthew, it was claimed,

> was not accustomed to attend or serve in his shop. But . . . his Wife by his desire and on his Behalf usually attended therein and did alone or with the Assistance of some Servant serve the Customers or persons applying there for any Goods or Articles And the said Matthew Lofthouse's wife since the commencement of the said Action hath Acknowledged or declared to several Persons and particularly to Your Orator's Wife that all the Articles which had been sold at the said Shop to your Orator or any person on his account or sent from such Shop to your Orator's house had been paid for . . . and that the said Matthew Lofthouse hath himself been informed by his said Wife to the same effect . . .[86]

Mary Hill, the wife of a Sheffield innkeeper, Thomas, also appears to have played a key role in her husband's business dealings, as did the wife of Thomas Gilkes, a Manchester coachmaker. In 1776, Mary and Thomas Hill were accused by Joseph Milner in the Court of Exchequer of refusing to pay a debt owed by Hill and his father-in-law for malt valued at over £60. Thomas Hill had apparently told Milner that he would consult his wife about the business and she advised him to sell some property to Milner in order to pay off the debt. Hill and his wife met Milner on 19 January 1769, ostensibly to execute deeds of conveyance, but instead Thomas made a violent attempt to seize Milner's papers containing proof of their debt.[87] In 1809 the Court of Exchequer also heard a case concerning the bankrupt coachmaker, Thomas Gilkes. In November 1808, Gilkes had been employed making a carricle for Matthias Morgan, an attorney. Yet Gilkes was so 'embarrassed' financially that he could not pay his workers, so he approached John Curtis,

---

[86] National Archives (NA), E112/1533/311.   [87] NA, E112/2064/264.

a farrier who supplied him with leather for his coaches, for a loan of £20 to be repaid when the carricle was finished. Curtis reportedly said that he could not spare the money, yet on 25 November, he was approached again by Gilkes's wife, who informed him 'that her husband could not shew himself to his work men and was obliged to secrete himself' (although subsequently Curtis denied he was told this). After Mrs Gilkes's intervention, Curtis applied to Morgan who agreed to lend Gilkes between £30 and £40. Later Curtis lent Mrs Gilkes further small sums of money himself. 'The wife of the said Thomas Gilkes', it was claimed, 'was often in the habit of applying to this defendant [Curtis] for the loan of small sums of money for the use of the said Thomas Gilkes.' By this time, Gilkes was in debt to several creditors, owing almost £250. Mrs Gilkes pleaded with Curtis not to reclaim his debt through the courts, telling him that her husband was apprehensive that his creditors would try to enforce a warrant against him. Although Curtis assured her that they did not plan such a course of action, Gilkes was soon after declared bankrupt and a complicated legal tussle over debts ensued.[88]

So far this chapter has concentrated on the importance of family and familial connections to women in business. Yet although female commercial activity was most likely to have been linked to the family firm, as has been noted women also ran businesses which they set up independently or in partnership with others to whom they were not related. As Davidoff and Hall have argued, women might have had more problems than men in raising money for such purposes.[89] However, it seems likely that for the sort of small businesses described in this book, families were the main source of any loan—for men as well as women[90]—and that gender was less of an issue in such circumstances than it might have been for commercial banks and moneylenders. Newspaper advertisements often describe women starting up on their own in business. Miss West, who had been 'assistant in the dress and pelisse department of the late Mrs. Plint', announced that she was

[88] NA, E112/1539/531.
[89] Davidoff and Hall, *Family Fortunes*, 278 ff., 301–15.
[90] R. J. Morris, 'The Middle-Class and the Property Cycle During the Industrial Revolution', in T. C. Smout (ed.), *The Search for Wealth and Stability: Essays in Economic and*

'commencing business' in Leeds in 1826, after the death of her employer and sale of her shop.[91] Also apparently on her own initiative, in 1828 Mrs Gray advertised that she had opened a public library in Manchester.[92]

Those who wanted to establish themselves in business in Manchester, Leeds, and Sheffield during the late eighteenth and early nineteenth centuries would find no shortage of advertisements in the local press publicizing the sale of potential ventures.[93] Yet it is often difficult to trace the identity of purchasers. Here directories can be of some help. After Mary Deeley's entry in the 1817 Manchester directory as a manufacturer of china and earthenware at 1 Market Place, for example, it was noted that she was the successor to William Mason.[94] One cannot be sure of the relationship between Deeley and Mason, but it seems probable that they were not members of the same family and that the transfer of ownership was part of a commercial transaction. Other evidence from directories also suggests that businesses were purchased by unrelated individuals. The millinery firm run by Alice and Ann Burrows at 10 Old Bridge Street, Manchester, for example, which was listed in the 1804 Manchester directory, was being conducted by Sarah Platt in 1817; Elizabeth Lyon's tea dealers at 3 Lower Byrom Street, also listed in the 1804 Manchester directory, passed to Ann Walker, listed in both the 1817 and 1828 versions; and Sarah Wise's school at 15 Mulberry Street, listed under her name in the 1804 and 1817 Manchester directories, was under the control of Jane Wilson in 1828.[95]

Social History Presented to M. W. Flinn (London, 1979), 92; Hunt, *Middling Sort*, ch. 1. The Heywood diary, discussed in more detail in Ch. 5, describes how a journeyman grocer raised part of the money to set himself up in a partnership from his family: John Rylands Library, Diary of George Heywood, MS 703 [63–7] and Ayrey's comments quoted above certainly suggest this. See also Wiskin, 'Women, Finance and Credit', 195–7, 211.

[91] *Leeds Intelligencer*, 18 May 1826. The sale of Mrs Plint's business is described ibid. Her husband, T. Plint, appears to have tried to continue the business 'under the Management of experienced Persons' earlier in the year, but failed in his endeavours: ibid. 30 March 1826.   [92] *Manchester Courier*, 27 September 1828.

[93] See e.g. *Sheffield Mercury*, 1 March; 27 December 1817; *Manchester Mercury*, 4 March; 19 August 1788; 21 February; 10 April; 5 June; 30 October 1804; 11 March 1817; *Leeds Intelligencer*, 4 May 1826.   [94] *Manchester & Salford Directory* (1817).

[95] *Deans & Co.'s Manchester and Salford Directory* (1804); *Manchester & Salford Directory* (1817); *Manchester and Salford Director* (1828).

Buying a business outright could be a costly and difficult task for any individual, regardless of gender.[96] An easier option was to set oneself up with a partner. This method was favoured by Misses Whitling and Naylor, who took over Elizabeth Barber's millinery business in Leeds in 1809. At the time that the pair assumed control, Naylor already possessed, it was noted, experience 'in conducting Miss Barber's Business',[97] presumably as an apprentice or assistant. Other examples of apparently unrelated women conducting businesses together appear in the trade directories. Ann Worsley and Mary Bouker, for example, were milliners at Bank Top in Manchester in 1788, Sarah Wells and Ann Smith were partners in a grocery business at 59 Moorfields, Sheffield in 1828, and Martha Carter, Sarah Burnand, and Elizabeth Mathers ran the Pleasant Dairy in Blackburn Lane, Leeds in 1826.[98]

Buying into an established business as partner to an existing owner was another option for those who could not afford to go it alone. This practice also offered the added advantage of providing the new entrant with informal training on the job. Despite the reassurance that entering into an established enterprise with an experienced partner offered, though, and in common with all business ventures, such an arrangement could still be fraught with difficulties. This was evidently the case in the partnership of Elizabeth Laycock and Christina Yeoman, which resulted in court proceedings in the early nineteenth century. The two women had run a millinery business in Leeds during the 1790s. In 1803, Elizabeth, now married to the ironmonger, John Hepworth, and acting with him, brought charges against Christina Yeoman in the Court of Exchequer. Elizabeth, it was noted, had been the 'apprentice or work-woman' of the milliners, Charles and Christina Yeoman. Sometime after Charles's death, the two women formed a partnership, and signed an agreement to this effect in 1793. The terms of their

---

[96] See R. Campbell, *The London Tradesman* (London, 1747), 331–40, on the costs of setting up in various trades and professions in mid-eighteenth-century London.

[97] *Leeds Mercury*, 18 November 1809.

[98] Edmond Holme, *A Directory for the Towns of Manchester and Salford* (Manchester, 1788); *Manchester & Salford Directory* (1817); *The Sheffield Directory and Guide* (1828); *General & Commercial Directory of the Borough of Leeds* (1826).

arrangement included the stipulation that if either one married or died then the partnership should end and the unmarried or surviving partner would take over the business and buy all the stock in trade at prime cost. When the partnership was formed, Yeoman was—apparently unknown to Laycock—already in debt. Laycock paid £300 to join her and they carried on in business together until 1796 when the younger partner married. At this point, the partnership owed over £1,252 to a London haberdasher, Samuel Barlow. It was claimed that Yeoman tried to get an account from Barlow, so that she could pay the partnership's debts, but he failed to provide it. However, he continued to trade with Yeoman in her own right, until her apparent bankruptcy, at which point Barlow took both women to the Court of King's Bench at Westminster for repayment of the all the business's debts. Barlow claimed that he did not know about the details of the original partnership agreement, and, moreover, that Christina had taken over her husband's business whilst owing him £675.[99]

Cases such as this remind us of the peculiar precariousness of business in the late eighteenth and early nineteenth centuries.[100] Both men and women in trade could experience failure as well as success, and despite the previous chapters' emphasis on the continued involvement of women in the commercial worlds of Manchester, Leeds, and Sheffield, not every woman was successful in business, and individuals could fall victim to their own incompetence, personal misfortune, or the effects of external economic forces. Directory entries reveal a degree of longevity amongst a significant, though small, proportion of female listings: 88.6 per cent of individual working women appeared only once in the directories sampled, 9.5 per cent secured two entries and 1.9 per cent were listed three times. Since the average chronological gap between the directories sampled for any one town is 12.5 years,

[99] NA, E112/2078/650.

[100] Sheila Marriner, 'English Bankruptcy Records and Statistics before 1850', *Economic History Review* 33/3 (1980), 351–66; Julian Hoppit, *Risk and Failure in English Business 1700–1800* (Cambridge, 1987); David A. Kent, 'Small Businessmen and their Credit Transactions in Early Nineteenth-Century Britain', *Business History* 36/2 (1994), 47–64; Margot C. Finn, *The Character of Credit: Personal Debt in English Culture, 1740–1914* (Cambridge, 2003). Small firms may have been particularly vulnerable, see Berg, 'Small Producer Capitalism'; S. Nenadic *et al.*, 'Record Linkage and the Small Family Firm: Edinburgh 1861–1891', *Bulletin of the John Rylands University of Manchester* 74 (1992),

appearing in more than one was clearly an achievement, and we can speculate with some confidence that the proportion of individual women appearing in multiple editions would have been much higher if directories had been sampled more frequently. Those women who appeared only once in the sample may have failed, retired, or changed business. It is also likely that directory compilers simply missed some people out of one edition, whilst including them in another, while significant changes in the way in which individuals were listed from one directory to the next (such as a name change or an alteration in both trade and address) make tracking them over time impossible. Still, the evidence presented here suggests, significantly, that over 10 per cent of businesses headed by women lasted for over a decade, although the majority of female-run enterprises—in common with most small family firms run by men—appear to have been short-lived.[101] Among the group of women who headed long-running businesses were Hannah Pattern, who worked as a penknife cutler in Silver Street, Sheffield between 1774 and 1797, Alice Swindell, who ran a printing, stationery, and bookselling business from various addresses on Manchester's Hanging Bridge between 1804 and 1828, and who also sold tickets for the circus at the same address,[102] and Hannah Stonehouse, who operated as a confectioner and pastry cook in Leeds from 1809 until her death in 1826 at the age of 72.[103]

Directories provide good evidence that a sizeable proportion of women's businesses were successful, but also indicate that very many may not have been. Other, and more conclusive, evidence of the failure of female-run businesses is not difficult to find. Court records and newspaper advertisements are particularly good sources for tracing

169–95; R. Lloyd-Jones and A. A. Le Roux, 'Marshall and the Birth and Death of Firms: The Growth and Size Distribution of Firms in the Early Nineteenth-Century Cotton Industry', *Business History* 24 (1982), 141–55; though see Owens, 'Inheritance and the Life-Cycle of Family Firms', for an alternative view of the relative success of family firms.

[101] Nenadic, 'The Small Family Firm in Victorian Britain'; Owens, 'Inheritance and the Life-Cycle of Family Firms', 27–9.

[102] *Manchester Mercury*, 18 September 1804.

[103] *Manchester and Salford Directory* (1804); *Manchester and Salford Director* (1828); *Sheffield Directory* (1774); *Directory of Sheffield* (1787); *Directory of Sheffield* (1797); *Leeds Directory for 1809* (1809); *General & Commercial Directory of . . . Leeds* (1826); *Leeds Intelligencer*, 28 December 1828.

business collapse. The records of the Lancashire Court of Quarter Sessions include the cases of Elizabeth Wolsencroft, a Manchester victualler, who was languishing in Lancaster gaol for debt in 1772,[104] as well as those of Mary Booth, who had operated as a draper in Manchester, and in 1809 owed almost £50 to a Joseph Pickering,[105] and Margaret Drummond, a victualler and wife of James, also a victualler and reedmaker, whose debts were listed separately to her husband's in 1812.[106] Frances and Martha Ogden, sisters and Manchester milliners, were also accused at the Lancashire Quarter Sessions of owing almost £100 to various—exclusively female—traders and manufacturers in Manchester, Stockport, and Liverpool in October 1812.[107]

Advertisements in the press announcing the bankruptcy of female traders and subsequent creditors' meetings, or the sale of bankrupt stock, were also not uncommon. The bankruptcy of Martha Holdsworth, a Sheffield-based Britannia metal manufacturer, was announced in a local paper in 1817,[108] as was that of Mary Marsden, a Manchester upholsterer,[109] and Ann Sheppard, a Leeds milliner.[110] Sheppard's business on Commercial Street was listed in the 1809 Leeds directory and advertisements for it appeared regularly in the *Leeds Mercury* that year. In May, she returned her 'Thanks to the Ladies of Leeds and its Environs, for Favours already conferred', and expressed her hope that 'by continual Exertions' she might 'ensure their future Patronage'.[111] On 18 November, she announced that 'she is on her Return from London with a Fashionable Assortment of MILLINERY, DRESSES, &c. &c. Which will be ready for . . . inspection on Thursday' and advertised for two apprentices to start immediately. Yet four weeks later, on 16 December, she was declared bankrupt in the same paper, with the sale of her entire stock being advertised at the end of the month.[112]

---

[104] Lancashire County Record Office (LCRO), QJB/39
[105] LCRO, QJB/55/1.   [106] LCRO, QJB/57/19 & 20.
[107] LCRO, QJB/57/68.   [108] *Sheffield Mercury*, 25 January 1817.
[109] *Manchester Courier*, 23 February 1828.
[110] *Leeds Mercury*, 16 December 1809.   [111] Ibid. 13 May 1809.
[112] Ibid. 30 December 1809.

Mary Farrar's foray into the timber trade in 1778 also ended in disaster and resulted in cases being brought before the Courts of Exchequer and King's Bench between her and a Leeds carpenter, William Bottomley, with whom she contracted to buy 115 ash timber trees.[113] Similarly unfortunate was Hannah Haslehurst, owner of a successful grocery business in Sheffield in the late eighteenth century, left to her by her husband, which she ran with her son. In 1782 she established the Sheffield Old Bank, which operated from the rear of her grocer's shop in Market Place. Her venture into the world of commercial banking lasted only three years until 1785 when, in common with two other newly founded banks in the town, Haslehurst's enterprise collapsed. The grocery side of the business, however, continued to run and was passed to her son some years later.[114] Not everyone in business was as fortunate as the Haslehursts when faced with financial problems, and the failure of one family business could have knock-on effects for others. In 1817, two businesses run by the Iredale family of Sheffield collapsed in apparently related incidents. Mrs Iredale was a milliner who advertised the launch of her millinery and dressmaking business on the High Street at the corner of George Street on 10 May 1817, 'in which', she claimed, 'from her experiences and connexions in London, she feels no doubt in meeting the . . . sanction and support' of the Ladies of Sheffield. The advertisement noted that she had already engaged a 'person . . . from Town' as a dressmaker and was looking for two apprentices.[115] Three months later, Mrs Iredale announced 'her intention of deposing of all her new and elegant assorted Stock'.[116] The following month, in September, the stock of the mercer and draper, William Brown Iredale, also of High Street, was being auctioned following his bankruptcy, along with 'a very large

[113] NA, E112/2069/414.

[114] A. W. Goodfellow, 'The Development of Banking', in D. L. Linton (ed.), *Sheffield and its Region* (Sheffield, 1956), 168; R. E. Leader, *The Sheffield Banking Company Limited: An Historical Sketch, 1831–1916* (Sheffield, 1916), 5; and Leader, *The Early Sheffield Banks* (London, 1917), 5.

[115] *Sheffield Mercury*, 10 May 1817.   [116] Ibid. 16 August 1817.

and elegant, and valuable Assortment of MILLINERY and DRESSES of the newest fashion': his wife's remaining goods.[117]

Elizabeth Raffald, the Manchester-based cookery-book writer, directory compiler, and grocer, also suffered serious financial problems in the early 1780s seemingly linked to her husband's failings. In 1780 John Raffald was declared bankrupt and the family had to leave the King's Head Inn where they had been based for eight years. As we saw in the previous chapter, Elizabeth's business interests had expanded rapidly during the preceding two decades, and it is possible that she overstretched herself. At the time of his bankruptcy, Elizabeth Raffald's husband, John, had become a heavy drinker and was said to have been deeply depressed, even suicidal. Whether this was the cause, or the result, of the couple's money problems is unclear, although Elizabeth reportedly told her husband at one point that killing himself might be a good idea since he harassed her so much.[118] Despite falling on hard times though, she remained irrepressible. During the Manchester race season she ran a refreshment stall selling strawberries near the Ladies stand on Kersal Moor.[119] When John was appointed master of the Exchange coffee house, Elizabeth began to sell soup there, even though it had not formerly served food.[120] She also compiled and published the third edition of her Manchester directory. Yet her frantic activity was cut short on 19 April 1781, when, aged just 48, she died of what appears to have been a stroke.[121] Within a week John Raffald's creditors, now lacking, it would seem, the security of Elizabeth's industry, took steps to remove him from the coffee house and the Raffald's minor business empire was at an end.[122]

As we have seen, female involvement in small businesses could take a variety of forms, and Elizabeth Raffald herself operated as both an

[117] *Sheffield Mercury*, 6 and 20 September; 8 November 1817.
[118] Barker and Harvey, 'Women Entrepreneurs and Urban Expansion: Manchester, 1780–1820'. See also Roy Shipperbottom (ed.), 'Introduction' to *The Experienced English Housekeeper* (Lewes, 1997).   [119] *The Manchester Directory for the Year 1773*, p. viii.
[120] Shipperbottom (ed.), *The Experienced English Housekeeper*, p. xvi
[121] Ibid.   [122] See *Manchester Mercury*, 1, 22 May 1781.

independent trader and in partnership with her husband. The majority of women identified in this study traded in their own right: either as head of a family business, or as an independent trader and generally an employer of others. Many more women, of course, were likely to have been hidden from view as less senior members of family firms or as employees. Most businesses appear to have been operated by families, and were run by husbands and wives, siblings, or parents and their children, but they could also be established by unrelated individuals forming partnerships. Within all such enterprises, hierarchies of power were not necessarily gendered, since women not only employed men, but were commonly the senior partner in businesses run with their adult children. As has been shown, both age and wealth were important factors in the power dynamics of small businesses, often overriding considerations of gender. It is certainly true that when wives worked with their husbands, the man would almost always assume the position of head of the business. However, the smooth manner in which widows could take control of familial concerns suggests their deep involvement prior to their husbands' deaths. The level of female skill and commercial knowledge in such cases is emphasized by the number of widows who remained in charge of family businesses even after their sons came of age and worked alongside them. None of this suggests that women in Manchester, Leeds, and Sheffield were economically sidelined by men during the late eighteenth and early nineteenth centuries. Female enterprise was clearly key not only to the economy as a whole—most visibly through the direct contribution of businesses run by women—but also in terms of women's input into partnerships, and more importantly, family concerns. As we shall see, in the next and final chapter, it is evident that women felt particularly committed to family businesses, working hard both to maintain them and to further their success.

5

Family, Property, and Power

MOST firms in Manchester, Leeds, and Sheffield between 1760 and 1830 were familial concerns. Exploring the complex nature of female involvement in small businesses thus means focusing heavily on families, although partnerships between non-relatives were also significant, if less common. As we shall see in the discussion of individual businesswomen that follows, those factors commonly thought to discriminate against women in business—principally the laws of property and ideas about a woman's place—could affect female enterprise in important ways. Yet it is also apparent that women were not necessarily economically and socially marginalized as a result, for not only were legal restrictions on female property ownership less rigorous than has been thought, but, as we saw in Chapter 3, prevailing ideas about respectable femininity did not automatically preclude women from openly engaging in business. Women could experience a wide variety of opportunities and obstacles in their struggles to achieve financial security. Being female might have a significant impact on women's commercial activity, but this does not mean that gender predetermined the nature of this involvement, nor that all women shared the same experiences. In Manchester, Leeds, and Sheffield, evidence of female agency is as common as material describing their subjugation. Indeed, many middling women of business were able and willing to assert themselves and to manipulate the law and their familial and wider relationships to the advantage of both themselves and their family.

WOMEN AND THE LAW

In 1820, 'Sarah Richardson of Manchester, Hat manufacturer', took William Gamon of Chester, heir to 'Elizabeth Towsey of Chester, Hatter and Hosier', to the Court of Exchequer. Towsey had died in June 1819, owing Richardson over £71 'for goods sold and delivered by your Oratrix in the way of her trade or business'. According to her plea, Richardson had 'frequently and in a friendly manner' applied to Gamon for the money he owed her, but no payment had been forthcoming.[1] Richardson had therefore taken Gamon to court to pursue the debt. She appeared as sole complainant in the court records, without the support of a male relative or 'friend', and asserted her legal rights just as any man might have done. This apparent gender-blindness on the part of the law was not unusual. The legal system did not necessarily discriminate against women at this time. The belief that it did is largely drawn from descriptions of married women's property rights, which, in theory, were severely restricted under common law. Widows and spinsters, in contrast, appeared much freer from legal constraint. Widows, in particular, have been depicted as uniquely independent amongst women if they were in control of any sort of inheritance,[2] but since primogeniture tended to affect only the elite, and daughters commonly inherited on a remarkably equitable basis with their brothers,[3] some spinsters also enjoyed a high degree of freedom.

[1] National Archives (NA), Court of Exchequer Pleadings, E112/2184/238.

[2] Amy Erickson, *Women and Property in Early Modern England* (London, 1993), 153–86; Barbara J. Todd, 'The Remarrying Widow: A Stereotype Reconsidered', in Mary Prior, (ed.), *Women in English Society, 1500–1800* (London, 1985); Christine Churches, 'Women and Property in Early Modern England: A Case Study', *Social History* 23/2 (1998); Maxine Berg, 'Women's Property and the Industrial Revolution', *Journal of Interdisciplinary History* 24 (1993); David Green, 'Merry Widows and Sentimental Spinsters', in Jon Stobart and Alistair Owens (eds.), *Urban Fortunes: Property and Inheritance in the Town, 1700–1900* (Aldershot, 2000). Although see Alistair Owens's recent questioning of the degree of financial independence enjoyed by widows, based on a study of early nineteenth-century Stockport: Alistair Owens, 'Property, Gender and the Life Course: Inheritance and Family Welfare Provision in Early Nineteenth-Century England', *Social History* 26/3 (2001), 299–317, p. 300.

[3] Erickson, *Women and Property in Early Modern England*, 71; R. J. Morris, *Men, Women and Property in England, 1780–1870: A Social and Economic History of Family Strategies Amongst the Leeds Middle Classes* (Cambridge, 2005), 109–19.

Married women, on the other hand, were technically subject to 'coverture' and had their legal identity subsumed into that of their husband. Contemporary legal theorists, and most famously, William Blackstone, described the suspension of a woman's legal existence during marriage as rendering her unable to own property, make contracts, sue or be sued.[4] Yet it was clearly not the case that married women were always constrained to this extent.[5] As Margot Finn has explained, coverture 'in this period is best described as existing in a state of suspended animation', while 'wives' legal inability to contract and litigate debts was often ignored or attenuated in practice'.[6] Moreover, coverture was not entirely detrimental to women, and was often portrayed as a reciprocal arrangement, where in return for property benefits, men took on the maintenance of wives and children.[7] Indeed, Margaret Hunt has explained that married women believed they had the right to expect maintenance, protection, and freedom from assault from their husbands, as well as a say in the family finances commensurate with the property that they brought into the marriage.[8] Moreover, other jurisdictions such as equity, customary, and ecclesiastic law gave women individual legal rights that could challenge aspects of common

---

[4] William Blackstone, *Commentaries on the Laws of England*, 4th edn., 4 vols. (Dublin, 1771), i. 442–3. For modern historical views that echo this reading of the law see Janelle Greenberg, 'The Legal Status of the English Woman in Early Eighteenth-Century Common Law and Equity', *Studies in Eighteenth-Century Culture* 4 (1975), 171–81; Lawrence Stone, *Road to Divorce: England 1530–1987* (Oxford, 1990), 13.

[5] Erickson, *Women and Property*, 150–1; Margot Finn, 'Women, Consumption and Coverture in England, c. 1760–1860', *Historical Journal* 39/3 (1996), 702–22; Margaret Hunt, 'Wives and Marital "Rights" in the Court of Exchequer', in P. Griffiths and M. S. R. Jenner (eds.), *Londinopolis: Essays in the Cultural and Social History of Early Modern London* (Manchester, 2000), 125; M. Berg, 'Women's Consumption and the Industrial Classes of Eighteenth-Century England', *Journal of Social History* 30/2 (1996), 415–34; Hannah Barker, 'Women, Work and the Industrial Revolution: Female Involvement in the English Printing Trades, c. 1700–1840', in Hannah Barker and Elaine Chalus (eds.), *Gender in Eighteenth-Century Society: Roles, Representations and Responsibility* (London, 1997), 99; Nicola Pullin, ' "Business is Just Life": The Practice, Prescription and Legal Position of Women in Business, 1700–1850', Ph.D. thesis (London, 2001).

[6] Finn, 'Women, Consumption and Coverture', 707.

[7] Joanne Bailey, *Unquiet Lives: Marriage and Marriage Breakdown in England, 1660–1800* (Cambridge, 2003), 62.

[8] Hunt, 'Wives and Marital "Rights" ', 118–21. See also Alexandra Shepard, *Meanings of Manhood in Early Modern England* (Oxford, 2003), 80–6.

law. As Nicola Pullin has argued, histories of women and trade need to 'separate narratives of women's legal *rights* from those detailing their *ability* to trade under the legal system'.[9]

In Manchester, Leeds, and Sheffield, it is clear that some women did trade independently of their husbands, and while married women did not enjoy the same trading rights as men or single women, the existence of numerous exceptions and differing interpretations of the law left them 'legal spaces' in which to conduct business.[10] One way in which married women could escape the supposed confines of coverture was by invoking borough custom and trading as 'femes soles'. Some historians describe custom as an important privilege for trading women, yet it is unclear how long feme sole custom continued from the medieval to modern periods,[11] and a decline in custom, coupled with the growth in common-law jurisdiction, has been described as adversely affecting both the legal and economic status of women during the eighteenth century.[12] Yet it is debatable how helpful the custom of feme sole trading was to married women anyway, since it made them fully liable for trading debts and subject to bankruptcy laws. Feme sole status offered little protection to married women whose husbands could hide behind their wives' liability.[13] Indeed, Pullin argues that 'in practical terms, the custom seems to have been primarily concerned with debt recovery and personal libability rather than

[9] Pullin, 'Business is Just Life', 30; Finn, 'Women, Consumption and Coverture'; Joanne Bailey, 'Favoured or Oppressed? Married Women, Property and "Coverture" in England, 1660–1800', *Continuity and Change* 17/3 (2002), 1–22.

[10] Pullin, 'Business is Just Life', ch. 2. See also Erickson, *Women and Property*, 19.

[11] Mary Prior, 'Women and the Urban Economy', in Prior, *Women in English Society*, 103. See also Mary Bateson (ed.), *Borough Customs*, 2 vols. (London, 1904–6), i. 227–8; Erickson, *Women and Property*, 30, 246–7; M. Kowaleski, 'Women's Work in a Market Town: Exeter in the Late Fourteenth Century', in B. Hanawalt (ed.), *Women and Work in Pre-industrial Europe* (Bloomgton, Ind., 1986), 146; Pullin, 'Business is Just Life', ch. 3; Richard Grassby, *Kinship and Capitalism: Marriage, Family, and Business in the English-Speaking World, 1580–1740* (Cambridge, 2001), ch. 8.

[12] Prior, 'Women and the Urban Economy', 103; Erickson, *Women and Property*, 6.

[13] Judith Bennett, 'Medieval Women, Modern Women: Across the Great Divide', in David Aers (ed.), *Culture and History, 1350–1600: Essays on English Communities, Identities and Writing* (Hemel Hempstead, 1992), 154–5; Margaret Hunt, *The Middling Sort: Commerce, Gender and the Family in England, 1680–1780* (1996), 139.

conferring the "right" to trade in itself'.[14] Moreover, whilst coverture is usually seen as detrimental to women, it could be used as a means to avoid liabilities conferred by their feme sole status, as we shall see. Another legal device available to married women was the use of a 'separate estate'. Such prenuptial contracts were not uncommon, and women fairly low down on the social scale might hold property in this way, supposedly immune to the laws of coverture and the grasp of greedy or penurious husbands.[15]

The legal position of women, and married women in particular, was clearly complicated. Men and women of the middling sort had access to a number of courts, both local and national. Local courts of record recognized certain types of customary law, such as feme sole status, while the national courts of Chancery and Exchequer operated common law and would generally enforce coverture. Not surprisingly litigants, well aware of the pluralistic nature of the legal system, would take their case wherever they believed they had most chance of winning. Thus, Pullin notes, women wanting to sue as feme sole traders were more likely do so in a local court, while those seeking a defence against being sued would prefer a superior common-law court in order to plead coverture in their defence.[16]

Yet while the law played a crucial role in determining women's rights over property, whether or not certain laws, or interpretations of the law, affected individual women could depend on factors as diverse as the personalities and behaviour of those involved, the degree of power which they felt they had and which others believed they possessed, their location, wealth, and connections.[17] Thus while the

[14] Pullin, 'Business is Just Life', 71. See also Marjorie K. McIntosh, 'The Benefits and Drawbacks of *feme sole* status in England 1300–1630', *Journal of British Studies* 44 (2005), 410–38.

[15] Amy Erikson, 'Common Law versus Common Practice: The Use of Marriage Settlements in Early Modern England', *Economic History Review* 43 (1990), 21–39; Susan Staves, *Married Women's Separate Property in England, 1660–1833* (Cambridge, Mass., 1990); Berg, 'Women's Property and the Industrial Revolution'; Hunt, *Middling Sort*, 157–62.   [16] Pullin, 'Business is Just Life', 60.

[17] Staves argues that in provincial towns, inhabitants might have been less aware of legal developments than in the capital, so that the law in such instances would have less role in shaping social practice: Staves, *Married Women's Separate Property in England*, 205.

pitfalls of coverture could be neatly avoided by some women, it could result in disaster for others, and feme sole traders might appear particularly independent in one instance, but vulnerable to husbands taking both goods and profits in another.[18] Susan Amussen has observed that in early modern England, marital arrangements favoured stability over strict legality,[19] and this generally appears to have been the case in our three towns. Family breakdown and the disruption of personal relationships, however, could result in both women and men either flouting the law or asserting their rights under it. The tendency for men to gain the upper hand in such situations is evident, but was not inevitable. According to Earle, the depositions of middling Londoners in cases of marital breakdown suggest that wives 'often gave as good as they got, or better. They were independent individuals . . . [who] would say that they would do as they please and then proceed to do as they pleased. Mild and meek they were supposed to be, but in reality the women of the middle station were quite capable of holding their own on the battlefield of marriage.'[20] Erickson is less optimistic, but notes that whilst 'The reality of women's receiving large amounts of property and exerting power over it in a distinctive way does not change the fact of oppression . . . it does highlight the disjuncture between theory and practice. It also exhibits the ingenuity of many ordinary women in working within a massively restrictive system.'[21]

The study of middling women and the law that follows supports both these claims. It is based on the particularly rich and detailed records of the superior courts of Exchequer and the Chancery court of the Palatine of Lancaster. Both Chancery and Exchequer were courts of common law and equity. Judges in these courts often upheld the contractual obligations of married women and imported equitable principles into the operation of common law, particularly in the interests of commerce.[22] The records of these courts are organized by county, and allow those exploring particular regions relatively easy

[18] Cited in Hunt, *Middling Sort*, 125, 139–42.
[19] Susan Dwyer Amussen, *An Ordered Society: Gender and Class in Early Modern England* (Oxford, 1988), 128.   [20] Earle, *Making of the English Middle Class*, 204.
[21] Erickson, *Women and Property*, 19.   [22] Pullin, 'Business is Just Life', 40–2.

access to some of the vast numbers of lawsuits handled each year in
equity courts.[23] Although the proportion of cases brought in
Exchequer from outside London during the eighteenth and early
nineteenth centuries declined, the numbers emanating from northern
English counties rose significantly.[24] In addition, Exchequer was a
popular choice for those of the middling orders. Horwitz has calculated that 'commercial/artisanal' litigants constituted perhaps half of
all first-named plaintiffs and defendants from 1735 onwards, with
women making up between 8.5 and 16.1 per cent of first-named litigants during this period.[25] Margaret Hunt has estimated that 69,000
women appeared as plaintiffs in central equity courts during the eighteenth century, and although the majority of these would have been in
Chancery, her calculations still suggest that well over 10,000 women
were plaintiffs in the Court of Exchequer.[26]

   An examination of Exchequer pleadings originating, or concerned
with events, in Manchester, Leeds, and Sheffield between 1760 and
1830 uncovered thirty-two cases in which women involved in business played a central role. A further nine such cases were found
amongst the Palatine of Lancashire Chancery Court pleadings. All the
cases concerned disputes over property, and detailed battles over
inheritance and business debts. Only two of the cases examined in
pleadings appear to have made it further to the deposition stage.[27] It
was common for Exchequer cases not to proceed beyond an initial bill
of complaint or pleading, which suggests that settlement was made

   [23] Especially compared to the records of Chancery: J. Milhous and R. D. Hume,
'Eighteenth-Century Equity Lawsuits in the Court of Exchequer as a Source for Historical
Research', *Historical Research* 70 (June 1997), 231–46, p. 236.
   [24] Henry Horwitz, *Exchequer Equity Records and Proceedings, 1649–1841* (Richmond,
2001), 37–8.   [25] Ibid. 47–52. These figures exclude tithe cases.
   [26] There were 200,000–250,000 equity cases brought in Chancery in the eighteenth
century, and roughly 40,000 in Exchequer. Hunt estimates that 69,000 women plaintiffs
appeared in the two courts: 'Wives and Marital "Rights" ', 110–11.
   [27] Cases involving Hannah Sheldon and the Beswicks: NA, Court of Exchequer
Depositions, E134/27Geo 3/Hil 2 and E134/47Geo 3/Mich 5. On the workings of the
Court of Exchequer, see Horwitz, *Exchequer Equity Records and Proceedings*, ch. 1; on the
Palatinate of Lancashire see Horwitz, *Chancery Equity Records and Proceedings, 1600–1800*
(London, 1995), 34; T. Rath, 'Business Records in the Public Record Office in the Age of
the Industrial Revolution', *Business History* 17/2 (1975), 189–200, pp. 195–8.

soon after legal action was instigated, or one of the parties gave up or died, or records are incomplete.[28] It is clear from this sample that women were not averse to going to law in order to seek redress for their grievances: twenty-nine of the cases in the sample of forty-one were brought by women, usually with male family members, family friends, or the executors of disputed wills,[29] but in ten cases, women acted alone or with female relatives.[30] As other historians have shown, women could be active participants in civil legal action.[31] Typical in this respect was Mary Hobson, the widow of Samuel, who in 1811 claimed to be entitled to the estate of John Hoole, a Sheffield button manufacturer, who had left his business to Samuel in his will.[32] Although the case appears to have gone no further than the pleadings stage, Mary Hobson evidently won out, and is listed in the 1817 Sheffield directory as a 'horn button manufacturer'.[33]

Other examples of the assertion of female property rights include the case of Elizabeth Alkinson, wife of a Manchester silver plater, who made a claim on the estate of John Wilson in 1813,[34] and Betty Bond, the wife of a Manchester innkeeper, who in 1827, along with several other creditors, took action against Thomas Binks, a slate merchant who had borrowed £100 from her in 1820 when she had been married

[28] Hunt, 'Wives and Marital "Rights"', 112; Horwitz suggests that around of 80% of equity proceedings in Exchequer never went beyond pleadings: *Exchequer Equity Records and Proceedings*, 31.

[29] Equity conferred upon wives the ability to act as if they were individual agents, but did not give them the same legal rights as men and single women possessed. Thus equitable title to a separate property might be upheld under common law, but an individual woman could not claim legal title to that property herself, rather the trustees of the property had to act on her behalf: see Pullin, 'Business is Just Life', 43–4.

[30] NA, E112/1525/79, 1541/573, 2184/238, 2066/304, 2070/433, 2089/1081, 2257/73.

[31] Erickson, *Women and Property in Early Modern England*, ch. 7; Finn, 'Women, Consumption and Coverture in England', 714–22; Geoffrey L. Hudson, 'Negotiating for Blood Money: War Widows and the Courts in Seventeenth-Century England', in J. Kermode and G. Walker (eds.), *Women, Crime and the Courts in Early Modern England* (1994); Craig Muldrew, ' "A Mutual Assent of her Mind?" Women, Debt, Litigation and Contract in Early Modern England', *History Workshop Journal* 55 (2003), 47–71, pp. 54–7. On the role of individuals in outlining their own cases, see Joanne Bailey, 'Voices in Court: Lawyers' or Litigants'?', *Historical Research* 74/186 (2001), 392–408.

[32] NA, E112/2089/1081.   [33] *Sheffield General Directory* (Sheffield, 1817).

[34] NA, E112/2084/900.

to Thomas Openshaw, another innkeeper. Since Binks had died in 1823, the creditors were calling on his daughter, Esther, to repay his debts.[35] In 1814, Margaret Barton and William Vickers brought a joint case in the Chancery Court of the Palatine of Lancaster against John Hobson. All three had been involved in a firm of brassfounders and coppersmiths: Margaret inheriting her share from her husband, John Barton. After John's death in 1807, the partners 'did contrive to carry on the said Business and Copartnership' until it was dissolved two years later. Hobson had been charged with collecting in business debts of 'a very large and considerable amount' but had proved negligent. Although both he and Vickers owed Barton money, Vickers had apparently come to some agreement with Barton, so that it was Hobson who was taken to court.[36]

Women might also pursue claims against members of their own family. Mary Coward, the wife of a Manchester farrier, Thomas, brought a claim against her mother Ann Dixon in 1803. Her father Rowland Parkinson had apparently left Mary 'a considerable personal estate', to be inherited when her brother James came of age. However, Ann had remarried and her new husband Richard Dixon had assumed control of some of the estate due to Mary, who, despite her brother reaching the age of majority, had received no money. For their part, Richard and Ann Dixon claimed that there was not enough money in the estate to pay Mary.[37] Complaints that new husbands were misdirecting family inheritances willed by a previous spouse were common, but in some cases it was women who were accused of being obstructive. Abigail Lawton, wife of the Manchester cabinetmaker Samuel Lawton made a claim in 1781 on the estate of Mary Chandley, her mother. Chandley had died in 1779 and Abigail's sister Arabella had assumed control of all her property and was, apparently, refusing requests to share. Arabella claimed that she had already given Abigail her share in cash, and that she had used the money to purchase a house in Manchester with her husband.[38]

Cases such as those brought by Mary Coward and Abigail Lawton demonstrate not only the propensity for family relations to break

---

[35] NA, Chancery Court of the Palatine of Lancaster, PL/6/118/25–6.
[36] NA, PL6/105.   [37] NA, E112/1538/477.   [38] NA, E112/1527/160.

down over issues of property, but also the ability of individuals to get, or to lay claim to, more than their fair share of family wealth. Legal cases often resulted from such greed, but it is also likely that many more instances existed where people were allowed to assert their own wishes to the detriment of others and simply got away with it. For many, going to law would have been considered too expensive or too stressful. For others, it was a more common experience. The Beswick family provides a case in point: in 1806, Ann Beswick and her brother Samuel were pursued by the creditors of their deceased father James, who had died in 1792. Ann and Samuel had taken over his Manchester shop on his death but appeared unable to honour all their father's debts, or his funeral expenses. Samuel had since been declared bankrupt.[39] The pair later denied they had received anything from James Beswick's estate.[40] The actions of James Beswick's creditors followed an earlier one in 1803, brought by Ann Beswick and Margaret Beswick, her niece, who had claimed ownership of a plot of land apparently loaned to James prior to his death.[41]

As we have seen, disputed property claims were often the result of a death in the family. In three cases, action was brought to try and force widows to pay their husband's debts. In 1775, Thomas Hudson accused the widow of Richard Bingley, former partner in a Sheffield firm manufacturing silver and silver-plated goods, of refusing to pay back a loan of £1,000 after her husband's death.[42] Several Manchester brewers acting together in 1809, accused Alice, widow of the deceased alehouse keeper Jones Wrigley, of defaulting on debts totalling almost £100.[43] In 1776, Sarah Willatt was charged with refusing the pay the debts of her late husband John incurred during his partnership in a lacemaking firm.[44] Other cases were brought by widows pursuing money due to the estates of their dead husbands. Hannah Sheldon, widow of the Sheffield miller John, demanded moneys from the estate of George Eyre for this reason in 1779,[45] and Martha Dawson, widow

[39] NA, E112/1537/442.
[40] NA, E134/47Geo 3/Mich 5, and (1808), E134/48Geo 3/East 14.
[41] NA, E112/1534/372.   [42] NA, E112/2064/248.
[43] NA, E112/1539/524.   [44] NA, E112/1526/117.
[45] NA, E112/2066/304. See also E134/27Geo 3/Hil 2.

of a Manchester linen merchant, also John, pursued William Craven in court in 1817 for a debt owed to her husband since 1805.[46] In 1810, Eleanor Welsh, the widow of Anthony, who had been co-partner in a carrier service between Manchester, Glasgow, and Edinburgh, took the other partners (one of whom was also a woman) to court for their failure to compensate her for her husband's share of the business, which she estimated at almost £10,000. In addition to not paying her for her share, the other three partners had, it was claimed, refused to show Eleanor the company accounts.[47]

Uncertainties over inheritance could also allow widows to lay claim to money or property less legitimately. In 1776, John Corbett, a Manchester gentleman, brought a complaint against Catherine Hall, the widow of the slater Richard Hall, who had died five years earlier. Just after his death, Corbett had rented two houses in Great Turner Street from Catherine, but soon after moving in, he discovered that she might not be the legal owner of the buildings. Richard Hall had apparently died intestate, and competing claims on his property came from 'several sons and daughters' as well as the owner of a mortgage on the houses, a painter from Cheadle named John Chandley. The issue was probably clearer than Corbett suggested, since under ecclesiastical law a widow was legally entitled to administer her deceased husband's estate and was allowed to enjoy one-third of her husband's real property during the remainder of her life. She was also, according to Erickson, likely to receive as much as the widows of men who left wills.[48] Alistair Owens has argued that intestate succession could be a deliberate ploy on the part of some property owners to avoid the expense of a will whilst still ensuring an equitable transmission of property to heirs according to the rules governing inheritance.[49]

---

[46] NA, PL/6/108/92.   [47] NA, E112/1541/573. See also E112/1541/586.

[48] Erickson, *Women and Property*, 174, 178, 186. These dower rights may have been increasingly unclear in the eighteenth century, however, and were not always respected, although it should be noted that husbands often left their wives rather more than this by the more modern practice of jointure: Staves, *Married Women's Separate Property in England*, chs. 2 and 3; Morris, *Men, Women and Property in England*, 101–9.

[49] Alistair Owens, 'Property, Will Making and Estate Disposal in an Industrial Town, 1800–1857', in Stobart and Owens, *Urban Fortunes*, 82–3.

Corbett was, apparently, threatened both by the mortgagers, with eviction, and by Hall's son, also Richard, who was called from London by his mother and allegedly said he would 'cause a Distress' to Corbett if he did not pay his rent. An informal agreement was reached whereby Corbett would pay his rent to Catherine, who would then pay Chandley. This continued until 25 December 1775, when Hall demanded rent early and being of a 'desponding, Covetous Envious and ill natured temper' sent a bailiff to the houses. This action appears to have had little effect, and the bailiffs were dispatched again the following April. Hall then appears to have taken legal action against Corbett, as his pleading demands that her attorneys stop harassing him. He also claimed that Hall had stopped maintaining the buildings properly since the dispute escalated, and that they were now leaking, resulting in Corbett and his family contracting 'coughs and colds' and furniture and clothing being spoilt, whilst an infestation of bugs had also destroyed more of his possessions.

Catherine Hall, whatever her legal rights, was clearly no pushover. Assertive female behaviour is also evident in a case involving the fate of a widow's inheritance once she had remarried and competing claims between the custom of a wife's 'portion', the establishment of a separate estate and the principle of coverture. In 1780, William and John Greenwood, the children of John Greenwood, painter, chapman, and dealer,[50] brought a case against James Walton, their stepfather. Joining them in their action was Thomas Cooper, the husband of their dead sister Alice, and their mother Elizabeth.[51] Elizabeth had inherited real estate worth over £60 a year upon her first husband's death in 1769 in addition to money and his stock-in-trade worth over £3,000. The terms of John Greenwood's will allowed his 'dearly beloved wife' to take as much of the moveable property 'as she should think suitable in her own reason and capacity to manage' up to the value of £200, as much of the household goods as she needed to furnish a house and live comfortably, and to keep in the shop 'such goods as she in her own discretion shall chuse and think fit to deal in for the Procuration of her and Childrens maintainance bringing up and Education'. She was also to receive half the rental interest on the real estate, with the remaining interest to be placed in trust for her children. An additional clause stated that in the event of Elizabeth's remarriage, she was to lose all of her inheritance 'but that part only given her for the Stocking of her Shop'.[52]

Elizabeth duly did remarry, a year later. Her unfortunate choice was James Walton, a former employee of John Greenwood. Soon after the marriage, Walton was accused of assuming control of all the business's stock, valued at £1,423, and receiving debts due to John's estate of £1,578, despite having signed a prenuptial agreement in which he promised to leave Elizabeth's inheritance untouched. While marital disharmony increased, and the pair separated, Walton, it was alleged, proceeded to squander the Greenwood estate.[53] The current action was therefore aimed at preventing Walton having any further access to the family's property and business. The case against Walton centred on upholding the clause in John Greenwood's will that threatened to cut Elizabeth off from most of his estate if she remarried (a clause Walton was no doubt aware of since he was one of the witnesses to the will).[54] On face value, such conditions could be seen as constraining women's choice of action and 'locking' wives into widowhood,[55] but as Amy Erickson has pointed out, restrictions imposed in bequests on widows remarrying were primarily aimed at ensuring that family property remained in the hands of chosen heirs and could not be squandered by a feckless new husband.[56] This clause was therefore called on in an attempt to protect both Elizabeth's wealth and that of the Greenwood family.

Yet it is also clear that prior to her remarriage, Elizabeth had planned to ignore this part of her husband's will, since she formed a prenuptial agreement with Walton in which she clearly stated her intention to retain much of her inheritance. Elizabeth and her family

[52] Lancashire Record Office (LRO), Will of John Greenwood (1769).
[53] NA, E112/1527/155.   [54] Will of John Greenwood.
[55] Owens, 'Property, Gender and the Life Course'; Todd, 'The Remarrying Widow', 72–5.   [56] Erickson, *Women and Property*, 168–9.

thus attempted to use both custom and the formulation of a separate
estate in an attempt to circumvent the common-law practice of coverture. In addition to taking him to the Court of Exchequer, she also
secured her husband's arrest and temporary imprisonment in 1780.
James Walton appeared before the Lancashire Quarter Sessions on
11 July accused of 'assaulting and abusing' his wife 'in a most brutal
and violent manner' and was bound over to keep the peace for a period
of twelve months. According to the court record, he had 'threatened to
shoot her and repeatedly put her in fear of her life in so much that she
dare not Live with him and has been Obliged to seek Relief and
Refuge at Neighbours Houses'.[57] Walton, in turn, pursued Elizabeth
and her supporters through the Court of Common Pleas, claiming
ownership of the business and its stock, and forced her to return to the
Court of Exchequer in an attempt to restrain him in 1782.[58]

The issue of a woman's separate property was central in two other
cases from the Exchequer and Chancery courts. Sarah Wood took action
against her estranged husband, John, a chapman of Manchester and
then Bradford. Sarah and John had married in 1750, but not before she
and her brothers had made him sign a prenuptial agreement that guar-
anteed John a 'considerable marriage portion' of over £1,000 in return
for £40 per year for Sarah and £100 on his death, plus the provision that
if she died first and childless she could leave £100 as she wished. In 1762
the couple formally separated, but John, it was claimed, despite acquir-
ing 'a considerable fortune in Trade' had failed to support his wife who
had been forced to move to a remote house in Yorkshire.[59]

The second case featured one woman contesting the legality of the
separate estate of another. Sarah Coe, of Leeds, the sister and sole
beneficiary of Thomas Wallworth, a Leeds husbandman, made a
claim on the estate of Thomas's estranged wife Elizabeth, who had left
him several years previously and gone to live in Stockport. According
to Coe's claim, Elizabeth had run a lucrative ale-selling business
'wherein she acquired a considerable Property or Fortune' to which
Thomas Wallworth 'as Husband of the said Elizabeth Wallworth

[57] LRO, QSO/2/149.   [58] NA, E112/1528/164.   [59] NA, E112/2061/152.

become well intitled'. Elizabeth, however, was accused by Coe of having 'secreted and concealed such of her Money Property Fortune and Effects from him' by placing it in the hands of her brother-in-law, Thomas Haigh, another aleseller. Haigh and his wife Ellen, Elizabeth's sister, disputed this version of events, and claimed that soon after separating from Thomas, his creditors took all Elizabeth's goods and chattels. Her father James Massey then provided for her and took her and her children in. When he died, he left his estate to Ellen 'for her sole and separate use', and it was this that formed the basis for her business (which they claimed made little money, and most of what was left was taken by her daughter Margaret anyway).[60] The Haighs were depending on the fact that under equity, a husband who deserted his wife while her friends or family had given her the means to support herself and carry on a trade could not lay claim to her property at a future date.[61]

Most wills appointed widows as executors, or at least co-executors, of their husband's estate.[62] Widows could be vulnerable when this did not happen, as is illustrated by the case of Elizabeth Townley, the widow of a Manchester bricklayer George Townley. She took action in 1786 on behalf of herself and her children against the executor of George's will, his father Thomas. He was accused of selling property that should have gone to her son John.[63] In a similar case, Mary Braithwaite, widow of James, who had been a maltser in Leeds, also took his executors to court. Upon his death in 1788, Mary took over his business, but her husband's will, while encouraging her to continue to trade, had instructed that her commercial activities were to be supervised

[60] NA, E112/1525/79.   [61] Pullin, 'Business is Just Life', 48.

[62] Leonore Davidoff and Catherine Hall, *Family Fortunes: Men and Women of the English Middle Class, 1780–1850* (London, 1987), 211; Amy Louise Erickson, 'An Introduction to Probate Accounts', in Peter Spufford (ed.), *Guide to the Probate Accounts of England and Wales* (London, 1999); Berg, 'Women's Property and the Industrial Revolution', 237–9; Owens, 'Property, Will Making and Estate Disposal', 100. By contrast, Amy Louise Erickson found women were increasingly less likely to be named as executors in men's wills from eighteenth-century Cheshire, and that only 41% of wills had widows as executors by the 1780s, compared to 57% in the 1720s: 'Property and Widowhood in England 1660–1840', in Sandra Cavallo and Lyndan Warner (eds.), *Widowhood in Medieval and Early Modern Europe* (Harlow, 1999), 157.

[63] NA, PL/6/89/38.

by his executors William Sayer and William Braithwaite. These two men had been left his property in trust, with the instruction that:

if they found she reaped not a sufficient benefit therefrom then they should have the Liberty to prevent her further trading therewith, but in case it turned out to leave her a sufficient profit then they should permit her to have the use thereof for so long time as they should think proper and he thereby requested them to lend her all the assistance they possibly could

Mary Braithwaite took Sayer and William Braithwaite to the Court of Exchequer in 1789 on behalf of herself and her daughters, claiming malpractice on the part of the executors, and William Braithwaite in particular. Her brother-in-law, she claimed, was trying to defraud her of her husband's 'considerable Personal Estate', which consisted mainly of a malthouse and his stock-in-trade. The executors were accused of selling off part of the estate and taking in debts owed to James soon after his death, placing 'the Monies so received by him or some part thereof at Interest or in some manner made considerable advantage thereof for which they and particularly the said William Braithwaite ought to account to your Oratrixes . . .'[64]

Moreover, Mary accused William of taking her husband's account book as he lay dying, and tearing out 'the leaves or leaf in which the account between the said Testator and him was entered and destroyed the same and the said William Braithwaite afterwards wrote in the same book with his own hand that the account between him and the said Testator was balanced'. James had also lent his brother money, but William was accused of stealing the promissory note which proved the debt. Since then, William Briathwaite had refused to give Mary full accounts of the estate, claiming instead that James's estate was 'very small and inconsiderable and not more than sufficient to pay his just debts and funeral expenses'. William Braithwaite's answer contains the supposed accounts of James's estate that valued it at just over £33 at his death. He claimed he had never sold any part of the estate, he had not received debts on its behalf nor did he owe his brother money

---

[64] NA, E112/2070/433.

at his death. Unlike Sayer, whose answer stated that Mary 'had carried on the Malting Business much to the Advantage of the said Testator's Estate', William Braithwaite claimed that she had proved incompetent in this role.[65]

Women were not always the victims of unscrupulous relatives, and, as we have already seen, were also capable of breaking or bending the laws and customs governing inheritance. In 1775, John Pickford, a bricklayer, and Robert Lees, a whitster, both executors of the will of Ralph Smethurst, a Manchester whitster, took action against Smethurst's widow, Mary. The executors claimed that following Ralph Smethurst's death in 1774, Mary, without their permission, had

possessed herself not only of the said Testator's Household and other Goods plate Linnen and furniture but of all his Mortgages Bonds Notes and Securitys for Moneys and of his Books of Accounts receipts papers and vouchers and has since got in a considerable part not only of the moneys which were due upon securitys but other Debts which were owing to the said Testator at his Death and has converted the money so by her received to her own use.

The executors claimed to have asked Mary 'in a friendly manner' to give them details of the estate, but she had refused to comply. Although Mary had been left most of the estate, the executors complained that they would be liable to be charged by creditors for evading payment.[66]

Female malpractice was also alleged in 1773, when William Hancock, a Sheffield cutler, took his father and sister-in-law to court, claiming that they had conspired to deny him a fair share of the family cutlery and silversmithing business following the death of his brother Joseph. Although Joseph had died intestate, Hannah, his wife, was demanding a share in the partnership that the three men had formed in 1769, after a three-year period when the brothers traded independently of their father. William not only questioned her right to claim Joseph's share, but argued that she was also demanding more than Joseph's part, by ignoring money that Joseph had taken from the

[65] NA, E112/2070/433.   [66] NA, PL/6/86/53.

business and a payment of £70 that William had made directly to Hannah. These accusations were denied by the defendants, although Hannah admitted to receiving just over £36.[67] In another case, Sarah Law, the widow of Thomas Law, was accused of conspiring with Jonathan Bingley to defraud Thomas Hudson of money owed him following loans to support Bingley and Law's Sheffield-based silver and silver-plated goods manufacturing company. Not only did Hudson claim that the pair owed him money, but he also accused them of starting an action in the Court of King's Bench which claimed that the loan had been repaid in Thomas Law's lifetime 'with a view to defraud and harass your orator'.[68]

It is clear that women such as Sarah Law would take legal action to assert their own and their family's claims to property. It is also evident that the law could work very differently for women in different circumstances and, moreover, that some women were more than willing to circumvent or evade the law, or to pursue rulings under different legal systems, for personal or familial gain. Women might have suffered from numerous ideological, legal, and practical constraints on their business activities that severely hampered individuals in certain circumstances, but patriarchal power was less pervasive than has often been presumed and businesswomen were able to act more freely than has been believed. This was particularly true if women had control of property, while female agency was even more likely to be apparent when the individual women concerned were strong-willed, smart, and commercially astute.

BUSINESSWOMEN, MARRIAGE, AND THE FAMILY

Court cases concerning property reveal intimate details of both the familial and non-familial relationships of middling men and women in business. However, by their very nature, such sources tend to depict

---

[67] NA, E112/2062/105.   [68] NA, E112/2064/248.

relationships at their most fraught and problematic. Very little can be gleaned from court records about more contented relationships, although it is likely that these would have been more common. Many lawsuits hint at happier times, such as that brought by Andrew Gumbridge, an ironfounder, in 1824. Gumbridge had been married to Mary Dorning and as a consequence worked in partnership with her two brothers, John and William, as Gumbridge and Dorning, ironmongers and whitesmiths, in Manchester. When Mary died in 1823 her brothers, it was alleged, excluded Andrew from the business, resulting in his legal action against them.[69] Clearly Mary's presence had been necessary to ensure cordial relations, although the legal record gives little clue as to what these had been like when she was alive. In order to explore less traumatic circumstances than those described by legal sources, we need other types of evidence, and it is to these that this chapter now turns.

As a means of gaining first-hand testimony of married or family life, diaries, autobiographies, and letters are generally more fruitful sources than legal accounts, and can provide detailed and intimate information, particularly concerning domestic, familial, or 'personal' matters. Yet it is unusual to find such material from middling men and women extant. However, the correspondence of the Wilson family of Sheffield and the memoirs and diary of a Manchester grocer, George Heywood, have survived. Both offer important insights into relationships between middling women and men of business prior to, and within, marriage. It must be said that these sources also tend to depict strained rather than calm familial relations, but the existence of affection and love, particularly in marriage, is also clear, as is the degree of independence that some women appear to have enjoyed.

The Wilson family were snuffmakers, who founded a snuff manufactory at Sharrow in Sheffield in the late eighteenth century, after Joseph Wilson inherited £1,900 from the estate of his father, a shearsmith and edge-tool maker.[70] Wilson had married Ann Greaves in

[69] NA, PL6/115/68.
[70] M. H. F. Chaytor, *The Wilsons of Sharrow: The Snuffmakers of Sheffield* (Sheffield, 1962), 1–2.

about 1752 and the couple had thirteen children during the course of their marriage, of whom eight survived to adulthood.[71] Joseph Wilson was the brother of Sarah Holy, the button manufacturer discussed in the previous chapter. Although Sarah did not convert to Methodism until after the death of her husband, their other brother John was described as an ardent follower of Wesley, and built a preaching-house in the town in 1746.[72] The entire family seems to have considered itself Methodist by the later eighteenth century, although, as we shall see, Joseph was less rigorous than others in his adherence to its moral codes.

Joseph Wilson was not a particularly successful businessman, and tried his hand at several trades before he settled on snuff, including steel drawing, silver plating, sawmaking, and tobacco manufacturing. Ann took part in running affairs when Joseph was away on his frequent business trips, and also had a shop selling haberdashery and household goods.[73] Despite their joint efforts, Joseph was declared bankrupt in 1775 and was bailed out both by his own relatives and those of his wife. At this point his diverse interests were sold off and the most successful part, the snuff manufactory, was retained. A family dispute rumbled on from this point for several years until in 1780 it was agreed that the business would be divided into six parts, with Joseph and Ann taking one part and the remainder going to their children.[74] Joseph continued to be active in the business until 1783, although his eldest son, also Joseph, played an increasingly prominent role after joining his father at Sharrow in 1775.[75] Relations between father and sons were not cordial and both Joseph's nephew Thomas Holy and the Methodist minister Alexander Mather intervened at various points during the 1780s and

[71] Chaytor, *Wilsons of Sharrow*, 6.
[72] James Everett, *Historical Sketches of Wesleyan Methodism in Sheffield*, 2 vols. (Sheffield, 1823), i. 149. See also Jabez Bunting, *Memoir of the Late Thomas Holy* (London, 1832).
[73] Joseph Wilson's account books are peppered with payments to 'the shop', for which it is also noted Mrs Wilson kept her own account book, now lost: Sharrow Mill, Sheffield, Wilson papers, Ledger 17, p. 37 ½ [*sic*].
[74] Wilson papers, Folder entitled 'Settlement of the dispute between Joseph Wilson and his family', 1780.   [75] Chaytor, *Wilsons of Sharrow*, 11.

1790s to try to settle a series of disputes over property.[76] Joseph senior later claimed that these quarrels had peaked in 1785, when his eldest son attacked him at the mill:

[he] Throttled me and made me unsinisible for Sum Time . . . Wen I Came To My Self Jo had his Hand against my Throate and The Other Two Hold of Each Arm Just as If I had been mad an I Was Quiet as a Lamb And Sayd I Never Wishd To See or Spoke to Jo again and Was Sorry to Be father To Such a Son.[77]

Joseph senior was finally forced out of the business entirely in 1788, when both he and Ann were given annuities of £100, plus £200 to spend on building a new house.[78]

No records survive charting the nature of Ann and Joseph's relationship prior to his enforced retirement. There is no doubt, however, that things took a turn for the worse after 1788, with the two living apart. Joseph moved to London and wanted to start a new snuff manufactory there as well as planning to build a house for himself and his wife in the capital.[79] Ann was in a particularly powerful position after Joseph's bankruptcy, since the bulk of the money used to pay his debts came from her family,[80] and it is notable that the agreement made in 1788 gave her an independent income and her own share in the family business.[81] Joseph made a concerted effort to reunite himself with his wife, trying to persuade her to move to London with him. He certainly could have gained financially from her joining him, but his affection for his wife, and the sense of longing and loneliness he experienced without her, appear genuine. They echo the sentiments expressed by other lone husbands, described by John Tosh in his study of middle-class marriage in the early nineteenth century.[82]

---

[76] Wilson papers, Folder entitled 'The late Joseph Wilson's affairs with his family'.
[77] Ibid. Joseph Wilson to A. Mather, 6 June 1789.
[78] Ibid. 'The late Joseph Wilson's affairs with his family'.
[79] Ibid. Joseph Wilson to Ann Wilson, 26 May 1789.
[80] Ibid. 'Joseph Wilson's debts at the time of bankruptcy'.
[81] Ibid. 'The late Joseph Wilson's affairs with his family'.
[82] John Tosh, *A Man's Place: Masculinity and the Middle-Class Home in Victorian England* (New Haven, 1999), 58–9.

Joseph addressed his letters to 'Dear Nanee' and frequently signed them with the note 'I remain Dear Nanee Thine till Death'.[83] Ann was far cooler towards her husband, replying to his entreaties that they build a house together in the capital that

I would not have you give your self the least Trouble about a Hose [*sic*] for me, as I am confident I shall never leave Sheffield, therefore you need send no plans of Houses it is too late in the Day for me to change my Situation and I think I can spend my Days happily where I am.[84]

Joseph may well have been reminded of his attempts in 1771 to persuade the wife of one of his employees, the filesmith James Vickers, to join him in Sheffield by providing a rent-free home. Like Mrs Wilson, Mrs Vickers had refused to move.[85] Ann's children were clearly united with her in their opposition to their father, and stopped at least part of the payment of his annuity, resulting in Joseph's (unrealized) threats to take them to court.[86] On 4 June 1789, Joseph wrote to Ann that

I See I have Dun With you all . . . I See by Thy Letter How Thy mind is Changd I have Long Done Contrary To Wat Was Wat [*sic*] Would have been much my Interest for Fear of Taking My Knowledge [presumably of snuff manufacturing] To an Other House. I Now Drop Those Thorts and Must Do the Best as a Faithfull Steward fare well.

The letter contained the postscript: 'I Think I have a Wife and Children Such as Can not be Sampled in Sheffield but The Lord is Mercifull To us.'[87] Ann was as unimpressed by her husband's rebukes as she had been with his earlier pleas. Her reply reminded Joseph of both his husbandly and paternal duties—specifically accusing him of failing to be a 'faithful steward'—and reveals her weariness after thirty years of frenetic scheming and overambitious business plans:

Your present scheme is all your own doing and very revers to my sentiments. I do not conceive your going into the Snuff trade can ever answer any good

<hr/>

[83] Wilson papers, 'The late Joseph Wilson's affairs with his family'.
[84] Ibid. Ann Wilson to Joseph Wilson, 26 May 1789.   [85] Ibid. ledger 17, p. 67.
[86] Ibid. copy of a letter from Joseph Wilson to A. Mather, 12 May 1789; A. Mather to Joseph Wilson, 2 June 1789.   [87] Ibid. Joseph Wilson to Ann Wilson, 4 June 1789.

purpose to you neather do I think it acting like a faitfull Steward to oppose in any degree your Children. You have such a Wife and Children as are the worst thought by him whose Duty it is most to cherish instead of horrofiing them as you perpetually done [*sic*]—and you should make a better use of those mercies that have been so abundantly bestowed on you. Who could ever have thought that you who as so comfortably settled would in so short a time be dissatisfied therewith. Your scheme of going to London I cannot account any other reason than that you wished to part again from your Family as you could never seriously think that I should, as was it ever likely for me to leave Sheffield.[88]

Joseph's lack of familial comfort also weighed on his own mind. He wrote to the family minister Mather on 6 June that

I Assure you I have So Little Liking To Live Without my Wife That If In my Power I Will Compel Her To Come, I have offered hear [*sic*] That She Shall have a Shay and a Horse and Two of Her Daughters With Her Constantly and They As They [*sic*] are Six of Them may Change as often as They please.[89]

Yet it seems that Ann was not convinced, and the two remained separated until Ann's death in 1795. Mather had pleaded in 1788 for 'unity, & Cordial Love . . . The way whereto you <u>all</u> know to be That Connubial bearing, & forbearing with each other; with that concern to please in <u>all</u> things, as far as can be Both which are at once the duty, and priviledge of <u>all</u> that are so connect[ed].'[90] But Ann had his support in her refusal to travel to London. Mather wrote to Joseph in 1789: 'you say Mrs Wilson will not come to live with you. You have it from her own hand that She will not I have already said that it is not reasonable to expect she should.'[91] Although he appears to have remained estranged from both his wife and sons,[92] Joseph remained on good terms with at least one of his daughters,[93] but never returned to

[88] Wilson papers, Ann Wilson to Joseph Wilson, draft letter, undated.
[89] Ibid. Joseph Wilson to A. Mather, 6 June 1789.
[90] Ibid. A. Mather to Joseph Wilson, 15 December 1788.
[91] Ibid. A. Mather to Joseph Wilson, copy of letter dated 9 June 1789.
[92] Ibid. Joseph Wilson to Joseph Wilson, jun., 5 January 1791.
[93] Ibid. Joseph Wilson to Mary Tennant, 1 and 15 December 1795.

Sheffield. Sometime after 1789 he appears to have invited a Mrs Andrews to live with him in London, the cause of some scandal, and in 1795, Joseph Wilson, jun. received a letter from his cousin Jonathan Watson, which described his father's London home: 'There seems to be every thing comfortable, & himself & Mrs. Andrews are the whole family.'[94] Deborah Wilson, presumably previously Deborah Andrews, is described as Wilson's wife in his will, written in January 1796, following Ann's death the previous year.[95] Neither spouse had shown themselves keen to live alone: Ann staying in Sheffield where she was surrounded by her children, while Joseph Wilson, having failed to win back his wife, sought another woman to act in her place and to ensure 'every thing comfortable'. Joseph clearly wanted to assert more control over his family, but his authority was challenged by both his wife and children. His apparent anxiety and sorrow about his separation from Ann illustrates the importance of affection and love within middling marriages: whether or not Joseph was expressing genuine emotions, he clearly hoped that similar feelings could be aroused in his wife.

Emotional turmoil is also evident in the memoirs and diary of George Heywood, who travelled from Huddersfield to Manchester in the early nineteenth century to learn the grocery trade.[96] Heywood left a record of his life in the form of a memoir, completed in May 1815, which he continued after that date as a diary. George Heywood went to Manchester with high hopes. Looking back on his arrival in 1808 at the age of 20, he noted 'I desired to see more business, to get more experience and thought Mancr. a busy place and a good deal to be seen and learnt there . . .'[97] Having started off with a Mr Hyde, where he became skilled in 'breaking sugar, scribing and turning out butter',[98] he left to work for a widow, Mrs Owen, in November 1809.

[94] Ibid. Jonathan Watson to Joseph Wilson, jun., 24 November 1795. See also A. Mather to Joseph Wilson, copy of letter dated 9 June 1789; Benjamin Eyre to Thomas Holy, 30 November 1790.

[95] Ibid. copy of Joseph Wilson's will, 1796. Wilson noted in his will that his eight children 'are already amply provided for by me' and left the bulk of his wealth to his new wife and other relations and friends in the form of small gifts.

[96] John Rylands Library, Diary of George Heywood, MS 703.   [97] Ibid. [11].

[98] Ibid. [13].

Heywood hoped to secure higher wages in his new post, and his ulti-
mate ambition was to have a shop of his own. At one point it seemed
as if he might achieve this through marriage to his employer. In July
1810, Heywood recorded that

when John Walker [Mrs Owen's brother] was gone to London Mrs Owen had
to go in the evenings to keep Mrs W. compy and I was in the habit of going
for her home after we had made shop up for several nights together I took the
key and we came home from 11 to 12; this circumstance made me quite a
favorite with hr, and by this means a connection was formed between us
which has lasted many years, a connection which is hardly yet broke off.[99]

George's excitement concerning his flowering relationship with Ann
Owen is evident in his writing, as are her actions in encouraging the
attentions of a much younger man:

The first evening anything of this happened or what lead to this Mrs O. went
into sitting room [*sic*] after we got home and begun reading, I went to Bed,
the next she ask'd me to sit down with her, the Family were gone to bed, and
the third I ventured to give her a salute as she made no refusal, I felt encouraged to repeat it another time, and this was the beginning of the practice
which has continued so long. From a spark thus kindled it was soon blown
into a flame which has continued to burn with ardour ever since.[100]

Despite Heywood's clear infatuation with Ann Owen, his mind was
also on the change of circumstances and status that a marriage might
bring. This would have affected them both, for it is clear from
Heywood's account that he planned to take over her business and
place Ann in the role of assistant:

From this time I begun to find great pleasure in her company and she in mine
which seem'd to increase continually I pictured to myself what pains I could
take with the business, how regularly I would have everything carried on,
what an improvement I could make in the premises, how comfortable and
happy it should be my study to make the family, and in doing all this how
happy I should be myself with an industrious managing and agreeable wife
like this to assist me.[101]

[99] Diary of George Heywood [15].   [100] Ibid. [15].   [101] Ibid. [15–16].

His pursuit of Mrs Owen was no mercenary activity, however, and his writing reveals his emotional tumult over their affair. Heywood described his relationship with Ann as a 'torment', 'a connection which has cost me many hours & days of anguish and uneasyness', and a year after it ended, in August 1815, he described the 'slavish passion of Love' which he had formerly felt for her.[102]

Not surprisingly, given his relative age and wealth, Heywood was met with hostility from amongst Ann Owen's friends and family:

by us keeping company the Family and relations begun to think and speak very disrespectfully to me, they imagined I wanted to do something wrong to take for myself what belong'd to the children, which was never my wish . . . When her friends saw and heard there was so much intimacy between us they were apperhensive [*sic*] of something serious and wish'd her to be without me.[103]

At one point Heywood was taken aside by a Mr Bingham, a family friend, who asked him what his intentions were concerning Mrs Owen. Heywood reportedly replied that 'I had no intention but what was just, honest and upright . . .'[104] Bingham was said to have told Heywood that 'I have no objection to you in the least, you are as good as any here and may look up to any Trademan's daughter . . .',[105] but warned Heywood at length of the dangers of marriage to a widow:

You know it is a very heavy undertaking, you know it is a very unruly family, you know there is property to the amount perhaps of 3 or £4,000, this property the children can by law claim two thirds this property, should you ever come to the place, must be entirely made over to the children [*sic*]. Then said I, if the property was taken away how could the Children be brought up and supported as they ought to be. No say he, the property would not be taken away, unless as Peter & Thomas are coming forwards, perhaps in a few years, 5 or 6, may want to begin business, then by giving proper notice, 6 or 8 months, may claim two thirds or perhaps it may not be wanted at all, be that as it may, the amount of what there is must be taken and remain in the business under proper inspection, that it be taken every year what is got

---

[102] Ibid. [15].   [103] Ibid. [16].   [104] Ibid. [18].   [105] Ibid. [19].

afterwards, you must have what there is now must be for the children in short what property there is now must be intirely made over to the children; that you must begin afresh in the world, as if you had not a shilling, with this property to work upon and this you must pay interest for.[106]

Bingham's hints that Ann's widow's inheritance was threatened if she remarried, and once her sons came of age, did not alarm Heywood, who noted that 'I did not know what to make of all this but I thought it was either to frighten me or get me to say something but it did neither of these . . . for I knew they could not do what they threatened.'[107]

Yet it was not Ann Owen's friends or family who seem to have prevented the marriage, but Mrs Owen herself who resisted Heywood's advances in her own interest. In an entry for early 1811 Heywood noted:

She advised me to get another situation and when they [her family] saw the loss of me they would be very willing and desirous for me to come back again, and she promised whether they were agreeable or not I should come again but not as a servant. I drew this up on paper as an agreement between us and wanted her to give it me with her name on it, but this she refused, in this she was not sincere, and it has sometimes led me to doubt whether she was sincere in other respects I have seen many things since to make me doubt of this.[108]

In 1812, Ann admitted that she had promised Heywood that he could return as a partner 'only to get me to leave her quietly'.[109]

After Heywood left Ann Owen's service on 9 April 1811, they continued to enjoy an on–off relationship. Owen broke off their affair on several occasions. A year after Heywood left her employment, she said that he should 'be a friend without being nearer to her than I ought or ever must be',[110] although two weeks later she visited him to renew relations.[111] Two months after that, on 29 June, she refused to see him, claiming that she was seeing another man, John Mabbott, in order, she

[106] Diary of George Heywood [18–19].   [107] Ibid. [19].   [108] Ibid. [16].
[109] Ibid. [22].   [110] Ibid. [21].   [111] Ibid. [22].

told Heywood, to 'wean myself off you'.[112] Heywood—who had by
this point taken to spying on Ann[113]—noted his confusion at her
behaviour in his diary:

Ever since I left Mrs Owen we have kept company as often as we could get
together at least as often as I could meet with her. Sometimes she would
behave with the greatest kindness and respect at other times she would be as
different, which I could not account for, so much so that I begun to make
memorandums in order to compare her conduct towards me at different
times.[114]

George's list-making and spying reveal his boyish inexperience in
affairs of the heart. In contrast, Ann Owen appears both more confident and more forward. This was not unusual, and Tim Hitchcock
has described the ways in which women might offer themselves to
men who remained largely passive, although usually on the understanding that serious sexual activity would result in marriage.[115] Ann
seems to have had no such plans, and was, rather, enjoying the thrill of
a risqué relationship with a much younger man of whom her family
disapproved, and perhaps using him to remind them of her power over
familial wealth in the process.

Heywood records that Mrs Owen proclaimed that she would not
commit herself to marriage. 'I'll not have any one', she told him, 'I see
no other chance but you looking out for and going with somebody
else. I shall see you nicely married and you shall see me just as I am.'[116]
'I have nothing against you but your youth,' he reports her saying,
and adding that 'Every letter I have from my Mother she says I shall
never have a shilling if I notice you': suggesting that it was not just
her marital property which she feared jeopardizing, but also a separate family inheritance.[117] The age difference between them was
apparently considerable, since Ann's brother Mr Walker wrote to
Heywood on 3 January 1813 that the match would be 'unlikely and

---

[112] Ibid.   [113] Ibid. [19].   [114] Ibid. [20].
[115] Tim Hitchcock, *English Sexualities, 1700–1800* (Basingstoke, 1997), 30–1.
[116] Diary of George Heywood [23].   [117] Ibid. [22–3].

inconsistent', especially since Owen was a woman with a large family and adult sons, whilst he was 'a young man to whom she might at least be mother too'. Walker claimed that if they married she would lose 'Family, reputation, connexion & friends'.[118] In spite of such resistance they did continue to see each other, but on 25 June 1814 she finally called it off, blaming the break-up on her mother and friends.[119]

George had spent four years in the fruitless pursuit of a woman who clearly held the upper hand in their relationship. It is not clear whether her family's threats to cut her off would have worked, had she really wanted to oppose them. However, she might well have found some—or all—of her inheritance endangered if she had formalized her relationship with Heywood by marriage, since her family would have had access to various forms of legal redress in these circumstances. Moreover, aside from concerns over her property, familial support would no doubt have been important to her, as it was for Ann Wilson. Instead of continuing her relationship with Heywood then, Mrs Owen chose to hang on to the considerable freedom that her relatively wealthy widowed state gave her. As we have seen from Heywood's plans for the business, Ann was right to suspect that marriage to George would have significantly curbed her independence. She appeared true to her word in not wishing to marry anyone else, and is listed in the Manchester directory of 1817 operating as a grocer from a premises at 19 Withy-Grove on her own, and as a grocer and tea-dealer at the same address in the 1828 directory along with P. Owen, almost certainly her son Peter.[120] It is not surprising that businesswomen were loath to hand over economic independence to new husbands,[121] and it is notable that widows were less likely to remarry than widowers in the eighteenth century.[122] Although some historians are pessimistic about the fate of widows, David Green has argued that middle-class widows

[118] Diary of George Heywood [26].   [119] Ibid. [29–30].
[120] *Pigot and Deans' Manchester & Salford Directory* (Manchester, 1817), 185; *The Manchester and Salford Director and Memorandum Book* (Manchester, 1828), 114.
[121] Bailey, *Unquiet Lives*, 69.
[122] Todd, 'The Remarrying Widow'; Jeremy Boulton, 'London Widowhood Revisited: The Decline of Female Remarriage in the Seventeenth and Early Eighteenth Centuries',

in early nineteenth-century London could be blessed with personal autonomy and legal and financial independence.[123]

After claiming to have abandoned all thoughts of marriage to Ann Owen by the start of 1815, Heywood considered the necessary conditions for a successful union:

I begin to think that equality in marriage is desirable [in terms of property brought into the marriage] for as they are perfectly equal after there should be some comparison before marriage, or it may give one the power of upbraiding the other if they should disagree afterwards—I find it very relieving to have a friend to relate my sufferings to, but it would be much more so if I had a comfortable partner to partake both of pleasures and sorrows. I begin to admire a married life if it can be supported with decency.[124]

Heywood's desire for economic and emotional 'comfort' was not new, and even in the last throes of his affair with Ann he claimed, 'I really thought we could live very comfortably together, I think I could have done almost anything to make her and myself comfortable . . .'[125] Heywood was clearly keen to find a wife. Not long after finally splitting from Mrs Owen, he noted a fondness for a Mary Lockwood in March 1815 and then in May declared 'I begin to feel a great attachment to B. Bowyer.'[126] Betty Bowyer was a domestic servant employed at the home of Mr Jones, George's employer after leaving Mrs Owen, with whom he lodged for several months. 'I think if she and I were placed together', Heywood mused,

we could make each other very comfortable. I have no means of shewing my respect for her at present but certainly feel it much. She is certainly no beauty, she has certainly no property, which are generally the first accomplishments,

---

Continuity and Change 5/3 (1990), 323–55; S. J. Wright, 'The Elderly and the Bereaved in Eighteenth-Century Ludlow', in Margaret Pelling and Richard M. Smith (eds.), *Life, Death and the Elderly: Historical Perspectives* (London, 1991), 106.

[123] David Green, 'Merry Widows and Sentimental Spinsters', in Stobart and Owens, (eds.), *Urban Fortunes*. Penelope Lane found that widows in the Midlands generally suffered an economic decline in comparison with their married state: Penelope Lane, 'Women in the Regional Economy, the East Midlands 1700–1830', Ph.D. thesis (Warwick, 1999), 62.

[124] Diary of George Heywood [45].   [125] Ibid [20].

[126] Ibid. [49–50].

but I have the evidence of my senses to say she is possesst of care, industry, sensibility, frugality, honesty, sincerity, these are much more durable than either riches or beauty.[127]

Compared with Ann, Betty was much closer to Heywood in age, there being only a year between them.[128] Heywood's decision to attach himself to a woman of sober character, after his affair with the flighty and inconsistent (though wealthy) Mrs Owen, was, according to Theodore Koditschek, a more usual choice for middle-class men, who generally looked for women 'who possessed feminized versions of the same qualities of character and industriousness that they valued in themselves'.[129] As we have seen from the Wilson correspondence, Heywood was not alone in seeking 'comfort' in marriage rather than pursuing some all-consuming passion.[130] Heywood noted disapprovingly of the relationship of an acquaintance in June 1815:

Mr Lord seems very fond of Miss Bell but I don't thing [*sic*] it would last long he will now squeeze and kiss her before company but this cannot be lasting, it would require some other charms than those of beauty or the <u>passion</u> of Love to preserve a man's affections, it requires a steady usefulness for that affection to grow into sincere esteem.[131]

That month Heywood set up in business with Robert Roberts, having purchased a share in a shop belonging to Roylance and Jones, for whom he had been working, with money borrowed from relatives and a loan from his past employers. Despite his new attachment to Betty Bowyer, and his own denials, his affair with Ann Owen evidently still rankled, and he noted that

I think this when it is known will fix many people's opinion of me who have hardly known what to think of me. Mrs Owen's family and relations have hardly known what to think of my judgement and abilities they will now look

---

[127] Diary of George Heywood [52].

[128] Betty was born in 1789, George in 1788.

[129] Theodore Koditschek, *Class Formation and Urban-Industrial Society* (Cambridge, 1990), 213. [130] See also Davidoff and Hall, *Family Fortunes*, 323.

[131] Diary of George Heywood [56].

upon this as a proof in my favour but they will be too late to receive any good from it.[132]

The following month he proclaimed that 'I cannot think it would be well for me to marry till I got a great deal more settled in business and show I can afford to live . . . but Religion must also be considered.'[133] Heywood worshipped at the Unitarian Cross St Chapel. Fortunately, Heywood noted, Betty was only a Methodist because her parents were: 'I was glad she had not choosed it from conviction.'[134] Despite his plans to wait, and the importance placed by the middling sort on a man's ability to provide for his family,[135] Heywood married Betty on 26 November 1815. He described this in his diary as 'the greatest day in my Life'.[136] After the marriage, Betty—with whom George was to have nine children—acted as a housekeeper for both George and his partner, in a plan that seemed to mitigate somewhat George's concerns about finances. Thereafter the diary reduced significantly in length and in the frequency of entries, although it was continued until 1832. It seems likely that nothing else matched the emotional intensity and importance of Heywood's years of courtship, and, moreover, that as the father of a large family and partner in his own business, George became too busy with other matters to sit and ponder his love life.

The courtroom battles and emotional struggles that this chapter has described might at first sight offer a rather depressing vision of marital and familial relations amongst women and men of business in the late eighteenth and early nineteenth centuries. However, within these narratives of strife and unhappiness are stories of companionship, affection, and romantic love, as well as tales of support, self-sacrifice, and duty. Women emerge from these sources in various guises: as powerless victims of patriarchal oppression, as valued co-partners in the family enterprise, and as independent agents with a significant degree of control over their own, and their families', lives.

---

[132] Ibid. [58].   [133] Ibid. [69].   [134] Ibid. [87].
[135] Bailey, *Unquiet Lives*, 63–4; Alexandra Shepard, 'Manhood, Credit and Patriarchy in Early Modern England c. 1580–1640', *Past and Present* 167 (2000), 75–106.
[136] Diary of George Heywood [97].

The experiences of Joseph and Ann Wilson and of George Heywood stress the importance of love, respect, and compatibility in the courtships and married lives of middling people of business.[137] It is notable, however, that the leading female characters in these stories—Ann Wilson and Ann Owen—appear to have been driven less by the desire for romance and spousal companionship, and more by a keenness to ensure financial and social independence for themselves and their children. The vision of hard-nosed, unemotional women and lovelorn men that could be drawn from these stories, is, however, likely to be misleading. We know from other sources that women were not immune to the potential pitfalls of romantic love in this period,[138] and we should accept neither Joseph Wilson's nor George Heywood's professions of love unquestioningly. Moreover, the relationships of George Heywood with Ann Owen and Betty Bowyer are presented entirely through male eyes, with Heywood eager to present himself as the victim of a deceitful, or at least inconsistent, woman, whilst Joseph Wilson's letters also reveal a tendency to present himself as hard done by. Although the cases discussed in this chapter provide insights into very few marriages and courtships, it is hard to escape the conclusion that married life offered more to men than to women of the middling sort. While few women would have wished to remain spinsters if this meant being poor or beholden to male relatives, the economic and social independence that widowhood and some types of marital separation could confer would have been attractive alternatives for many women, particularly those who had the support and companionship of their families, and especially their children.

[137] See Ralph A. Houlbrooke, *The English Family, 1450–1700* (London, 1984), 103–5; Hunt, *The Middling Sort*, 166–70; John Tosh, 'From Keighly to St. Denis: Separation and Intimacy in Victorian Bourgeois Marriage', *History Workshop Journal* 40 (1995), 193–206; Amanda Vickery, *The Gentleman's Daughter: Women's Lives in Georgian England* (New Haven, Conn., 1998), 39–86.

[138] See Amanda Vickery's account of Elizabeth Shackleton's disastrous second marriage: Vickery, *Gentleman's Daughter*, 73–7.

Conclusion

IN 1833, Betty Bohanna, who for many years had run a circulating library in Manchester, married the bookseller Daniel Heywood. Their marriage was not happy, and the couple were soon living apart. Following the split, Daniel was careless with both his stock and his shop, which he was in the habit of leaving open and unattended, 'while he strolled about the town or took a ride on the top of an omnibus'. Such lax behaviour led to disaster when his estranged wife 'employed a number of porters to cart away in sacks the largest portion of his best books, which she placed in premises nearly opposite, and where she commenced business on her own account'. While Daniel retired from business soon after, apparently a broken man, Betty became a successful bookseller. 'In her best days', it was noted, 'she was a very fine woman, rather masculine, and with a tendency to be "strong-minded".'[1]

This book has demonstrated that women such as Betty Heywood were not as rare as was once thought: either in terms of her involvement in commerce, or in her forthright dealings with family members. Clearly not all businesswomen in Manchester, Leeds, and Sheffield were as 'strong-minded' as Mrs Heywood, or as inventive in their response to marital disharmony, or in furthering their own enterprises. Yet it has become evident from this study that independence, entrepreneurship, and a strong sense of occupational identity were all features demonstrated by businesswomen in these towns, and, moreover, that the presence of middling women in urban commercial life showed little sign of dissipating in the early decades of the nineteenth century when Betty was active. In order to take into account the experiences of the sorts of lower middling women

---

[1] *The Shadow*, 16 January 1879, 254. I am grateful to Michael Powell for this reference.

considered here, and the ways in which they were perceived by society at large, we need to reconsider both prevailing narratives of historical change concerning women and our understanding of contemporary definitions of femininity.

Most obviously, this book offers a challenge to existing models of women's shifting economic and social status, and specifically the idea that the period of the industrial revolution witnessed the increasing marginalization of women, especially in (and from) the workplace. Historians such as Bridget Hill and Deborah Valenze have described the ways in which industrialization progressively sidelined female workers during the eighteenth and early nineteenth centuries.[2] Others have linked capitalism with patriarchy, describing them as dual structures in the creation of women's oppression. It has been claimed that the industrial revolution helped to promote separate spheres ideology, and with it such developments as restrictive labour practices and campaigns for the family wage, which acted to redefine and revitalize patriarchal forces.[3] Clearly the picture presented here of broad continuity in women's commercial activity does not fit with these models of decline and segregation. Indeed, if anything, the findings of this study suggest that businesswomen became increasingly prominent as economic development gained pace.

But while this book does not support a model that links female subordination (and male dominance) with modern industrial capitalism, neither does it sit comfortably with interpretations that have sought to emphasize continuity in women's experience by attacking the assumption that early modern capitalism robbed women of the work opportunities and public liberties formerly enjoyed under a 'wholesome family economy'.[4] The medievalist, Judith Bennett, for

[2] Bridget Hill, *Women, Work and Sexual Politics in Eighteenth-Century England* (Oxford, 1990); Deborah Valenze, *The First Industrial Woman* (Oxford, 1995).

[3] Catherine Hall, 'The Early Formation of Victorian Domestic Ideology', in S. Burman (ed.), *Fit Work For Women* (London, 1979); S. Walby, *Patriarchy at Work* (Cambridge, 1986); S. Dex, 'Issues in Gender and Employment', *Social History* 13/2 (1988), 141–50.

[4] Amanda Vickery, 'Golden Age to Separate Spheres? A Review of the Categories and Chronology of English Women's History', *Historical Journal* 36 (1993), 383–414, p. 402.

example, argues that women's work has always been low in status, skill, and pay from the thirteenth century to the present day.[5] Other historians have also stressed the profoundly second-rate nature of women's work and socio-economic status prior to the eighteenth century and into the modern era.[6] While this model of centuries-old social and economic female inferiority might hold true for many— indeed the majority of—women in the past, it was clearly not the experience of those examined in this book. In part, this difference is explained with reference to class, as this study has been concerned with the lower middling sorts, while other historians have tended to focus on the lives of labouring women whose experiences were, not surprisingly, quite different to those higher up the social scale.

But this is only a partial explanation of the differing conclusions arrived at, since we also know from the work of Maxine Berg and Pamela Sharpe that the development of capitalism during the eighteenth and nineteenth centuries could have contradictory effects for labouring women as well: with expanding niches of economic opportunity in some regions and trades, but contracting opportunities in others.[7] Women across a broad social range in Manchester, Leeds, and Sheffield were more likely than most to have been affected by the transformations associated with industrialization and consumer growth, and the experience of these towns' inhabitants undermines some of the arguments associated with the 'gradualist' schools of both economic and women's history: reminding us not to

[5] Judith Bennett, 'History that Stands Still: Women's Work in the European Past', *Feminist Studies* 14/2 (1988), 269–83.

[6] Louise A. Tilly and Joan W. Scott, *Women, Work and Family*, 2nd edn. (New York, 1987); Maxine Berg, 'Women's Work, Mechanization and the Early Phases of Industrialisation in England', in R. E. Pahl (ed.), *On Work: Historical, Comparative and Theoretical Approaches* (Oxford, 1988); Katrina Honeyman and Jordan Goodman, 'Women's Work, Gender Conflict, and Labour Markets in Europe, 1500–1900', *Economic History Review*, 2nd ser., 44/4 (1991), 608–28; Pamela Sharpe, 'Continuity and Change: Women's History and Economic History in Britain', *Economic History Review*, 2nd ser., 48/2 (1995), 353–69.

[7] Pamela Sharpe, *Adapting to Capitalism: Working Women in the English Economy, 1700–1850* (Basingstoke, 1996); Maxine Berg, 'What Difference Did Women's Work Make to the Industrial Revolution?', *History Workshop Journal* 35 (1993), 22–44.

underplay the economic and social transformations that were apparent in certain sectors of the economy and in particular regions.[8] This
study began with a strong assertion of provincial identity in the late
Georgian period and of the unique characteristics of northern 'industrial' towns. As has been suggested, it may well be that these environments offered women in business an unusual level of opportunity to
benefit from the early stages of modern industrial capitalism and consumer growth. Such findings echo recent research on other fast-
growing and expanding urban centres in this period, notably London
and towns in the Midlands, which has also described widespread economic activity on the part of middling women.[9] It seems likely that
further research on specific regions and sectors will emphasize yet
more both the possibilities and limitations for working women of all
classes in this period, according to where and how they worked.

The importance of the family firm in urban economies, and the role
of women within such institutions, is also likely to become more apparent in future examinations of women's work, and research on the
middling sorts in particular. Although studies of business and entrepreneurship have often viewed family firms in a negative light—as a
source of conservatism and particularly resistant to change[10]—we have
seen such enterprises at the forefront of rapid economic expansion in
northern industrial towns, and, moreover, as a crucial site for female
economic activity. Women's involvement in family firms could take a
variety of forms, in settings where age, wealth, and skill were important
factors in power dynamics, and could often override considerations of

---

[8] Maxine Berg and Pat Hudson, 'Rehabilitating the Industrial Revolution', *Economic History Review* 45/1 (1992), 24–50. On the importance of regional diversity in current understandings of the industrial revolution see Steven King and Geoff Timmins, *Making Sense of the Industrial Revolution: English Economy and Society 1700–1850* (Manchester, 2001), ch. 2.

[9] Nicola Pullin, ' "Business is Just Life": The Practice, Prescription and Legal Position of Women in Business, 1700–1850', Ph.D. thesis (London, 2001); Maxine Berg, 'Women's Property and the Industrial Revolution', *Journal of Interdisciplinary History* 24/2 (1993), 233–50; Christine Wiskin, 'Women, Finance and Credit in England, c. 1780–1826', Ph.D. thesis (Warwick, 2000); Penelope Lane, 'Women in the Regional Economy, the East Midlands 1700–1830', Ph.D. thesis (Warwick, 1999).

[10] Alastair Owens, 'Inheritance and the Life-Cycle of Family Firms in the Early Industrial Revolution', *Business History* 44/1 (2002), 21–46, pp. 21–2.

gender. Although wives who worked alongside their husbands were usually relegated to secondary positions within businesses, the smooth manner in which widows could take control of familial concerns upon a husband's death suggests the importance of their earlier involvement. The level of female skill and commercial knowledge in such cases is emphasized by the number of widows who remained in charge of family businesses even after their sons came of age and worked with them. The experiences of women such as Betty Heywood also suggest not just that women might wield considerable levels of power within family firms, but also the degree of legal agency that businesswomen could command. Far from filling the role of the timid and powerless 'femme couverte', Betty clearly felt able to assert her rights over marital property with some vigour. As we have seen, it was not uncommon for mid-dling women to take legal action in order to further their own and their family's property claims. While the law could work very differently for women in different circumstances, and women might have suffered from numerous legal as well as ideological and practical constraints on their business activities, patriarchal power under the law has been shown to have been less pervasive than has often been presumed, allow-ing businesswomen to act more freely than has been thought.

As this book's examination of women's status and activities has shown, we need to reconceptualize middling women in this period, in order to acknowledge their significance as producers and distributors, as well as their importance as consumers—the role to which they are traditionally ascribed. In Manchester, Leeds, and Sheffield, we have seen that female enterprise was likely to be both accepted and rewarded, and that businesswomen could wield consid-erable power and exercise significant levels of independence, not just in their dealings in the commercial world, but also within their own families. In line with much other recent work, this study therefore challenges, or at least complicates, our understanding of 'separate spheres'.[11] According to proponents of this influential historical

[11] Critiques of separate spheres theory include Jane Lewis, 'Separate Spheres: Threat or Promise?', *Journal of British Studies* 30/1 (1991), 105–15; Vickery, 'Golden Age to Separate Spheres?'; Lawrence E. Klein, 'Gender and the Public/Private Distinction in the

model, as middle-class men embraced and came to dominate a new aggressive economic world in the late eighteenth and nineteenth centuries, their womenfolk became increasingly dissociated from the workplace and retreated into 'graceful indolence' in a strictly domestic setting.[12] An emerging social ideology of female domesticity was encapsulated in the notion of separate spheres and dictated that women and men were naturally suited to different spheres. In the new moral world-view of the middle classes, femininity became equated with the 'private' sphere of the home, family, and emotion, while masculinity was linked to the public worlds of work, politics, and power.[13]

This model—at its most basic—conflates ideological precept and analytic category, so that, as historians such as Linda Kerber and Amanda Vickery have pointed out, prescriptive ideologies have been described by historians as fact and the experiences of actual women have been obscured.[14] In particular, the separate spheres model leaves little analytic space in which to consider women in business. Men's work has been linked by historians to independence, masculine self-respect, male authority, and respectability,[15] yet as we have seen, occupation was also a way in which women could define themselves and were defined by others, alongside those 'domestic' characteristics with which we are more familiar. For the individuals encountered in this study, gendered identities did not conform to a simple model of

Eighteenth Century: Some Questions about Evidence and Analytic Procedure', *Eighteenth-Century Studies* 29 (1995), 97–109.

[12] Vickery, 'Golden Age to Separate Spheres?'

[13] Leonore Davidoff and Catherine Hall, *Family Fortunes: Men and Women of the English Middle Class, 1780–1850* (London, 1987), 30.

[14] Linda Kerber, 'Separate Spheres, Female Worlds, Women's Place: The Rhetoric of Women's History', *Journal of American History* 75 (1988), 9–39; Vickery, 'Golden Age to Separate Spheres?'

[15] See Davidoff and Hall, *Family Fortunes*, ch. 5; Keith McClelland, 'Masculinity and the "Representative Artisan" in Britain, 1850–1880', in Michael Roper and John Tosh (eds.), *Manful Assertions: Masculinities in Britain Since 1800* (London, 1991); Sonya O. Rose, *Limited Livelihoods: Gender and Class in Nineteenth-Century England* (London, 1992), ch. 6; Anna Clark, *The Struggle for the Breeches: Gender and the Making of the British Working Class* (London, 1995); John Tosh, *A Man's Place: Masculinity and the Middle-Class Home in Victorian England* (London, 1999), chs. 1–3; M. Cohen and T. Hitchcock (eds.), *English Masculinities 1660–1800* (London, 1999), 234.

separate spheres, where women were defined solely by their roles as wives and mothers. Businesswomen—particularly those who controlled their own enterprises—could clearly carve out a respectable niche for themselves in the public sphere by virtue of their occupation, in addition to more predictable expressions of domestic femininity and moral worth.

Yet attacks on the notion of separate spheres as a way of describing either the lives of middling women, or the ways in which they perceived themselves and were perceived by others, should not lead us to ignore the importance and prevalence of gender differentiation altogether. As this study has demonstrated, gender remained a powerful defining concept for lower middling women and men, and businesswomen in particular were likely to have been profoundly affected by gendered ideas. This was seen most clearly in the degree to which they were clustered into certain areas of trade, and it has also been shown that women might find their actions severely constrained according to their sex. The variety of middling women's experiences evident in Manchester, Leeds, and Sheffield over a period of seventy years underlines both the complexity of female involvement in enterprise, and the dangers inherent in presenting a uniform picture of commercial women. Despite this, the woman of business remains a prominent figure in the life of northern industrial towns in the late eighteenth and early nineteenth centuries, and one far removed from traditional representations of middle-class women in this period. Here individuals such as Betty Heywood appeared not as oddities, but as representative of the women and men who inhabited and shaped the urban commercial world.

APPENDIX

Notes on the Methodology Used for Handling Occupational Data from the Directories

There appears to have been no standard usage in the way women's (and men's) names were expressed between 1760 and 1830. In both directory entries and newspaper advertisements, a woman—whether married, unmarried, or widowed—might appear with her first name or her initial listed, or with neither, and with or without an honorific title. The Leeds milliner Jane Plint, for example, appeared in various guises in directories and advertisements between 1797 and 1826 as 'Mrs Plint', 'J. Plint', and 'Jane Plint'.[1] This variation in practice inevitably means that women's entries have been overlooked and thus underrepresented in this study. This is particularly likely in the case of directories where the brevity of entries did not allow for any indication of gender aside from any first name given and the inclusion of an epithet.

As was described in Chapter 2, the number of occupations ascribed to women grew significantly between 1760 and 1830. In order to assess this development, occupational descriptions were standardized to some degree. This standardization was implemented particularly in terms of spelling: so that 'hairdresser', 'hair-dresser', and 'hair dresser', for example, were counted as one descriptor. However, the contemporary practice of listing several jobs together, for example 'bookseller, stationer, and circulating library owner', was retained. This not only maintained the integrity of the sources, but reflected different experiences of work and types of business operation.

Where a woman appeared without a listed occupation, but her address was, for example, given as an inn or coffee house, it was assumed that the individual concerned was an inn- or coffee house-keeper. Likewise, when a

---

[1] *The Leeds Directory for 1809* (1809); *Directory, General and Commercial, of the Town & Borough of Leeds* (1817); and see the discussion of Jane Plint's advertising in Ch. 3.

school was listed with no occupation given, it was presumed that the woman listed was a teacher. Sometimes women also appeared alongside husbands or relations, where the man—who usually appeared to be the husband—was given an occupational label but the woman was not, and was simply listed by her address. In this case, whether or not a woman was considered to be working in the same business as her (probable) husband depended on the nature of his employment. In the case of middling and lower middling manufacturers and traders—such as carriers, grocers, and butchers—the wives of these men were included in the final analyses on the basis that they were assumed to be working alongside their menfolk. Where more prosperous trades and professions were listed—such as bankers, doctors, and cloth merchants—it was assumed that these women may not have been working alongside the men they lived with, and they were not included in the final dataset. This did not affect the final analysis significantly, since only 32 entries were included, and 25 excluded, in this way.

Where more than one occupation was listed and these fell into more than one economic sector, e.g. 'hairdresser and fruiterer', the first listed occupation was generally used to determine the sector to which that the individual was assigned. The economic sectors into which trades were grouped were decided predominantly by type of product rather than type of work. Historians of work frequently organize occupations according to type of work, often using the Armstrong classification, which updates and reworks Booth's data. However, Armstrong is arguably less helpful for early industrial society when many employments straddled the retail–manufacturing boundaries, and so for this reason grouping by type of product was preferred in this study.[2]

[2] C. Booth, 'Occupations of the People of the United Kingdom, 1801–81', *Journal of the Royal Statistical Society* 44 (1886), 314–435, see also debate with William Ogle, ibid. 436–44; W. A. Armstrong, 'The Use of Information about Occupation', in E. A. Wrigley (ed.), *Nineteenth-Century Society* (Cambridge, 1972). However, the Armstrong-Booth model is still the basis for some extremely fruitful research into the social structure of eighteenth-century society: Charles Harvey, Edmund M. Green, and Penelope Corfield, *The Westminster Historical Database: Voters, Social Structure and Electoral Behaviour* (Bristol, 1998); Nicola Pullin, ' "Business is Just Life": The Practice, Prescription and Legal Position of Women in Business, 1700–1850', Ph.D. thesis (London, 2001), ch. 6.

ECONOMIC SECTORS AND
OCCUPATIONAL TITLES

1. Shopkeepers and dealers (excluding those listed under food and drink medicines, and clothing)
2. Agents, auctioneers, and pawnbrokers
3. Food and drink
4. Clothing
5. Gardening and livestock
6. Transport
7. Accommodation
8. Building and furnishing
9. Manufacturing
10. Teaching
11. Nursing and medicine
12. Other trades

1. *Shopkeeping and dealing*

baby linen warehouse and dealer in
     foreign and British muslins
basket and cooper's ware dealer
baskets dealer
binning, linen draper, etc.
bobbins dealer
bone and ivory dealer
bone dealer
bookseller
bookseller and circulating library
     owner
bookseller and stationer
bookseller and stationer,
     and dealer in patent medicines,
     stamp office
bookseller, and mistress of the
     post-office
bookseller, stationer, and
     circulating library owner

bottle warehouse
chandler
chandler and soap boiler
chandler and stationer
china and earthenware dealer
china and glass shopkeeper
cloth merchant
clothes and earthenware dealer
coal dealer
coal merchant
cotton dealer
cotton merchant
cotton, twist, etc. dealer
cotton waste dealer
cotton, weft, and twist dealer
dealer
draper
draper and smallware dealer
dresser and calenderer

dresser and dealer in cloth
drysalter and agent to the Leeds &
  Yorkshire Fire Assurance Co.
earthenware and glass dealer
earthenware dealer
factor and draper
factor and manufacturer of edge
  tools and wool shears
fellmonger
flock dealer
flower dealer
fustians dealer
glass and china dealer
glass-, china-, and Staffordshire-ware
  dealer
glass dealer
hardware dealer
horns, bones, tips, etc. dealer
huckster
ironmonger
ironmonger and iron merchants
ironmonger, hardware, jewellery,
  etc. dealer
jewellery, music, and toy warehouse
  keeper
lace and fancy articles dealer
leather dealer
linen and woollen draper
linen draper
linen draper and hosier
linen draper and mercer
linen draper and milliner
linen draper and silk mercer
linen draper and straw hat maker
mercer
merchant
old china dealer
rag and paper dealer

rag dealer
repository keeper
repository and childbed linen
  warehouse keeper
repository of polite literature keeper
rope and sacking dealer
seeds dealer
shop and post-office keeper
shopkeeper
shopkeeper and cork dealer
shopwoman
smallware dealer
stationer and bookbinder
stationer, bookbinder, and
  machine ruler
stiptics dealer
stone merchant
tallow chandler
timber dealer
timber merchant
timber merchant, chest- and
  trunkmaker
toy and hardware dealer
toy and hardware shopkeeper
toy seller
toy warehouse keeper and basket
  manufacturer
toys and hardware dealer
toys and perfumery dealer
twist, weft, etc. dealer
waste dealer
wholesale dealers in calico, jannet,
  and muslin mits
woodenware dealer
woodhouse keeper
woollen draper
woollen draper and tailor
woollen draper and man's mercer

woollen drapers, undertakers,
  tailors, etc.

worsted dealer

yarn merchant

2. *Agents, auctioneers, and pawnbrokers*

agent to the Phoenix Fire Office

auctioneer

broker

pawnbroker

pawnbroker and jeweller

register-office keeper

repository and register-office keeper

3. *Food and drink*

baker

baker and flour dealer

butcher

butter factor

cheesemonger

cheesemonger and flour dealer

coffee-house keeper

commercial eating house keeper

confectioner

confectioner and cheesemonger

confectioner and fruiterer

confectioner and tea dealer

confectioner, cork dealer, pastry
  cook, and fruiterer

confectioner, fruit dealer, and
  register-office keeper

confectioner, fruiterer, and keeper
  of register office for servants

confectioner, poulterer, etc.

cook

corn and flour dealer

corn chandler, baker, and tea dealer

corn dealer

corn factor

dairy

eating-house keeper

eggs and butter dealer

fishmonger

flour and tea dealer

flour dealer

flour, bacon, etc. dealer

fruit dealer

fruiterer

greengrocer

grocer

grocer and baker

grocer and chandler

grocer and corn dealer

grocer and draper

grocer and flour dealer

grocer and tea dealer

grocer, confectioner, and ginger
  beer manufacturer

grocer, tea and oil dealer

herb dealer

herring-warehouse keeper

keeper of cookshop

malster

malt-miller

meal and flour dealer

milk seller

milk-house

milkwoman

muffin maker

oatcake baker
oyster-rooms keeper
pastry cook
pie-shop keeper
pork butcher
pork butcher and eating-house
    keeper
pork dealer
potato dealer
poulterer
provision dealer
public bakehouse keeper
public baker
retail brewer
sausage-maker
ship biscuit baker
snuff merchant
tea and coffee dealer
tea and smallwares dealer
tea dealer

tobacco and snuff manufacturer
tobacco cutter
tobacco manufacturer and tea dealer
tobacconist
tobacconist and snuffmaker
victualler [default label when inn or
    hotel listed but no job description
    given]
victualler and wine and spirit
    merchant
victualler and billiards-room keeper
victualler and liquor dealer
victualler and liquor-merchant
victualler and wholesale and retail
    spirit dealer
vintner
wholesale and retail dealer in wine
    and spirits
wholesale grocer and tea dealer
wine worker

4. Clothing

blackworker
blackworker and burial-suit
    maker
blackworker and shroud maker
blackworker and straw bonnet-maker
bonnetmaker
boot- and shoemaker
breeches-maker and leather-seller
burial-suit maker
capmaker
clog- and pattenmaker
clogger
clothes broker
clothes cleaner and dressmaker
clothes dealer

clothes-warehouse keeper
dress- and pelisse-maker
dress- and shroud-maker
dress- and staymaker
dress- and straw bonnet maker
dressmaker
fancy dress-maker
feather dresser
glovemaker
glovemaker and black worker
glover and dealer in silks
glover and funeral furnisher
haberdasher
haberdasher, furrier, straw hat and
    stay warehouse keeper

haberdasher, milliner, and
    dressmaker
hat dealer
hat liner
hat manufacturer
hat manufacturer and dealer
hat manufacturer and dealer in
    foreign and British spirits
hatter
hatter, hosier, and glover
hat trimmer
hosier
hosier and glover
hosier and haberdasher
hosier and hatter
hosier and smallware dealer
hosier and tea dealer
hosiery dealer
lace embroiderer
ladies' feather dresser and furrier
laundress
leather hat and cap maker
leghorn and straw hat maker
list shoemaker
mangle keeper
mangler
mantua- and pelisse-maker
mantua-maker
mantua-maker and milliner
manufacturer of hosiery and gloves
milliner
milliner and blackworker
milliner and clear starcher
milliner and dealer in rotten stone
milliner and draper
milliner and dress- and straw hat
    maker

milliner and dressmaker
milliner and fancy dress-maker
milliner and furnisher of funerals
milliner and haberdasher
milliner and linen draper
milliner and mantua-maker
milliner and stationer
milliner and straw and leghorn hat
    and stay dealer
milliner and straw hat maker
milliner and straw hat manufacturer
milliner and toy dealer
millinery and stay
    warehouse keeper
old clothes dealer
pall and cloak hirer
peruke-maker and hairdresser
plain sewer
seamstress
shoe and stocking warehouse keeper
shoe binder
shoe warehouse keeper
shoemaker
silk stocking, feather, and muff
    cleaner
slopseller
stay- and dressmaker
stay- and corsetmaker
stay and straw hat manufacturer
staymaker
stay warehouse keeper
straw and chip hat manufacturer
straw bonnet maker
straw, chip, and leghorn hats,
    millinery, etc. dealer
straw hat and bonnet maker
straw hat and stay manufacturer

straw hat maker
straw hat maker, milliner, and
 dressmaker

tailor
tailor and draper
washerwoman

5. *Gardening and livestock*

cowkeeper
farmer
farmer and cattle dealer
gardener

gardener and dealer
gardener and seeds dealer
public gardens keeper

6. *Transport*

carrier
carter
hackney-coach keeper
hackney-coach proprietor
mule
news carrier

owner of ferry boats
packer
porter
quay-carter
stand coach owner

7. *Accommodation*

boarding-house keeper
governess of poorhouse
hall keeper
housekeeper
keeper of concert room
keeper of the post office
keeper of the White Cloth hall

lodgings keeper
lodging-house keeper
matron
matron of the Guardian Asylum
matron of the House of Recovery
matron of the infirmary
matron of the lunatic hospital

8. *Building and furnishing*

bricklayer
brickmaker
cabinetmaker
cabinetmaker and upholsterer
carpenter
carver and gilder
chairmaker
chair-bottomer
fancy chair warehouse keeper
furnishing ironmonger and lamp
 manufacturer

furnishing ironmonger, etc.
furniture and clothes warehouse
 keeper
furniture broker
furniture broker and register-office
 keeper
house and furniture painter
house milliner
house, sign, and
 furniture painter
joiner

joiner and builder
joiner and cabinetmaker
painter
plasterer and painter
plumber and glazier

shaggreen, and mahogany
  casemaker
stone-mason
upholsterer
upholsterer and cabinetmaker

9. *Manufacturing*

artificial flowermaker
baby-linen maker
band box- and trunkmakers
basketmaker
batting stick dresser
bellows-maker
blacksmith
blacksmith and farrier
blacksmith and wheelwright
blankmaker
bleacher
bookbinder
bracemaker
brass-cock founder
brazier
brazier and tinplate-worker
brazier and iron- and tinplate-
  worker
brazier, tinplate-worker,
  pewterer, etc.
brushmaker
button-mould manufacturer
calenderer
calenderer and velvet dresser
calico glazer
calico printer
calico glazier and
  hat-lining cutter
cap- and ferrule-maker
carder
carpet and coverlet manufactuers
casemaker

cast metal knife and scissor
  manufacturer
check and fustian manufacturer
check manufacturer
clasp manufacturer
clear starcher
cloth-presser
comb- and lantern light-maker
cooper
cooper and basketmaker
cooper and vatmaker
copper plate printer
coppersmith, brazier, and brass
  founder
cork manufacturer
cotton ball-maker
cotton ball winder
cotton band-maker
cotton manufacturer
cotton spinner
cotton throwster
coverlet manufacturer
currier
cut-glass manufacturer
cutler
cutler, and plate manufacturer
cutler, and vigo buttonmaker
cutter
desk knife manufacturer
dyer
dyer and clothes cleaner
dyer and dresser

edge-tool manufacturer
ender and mender
engraver and copperplate printer
filemaker
flymaker
fringe trimmer
fustian cutter
fustian- and check-maker
fustian calenderer
fustian calenderer and dresser
fustian cutter
fustian dyer
fustian manufacturer
geer- and slaymaker
glasscutter
heald knitter
hearthrug manufacturer
horn button manufacturer
horn button manufacturer and haft
    and scale presser
horn button manufacturer and scale
    presser
hourglass manufacturer
ink manufacturer
iron and brass founder
iron founder
iron-liquor, starch, and British gum
    manufacturer
jack- and spring-knife cutler
jeweller
jeweller and silversmith
lacemaker
lace tagger
lamp wick manufacturer
lancet- and phlem-maker
lancetmaker
lantern light- and combmaker

letterpress printer, publisher, and
    stationer
linen and woollen manufacturer
listing-maker
machine-maker
maker-up of fustians, etc.
manufacturer
manufacturer of china- and
    earthenware
manufacturer of cut glass
manufacturer by power and
    commission agent
manufacturer of razors, table knives
    and forks
manufacturer of spades, shovels,
    and cut nails
manufacturer of table knives, razors,
    and pen and pocket knives, and
    factor
manufacturer of umbrellas and
    parasols
mattress-maker
metal spoon manufacturer
mill owner
musical instrument manufacturer
muslin dresser, dyer, and finisher,
    iron liquor, mordant maker, etc.
    for printers
muslin manufacturer
optician and beer machine
    manufacturer, maker of rollers
    for cotton machinery
paper ruler
papermaker
paper-stainer
patten- and patten-clog maker
pattenmaker

patten, patten ring and tie manufacturers, and boot and shoe warehouse keeper

pen-, pocket-, and sportsman's knife manufacturer

penknife cutler

penknife manufacturer

picker-maker

pipemaker

pocketbook and pattern card manufacturer

pocketbook-maker

pocketbook-maker, and dealer in jewellery, gilt, and plated metal

pocket-knife cutler

pocket-knife manufacturer

print glazer

print glazier and maker-up

printer and bookseller

printer and stationer

quilter

razor and jack-knife manufacturer

razormaker

reedmaker

reeler

roller-coverer

rope and twine manufacturer

ropemaker

rubber, shampooner, and electricioner

rugmaker

saddler

saddler and harnessmaker

sash cord, etc. maker

scissormaker

scissorsmith

scissorsmith and victualler

scythe, hay, and straw-knife manufacturer

sickle manufacturer

silk and cotton handkerchief and check manufacturer

silk dyer

silk weaver

silk winder

silk, cotton, and woollen dryer

silversmith and toy dealer

sizer

slay- and geer-maker

smallware and thread manufacturer

smallware manufacturer

smallware weaver

smith and farrier

spinner

spinner and manufacturer of sewing cotton, etc.

spinner and manufacturer by power

spoonmaker

spring-knife cutler

stocking grafter

stocking manufacturer

stuff manufacturer

table-knife cutler

table-knife cutler and victualler

tambourer

tinplate worker, brazier, etc.

tinner

tinplate worker

tippet knitter

tobacco pipe manufacturer

trunk- and packing case-maker

turner

twist reeler

umbrella maker

velvet dresser
vigo buttonmaker
watch- and clockmaker
watchmaker
weaver
wheelwright
whip-hook and mountmaker
whipmaker

whitesmith
whitesmith and ironmonger
whitster
winder
wire worker
wire-drawer and worker
wool comber
writing ink manufacturer

10. *Teaching*

mistress of the Catholic school
professor of music
schoolmistress [default label when
   school listed but no job
   description given]

teacher
teacher of dancing
teacher of the piano-forte and
   singing

11. *Nursing and medicine*

bleeder and dealer in leeches
bleeder with leeches
chemist and druggist
dentist
druggist
druggist, confectioner, and dealer in
   garden feeds
drugs dealer

hospital midwife
ladies' nurse
manufacturing chemist
medical botanist
midwife
monthly nurse
nurse
tooth drawer

12. *Other trades*

barber
bookkeeper
charwoman
chimney sweep
circulating library owner
commissioner
hairdresser and fruiterer
hairdresser and register-office keeper

hairdresser
higler
librarian
mistress of post office
new library owner
perfumer and hairdresser
undertaker
weighing machine operator

Index